Related Books of Interest

Do It Wrong Quickly
How the Web Changes the Old Marketing Rules

by Mike Moran
ISBN: 0-13-225596-0

For decades, marketers have been taught to carefully plan ahead because "you must get it right — it's too expensive to change." But, in the age of the Web, you can know in hours whether your strategy's working. Today, winners don't get it right the first time: They start fast, change fast, and relentlessly optimize their way to success. They do it wrong quickly...then fix it, just as quickly!

In this book, Internet marketing pioneer Mike Moran shows you how to do that — step-by-step and in detail. Drawing on his experience building ibm.com into one of the world's most successful sites, Moran shows how to quickly transition from "plan then execute" to a nonstop cycle of refinement.

You'll master specific techniques for making the Web's "two-way marketing conversation" work successfully, productively, and profitably. Next, Moran shows how to choose the right new marketing tools, craft them into an integrated strategy, and execute it...achieving unprecedented efficiency, accountability, speed, and results.

Listen to the author's podcast at:
ibmpressbooks.com/podcasts

Mining the Talk
Unlocking the Business Value in Unstructured Information

by Scott Spangler and Jeffrey Kreulen
ISBN: 0-13-233953-6

Two leading-edge IBM researchers introduce a revolutionary new approach to unlocking the business value hidden in virtually any form of unstructured data—from word processing documents to websites, e-mails to instant messages.

The authors review the business drivers that have made unstructured data so important– and explain why conventional methods for working with it are inadequate. Then they walk step-by-step through exploring your unstructured data, understanding it, and analyzing it effectively.

Sign up for the monthly IBM Press newsletter at
ibmpressbooks/newsletters

Related Books of Interest

The New Language of Marketing 2.0
How to Use ANGELS to Energize Your Market

by Sandy Carter
ISBN: 0-13-714249-8

From developing the right strategies to energizing your channels of communication, this book will serve as a useful guide to the new technologies that are driving change in marketing and unlocks the secrets to new methods of communicating: Blogs, wikis, video, viral marketing, e-mail, and web communications. Through the reach of the Internet, the marketer is not—and ought not to be—at the center of successful marketing. The customer is the center now. The Internet allows customers to opt-in or select the message that most clearly resonates with them. They choose to read an interesting blog, watch entertaining viral video, cruise Virtual Worlds, and speak through Avatars. What does this mean to us? It means that the previously separate worlds of marketing and communications are merging: Marketing 2.0 is about marketing through communication.

Reaching The Goal
How Managers Improve a Services Business Using Goldratt's Theory of Constraints

by John Arthur Ricketts
ISBN: 0-13-233312-0

Managing services is extremely challenging, and traditional "industrial" management techniques are no longer adequate. In *Reaching The Goal*, John Arthur Ricketts presents a breakthrough management approach that embraces what makes services different: their diversity, complexity, and unique distribution methods.

Ricketts draws on Eli Goldratt's Theory of Constraints (TOC), one of this generation's most successful management methodologies... thoroughly adapting it to the needs of today's professional, scientific, and technical services businesses. He reveals how to identify the surprising constraints that limit your organization's performance, execute more effectively within those constraints, and then loosen or even eliminate them.

 Listen to the author's podcast at:
ibmpressbooks.com/podcasts

Visit ibmpressbooks.com
for all product information

Related Books of Interest

The New Language of Business

Carter

ISBN: 0-13-195654-X

Executing SOA

Bieberstein, Laird, Jones, Mitra

ISBN: 0-13-235374-1

Enterprise Master Data Management

Dreibelbis, Hechler, Milman, Oberhofer, van Run, Wolfson

ISBN: 0-13-236625-8

Inescapable Data

Stakutis, Webster

ISBN: 0-13-185215-9

Irresistible! Markets, Models, and Meta-Value in Consumer Electronics

Bailey, Wenzek

ISBN: 0-13-198758-5

Can Two Rights Make a Wrong?

Reger

ISBN: 0-13-173294-3

Praise for *Intelligent Mentoring*

"A crucial part of my job is to help develop and retain the more than 200,000 members of IBM's global technical community. Over the years I have found that the true spirit of any organization is its people and unique, world-class mentoring programs play a crucial role in their success. What I really like about *Intelligent Mentoring: How IBM Creates Value through People, Knowledge, and Relationships* is that it is not an academic treatise on the theory of mentoring, but a series of practical solutions that can be used by virtually any organization to gain productivity, increase retention, and improve bottom-line results."

—Nick Donofrio
Executive Vice President, Innovation and Technology
IBM Corporation

"We have known about the importance of mentoring in developing people for decades. Yet few organizations have successfully leveraged it as part of their HR strategy. IBM is one of those companies. *Intelligent Mentoring* is about more than the mentoring initiative successfully implemented at IBM. It is a guide for how companies can leverage mentoring in a way that aligns with company strategy and supports organizational and individual development. It is a must-read for any executive considering a mentoring initiative as part of the firm's HR strategy. IBM's mentoring effort combined the best of what we know from mentoring research, career development theory, and change management to create a highly successful effort. There is much here for practitioners and scholars to learn."

—David A. Thomas, Ph.D.
Naylor Fitzhugh Professor of Business Administration
Harvard Business School

"Performance is the ultimate driver of this company. Even back in our earliest days, one of the keys to IBM's greatness was performance, along with top-notch technology. Since arriving at IBM in 2000, my goal has been to identify, develop, train, reward, and retain high-performing people, and one of the best ways to support these high performers is through mentoring. I believe that *Intelligent Mentoring: How IBM Creates Value through People, Knowledge, and Relationships* has done a phenomenal job of capturing the innovative and varied mentoring initiatives that IBM has used over the years. The authors really take you inside the company and show how mentoring has helped IBM preserve its corporate culture by passing on knowledge, not only between generations, but in all directions throughout our global community. This book is a must-read for anyone who wants to use the powerful tool of mentoring to its best and most productive advantage, and I recommend it highly."

—Randy MacDonald
Senior Vice President, Human Resources
IBM Corporation

Intelligent Mentoring

Intelligent Mentoring:
How IBM Creates Value through People, Knowledge, and Relationships

Audrey J. Murrell
Sheila Forte-Trammell
Diana A. Bing

IBM Press
Pearson plc

Upper Saddle River, NJ • New York • San Francisco
Toronto • London • Munich • Paris • Madrid
Cape Town • Sydney • Tokyo • Singapore • Mexico City

www.ibmpressbooks.com

IBM Press Program Managers: Tara Woodman, Ellice Uffer

Cover design: IBM Corporation

Associate Publisher: Greg Wiegand
Marketing Manager: Kourtnaye Sturgeon
Acquisitions Editor: Katherine Bull
Publicist: Heather Fox
Development Editor: Todd Brakke
Managing Editor: Kristy Hart
Designer: Alan Clements
Project Editor: Anne Goebel
Copy Editor: Paula Lowell
Indexer: Erika Millen
Senior Compositor: Gloria Schurick
Proofreader: San Dee Phillips
Manufacturing Buyer: Dan Uhrig
Published by Pearson plc
Publishing as IBM Press

IBM Press offers excellent discounts on this book when ordered in quantity for bulk purchases or special sales, which may include electronic versions and/or custom covers and content particular to your business, training goals, marketing focus, and branding interests. For more information, please contact:

U. S. Corporate and Government Sales
1-800-382-3419
corpsales@pearsontechgroup.com.

For sales outside the U. S., please contact:

International Sales
international@pearsoned.com.

Library of Congress Cataloging-in-Publication Data

Murrell, Audrey J.

  Intelligent mentoring : How IBM creates value through people, knowledge, and relationships /
Audrey Murrell, Sheila Forte-Trammell, Diana A. Bing.
    p. cm.
  ISBN 0-13-713084-8 (hardback : alk. paper) 1. International Business Machines Corporation—
Management—Case studies. 2. Mentoring in business—United States—Case studies. 3. Employees—
Coaching of—United States—Case studies. 4. Organizational learning—United States—Case studies.
I. Forte-Trammell, Sheila, 1948- II. Bing, Diana A., 1948- III. Title.
  HD9696.2.I54M87 2008
  658.3'124—dc22

                                    2008033455

  Pearson Education, Inc
  Rights and Contracts Department
  501 Boylston Street, Suite 900
  Boston, MA 02116
  Fax (617) 671 3447

ISBN-13: 978-0-13-713084-9
ISBN-10: 0-13-713084-8

Text printed in the United States on recycled paper at Courier Westford in Westford, Massachusetts.
First printing November 2008

Audrey Murrell would like to thank her original and most powerful mentors—her parents: timeless gratitude and admiration to her mother, Castella Burnley Murrell, for her insight as a researcher and teacher; and to her father, Irvin Maurice Murrell, for his passion for social justice and sincere belief that people can change the world.

Sheila Forte-Trammell would like to acknowledge the following members of her family: I'd like to express gratitude to my parents Dudley and Iris Miller (Montego Bay, Jamaica) who have inspired me with courage to uphold my values and to demonstrate commitment to excellence. Thanks to my daughters, Dr. Jamila Forte and Aisha Forte, for their steadfast love and to my husband, Gus Lee Trammell, for his kindness and encouragement. Finally, I'd like to acknowledge my sister Dr. Doreen Miller who embraces me with her love and generosity.

Diana Bing would like to give special thanks and acknowledgment to the following: her father Henry Bing Jr., for his great example of leading the way at IBM, as a pioneer for Diana and so many others; and her husband, Dr. Jerold Lawson, and her son, Tyler Bing-Lawson for their support and encouragement.

Lastly, we extend our personal gratitude to those who have mentored each of us throughout our careers, in different phases of our lives, and through challenges both great and small.

Contents

Foreword

Ted Hoff

Since its founding nearly a century ago, IBM has believed that the vitality of the next generation simply will not endure without mentors, without the guidance of experienced colleagues sharing their knowledge, wisdom, and experience with the newer members of our global community. You could say that mentoring has been part of IBM's DNA from the beginning. We know that providing inspiration to others enables all of us to reap the rewards of leadership. We know that our business has grown stronger over the years through collaboration and the practice of sharing information.

The world economy has today reached a turning point. For example, in less than a decade, the Internet has reached more than a billion people and has become the world's operational infrastructure. Open standards—widely adopted technical and transactional specifications—are spurring the creation of new kinds of products and services. Taken together, the Internet and open standards have enabled new business designs allowing all institutions to better integrate their operations and respond rapidly to global business challenges. As a result, businesses, governments, and institutions of higher learning can innovate in new entirely new ways, affording new growth opportunities in both economic and societal activity. Seizing the opportunities demands unique foresight, capability, and an employee base equipped with entirely new skills.

At IBM we foster a climate that promotes continuous learning, enabling our employees at all levels to become problem solvers, creative thinkers, and global citizens. We make it a priority to reexamine and reinvent our processes and practices through every aspect of our business. Mentoring is no exception. It helps us anticipate the needs of our global clients and enables us to provide them with twenty-first-century solutions and services.

To carry this out successfully, we offer our employees throughout the world the tools and resources to build their portfolio of expertise and experience. At the same time, they know that they are expected to leverage this knowledge to help build the skills of their colleagues, to make an impact on their immediate organization, and, overall, to drive success for IBM. Knowing how to respond rapidly to the needs of the client depends on the expertise of our employees, and mentoring is an important tool in the process.

A critical component of our mentoring program is **expert mentoring**, which is anchored on the premise that it takes many years of intense formal training and practical application for expert knowledge to develop—especially in areas such as information technology. To be competitive, companies must find ways of escalating the pace at which crucial knowledge is transferred to feed the constant development of new experts in their specific disciplines across the business.

It is an expectation pervasive across our company, and special emphasis is being placed on reaching out to technical IBMers in the emerging countries. Our approach to mentoring is that geographic boundaries should not be an inhibitor, or a barrier, to the transfer of knowledge and expertise vital to providing the kind of service our clients expect from us. As a globally integrated enterprise, we erase geographic lines of demarcation in all our transactions, including people and technology. Mentoring and knowledge-sharing must transcend borders in developing cultural competence, global leadership, cultural diversity, and the ability to work seamlessly in a virtual world.

I often remark to employees that if innovation is to truly matter, we must understand the changing nature of innovation and the shifts in the way it occurs. Human capital is central to that understanding. Innovation is happening more rapidly than ever, and it is far more dependent on collaboration across disciplines, specialties, and organizations than ever. There also is increasing emphasis on open sharing of intellectual capital as a platform for innovation, which is how I see mentoring as an enabler. The ability to innovate, reinvent, and adapt is a traditional strength of IBM and through expert mentoring and collaboration we are able to sustain our competitive advantage.

Mentoring and collaboration support the three IBM core values:

- Dedication to every client's success
- Innovation that matters—for our company and for the world
- Trust and personal responsibility in all relationships

Fostering a workplace climate that thrives on trust, that is focused on building individual and organizational capabilities, and that demonstrates intellectual curiosity are the necessary elements that move our innovation agenda forward.

Intelligent Mentoring: How IBM Creates Value through People, Knowledge, and Relationships is an admirable piece of work offering practical insights on mentoring as a way to preserve and transfer knowledge crucial to the success of an organization. It employs first-hand experiences to articulate how mentoring is relevant to global institutions of all types and sizes.

Overall, this book helps us understand that mentoring simply has to transform from a moral obligation to a personal and business imperative. It has the power to stimulate bold, new thinking—fertile ground for not only spurring innovation and creative problem solving, but living the IBM values.

—Ted Hoff
IBM's Chief Learning Officer and VP for Learning

Acknowledgments

This book represents the collective wisdom and experience of many individuals who willingly shared their time and have worked diligently to shape the IBM workplace as one that is welcoming. These individuals consistently find ways to creatively use mentoring as a means to share their knowledge with colleagues across the global enterprise.

The authors would like to extend special thanks to the following reviewers for their critical insights and constructive suggestions:

Dr. Diola Bagayoko
Dr. Stacy Blake-Beard
Dr. Faye Crosby
Bridgette Driver, Esq.
Dr. Regina O'Neill
Dr. David Porter
Dr. LaVerne Weldon
Richard Welty
Charlotte Wooten

The IBM mentoring story would not have been possible without the dedication and contribution of a team of individuals who exemplified the IBM values by volunteering their time and talent beyond their defined job responsibilities to promote mentoring at IBM. The following people must be commended for their contribution to the IBM Mentoring Program:

Jeanne Fraser
Brooke Price
Bob Slaney
Lisa Stein

Dr. Nancy Wall
Brenda Thompson
Olivia Robinson

Special thanks to Tobie Kranitz Walters who has given unwavering support and encouragement to the author team throughout the writing of the book, and to Mary Ann Bopp for her encouragement. We also would like to thank Margie Jonnet for her help and support throughout this process.

The authors would also like to thank Katherine Bull and Todd Brakke for their guidance, support, and expertise, without which our vision of this book would have not become such a wonderful reality.

About the Authors

Audrey J. Murrell, Ph.D. conducts research, teaching, and consulting that helps organizations better utilize and engage their most important assets—their human and social capital. She is an associate professor of Business Administration, Psychology, and Public and International Affairs at the University of Pittsburgh's School of Business and serves as the director of the David Berg Center for Ethics and Leadership. Audrey conducts research on mentoring, careers in organizations, workforce/supplier diversity, and social issues in management and has worked as a consultant for a number of Fortune 500 companies. Audrey has published more than 50 articles and is also the author (along with Crosby and Ely) of the book, *Mentoring Dilemmas: Developmental Relationships within Multicultural Organizations* published by Lawrence Erlbaum.

Sheila Forte-Trammell is a senior learning consultant at IBM and has many years of experience in human resources. She is responsible for designing and leading human resources initiatives that have global impact. Sheila's many years of experience includes diversity and multiculturalism, mentoring, organizational development, employee and industrial relations, compensation, and talent management. She is the recipient of several IBM awards and external awards, and was selected from a field of almost 200 professional women from Fortune 500 companies and academia to receive the 2004 National Woman of Color Award for Workplace Educational Leadership.

Diana A. Bing recently retired from IBM. She was IBM's director responsible for Employee Development and Enterprise Learning. As part of IBM's mission to attract, motivate, and retain its highly talented workforce,

Diana's overall vision was to enrich and develop IBM's employees, both technically and professionally, so that they meet IBM's business goals as well as the employees' personal career-development needs. To achieve this vision, she led the efforts in IBM Learning for the planning, design, development, and delivery of employee learning programs. These programs begin with new hire orientation and continue through mentoring and technical and professional development for all 355,000+ IBM employees worldwide.

I

Introducing IBM's Mentoring Portfolio

Chapter Contents

The past two decades have witnessed an explosion of interest across a variety of organizations, disciplines, demographic segments, and professions in the topic of mentoring.[1] One recent annual benchmark by a leading management consulting firm noted that companies are increasingly using mentoring as a key technique for attracting and retaining high-potential employees, new hires, as well as senior executives.[2] There is also clear evidence that interest in mentoring is not only pervasive in the United States, but also extends around the world within many global organizations.[3] Ironically, as our interest in mentoring continues to grow, our ability to understand how to unlock the power of mentoring relationships has not kept pace with this expanding curiosity. Issues such as the benefits of formal versus informal mentoring, how to structure formal mentoring programs to increase effectiveness, and what tools and techniques can be used to measure the impact of mentoring efforts, are just a few of the critical questions that persist.[4] While most agree that mentoring is important, there is still a crucial need to understand how to unlock the power of this valuable tool.

Throughout the pages of this book, we argue that a well-designed and diverse portfolio of mentoring programs and activities can provide a powerful and strategic tool for organizations that must face the rapidly changing demands of attracting, developing, and retaining talent within their global workforce. The examples of mentoring throughout IBM are used to illustrate how one organization can leverage new and existing skills/expertise as well as foster knowledge sharing across traditional boundaries such as function, geography, demographic group, and culture. We describe how IBM uses a broad portfolio of both formal and informal mentoring efforts to support three core components of its global business strategy:

- **Building organizational intelligence**, which allows IBM to bridge skill, leadership, and knowledge gaps while creating a climate where collaboration leads to innovation
- **Connecting across people**, which focuses on providing support and development across all employee segments
- **Sustaining business impact**, which involves integrating mentoring within the overall strategic goals and objectives of the organization

As illustrated in Figure 1-1, these three components are part of IBM's global strategy, and each helps to frame the selection and design of mentoring tools used within its portfolio approach. The need to develop this global business model was articulated by IBM CEO, Samuel Palmisano, stating that, "In a world where the means of production and distribution are increasingly available to anyone, the only way to differentiate yourself is to have better skills, to have a better idea, to come up with a more innovative solution, to know more than the next guy, and to apply it more effectively."[5]

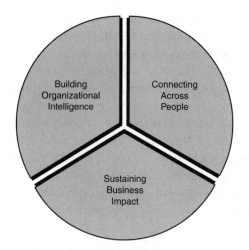

Figure 1-1   IBM's strategic business model.

The catalyst for this book was born out of the experience of IBM in using mentoring to address critical issues such as how it competes within the global "war for talent" and meets the demand for innovation within the dynamic technology industry. Benchmark and trend analyses provided evidence that IBM, like a number of other firms, was facing an aging workforce, a pipeline shortage, and the growing need to retain and transfer cutting-edge knowledge. In addition, internal analyses revealed that shifts in the IT industry would demand people who not only had deep technical knowledge and professional skills, but also the ability to collaborate in increasingly diverse and virtual environments. In attempting to address the needs of talented employees who are seen as the knowledge capital for IBM, the realities of shrinking training budgets, limitations of traditional classroom training, and the need for accessible and flexible learning systems presented some real challenges for the industry giant. These were all factors that led IBM to invest in and to revitalize mentoring as a strategic tool to attract, develop, retain, and energize employees throughout its global business enterprise.

We share and reflect on best practices developed within the global port-folio of IBM's mentoring initiatives. In the following chapters, we explore some of the emerging research on and innovative applications of mentoring as well as how the very nature of mentoring is being transformed by these efforts. To provide concrete illustrations of the power of mentoring, we present several best practices from IBM's mentoring portfolio to illustrate some simple but creative ways IBM uses these practices to address issues related to mentoring as well as key lessons learned. While the development and innovative use of formal and informal mentoring within IBM is an ongoing and continuous process, our discovery is that the activities highlighted in this book have strengthened and energized attention to mentoring throughout the IBM community worldwide. Our goal is to extend this energy and expand the dialog to other organizations. While there are ongoing discussions and communication about how to make mentoring effective and how to cultivate a stronger mentoring culture within IBM, sharing its portfolio approach may provide a catalyst for other innovative uses of mentoring that can not only transform organizations but can also transform the way we think about and utilize mentoring as a valuable and strategic management tool.

Mentoring Transformations

Traditional approaches to mentoring were developed during a period of time where the expectation for stable, long-term, full-time employment within a single organization was still the norm for people throughout their careers.[6] On the individual's side, the need for flexibility, mobility, and life-long learning are some of the dominant themes that have altered expectations about careers and employees' relationships to the firm.[7] On the organization's side, the use of restructuring, cross-function integration, and demands of the global supply chain have created new organizational structures, processes, and requirements.[8] Both of these dynamic trends have led to what researchers call a change in the "psychological contract," or the expectations that employees and employers have concerning mutual relationships and obligations within the business enterprise.[9] Others argue that the changing nature of individuals' careers and organizational demands requires a fundamental shift toward a new type of employability that is market-driven rather than employer- or employee-driven.[10]

Thus, changes in the employer-employee relationship coupled with the demands of market-driven employability mean that resources and support that are needed within organizations are more complex. In addition, a market-driving employment relationship requires that individuals take a more active role in managing their careers than was true decades ago.[11] Recognizing the importance of these dynamics, a great deal of research has focused on the increasing need for employees and employers to change their approach to mentoring from traditional forms such as senior-to-junior informal relationships or one-on-one formal relationships (for example, supervisors) provided by the organization, to thinking about mentoring as a diverse network of career and personal support.[12] The traditional definition of a mentor as a more senior individual who uses his or her influence and experience to help with the advancement of a single protégé or mentee is still relevant. However, the transformation of mentoring as experienced by IBM and captured by scholars examining other organizations is now expanding the types of relationships beyond this traditional senior-junior relationship to include a broad portfolio of mentoring forms such as peer mentoring, virtual mentoring, group mentoring, and reverse mentoring.[13]

To fully appreciate the need for such an expansive and complex view of mentoring, we must first understand the various challenges facing organizations like IBM. These challenges not only set the context for the mentoring portfolio developed by IBM, but they also provide the blueprint for similar issues being faced by other global companies. The responses to these concerns can then point us toward the best fit between specific global challenges and unique mentoring solutions.

IBM's Challenge

IBM's global business strategy (refer to Figure 1-1) was created in response to key challenges faced by the firm and similar global companies. Issues of talent development and retention, knowledge creation and transfer, and sustaining business impact can each be tied to clear trends facing the company.

The well-noted "War for Talent" concept as articulated by the McKinsey & Company[14] report reflects the increasingly competitive market for talent, leaders, and innovative knowledge workers. This report declared that knowledge or talent is now the key factor in driving the effectiveness of many organizations today and in the future. Thus, a company's capability to attract, develop, and retain talented individuals provides a competitive advantage as the war for talent persists. Issues such as social capital, communities of knowledge, and talent management have replaced some traditional human resources topics of hiring, staffing, and performance evaluation. The

McKinsey research included surveys of 13,000 managers and executives across more than 120 companies, along with case studies of 27 leading companies. It found clear evidence that better talent management leads to better performance. On average, companies that did a better job of attracting, developing, and retaining highly talented managers earned 22 percentage points higher return to shareholders. Unfortunately, as the authors noted in the report, organizations have a long way to go in being prepared for the ongoing talent war. Thus, organizations like IBM needed to face several issues impacting its current and future pipeline of knowledge within the organization—its people.

The first clear challenge is that the global war for talent means that top organizations around the world must pay more attention to the impact of high employee turnover, particularly among diverse employee segments. For example, Ernst & Young discovered that a lack of retention of women was costing the firm about $150k annually, in addition to causing a decrease in client satisfaction because the people responsible for their projects frequently changed.[15] Nortel Networks faced difficult challenges after three years of widespread layoffs and a decline in share values. It made the retention of the remaining talent within the company a strategic priority to help stem the negative trend. Deloitte management made the decision to focus more strongly on developing its international talent in the late 1990s but could only recruit about 1% of the organizational global workforce to participate. To meet this challenge, they created a Global Development Program, which began by understanding what attracted potential candidates to work at Deloitte internationally. Its focus on global retention helped Deloitte design an effort to double the number of participating countries and employees in these efforts. Deloitte executives see this strategic focus on global workforce development as a factor in the company's 2002 11 percent growth in global revenue.[16]

The significant impact that employee turnover has on key performance metrics is not unique to these few companies nor to IBM. This disturbing trend was highlighted by the findings of the most recent "corporate leavers survey." Conducted by the Level Playing Field Institute, this study showed that each year across the United States, more than 2 million professionals and managers voluntarily leave their job because they feel that they are treated unfairly.[17] This study concludes that voluntary turnover costs for U.S. firms in 2007 reached a staggering $64 billion dollars. This research also showed how employees who left their firms later provided information that discouraged potential customers and job applicants from working with their former employer. Thus, ignoring retention issues may impact future recruitment of talent and new customers into the organization. Also disturbing was the finding that people of color were three times more likely to report that workplace unfairness was a key reason for their voluntary exit compared to white males. The clear message from these studies and other corporate examples for IBM is that turnover and the loss of human capital is an expensive proposition that negatively impacts an organization's competitiveness.

The second challenge involves generational differences that are causing a dramatic change in what employees expect from their employer, as well as how they view the meanings of work and career. A great deal has been written, particularly in the United States, about the impact of "Generation X" and the emerging "new millennials" and their requirements for a satisfactory workplace environment.[18] These changing demographics are providing a talent pool of potential employees who expect a very different workplace than traditional organizations may provide. For example, members of Generation X have the following expectations about the work environment:

- Bureaucracy will be replaced with more participatory management
- The value of the employee shifts from being defined by tenure toward an emphasis on accomplishments, and open communication is facilitated throughout the organization
- An employee-friendly work environment is cultivated that includes respect, learning, collaboration, work-life balance, and a sense of purpose[19]

Similar observations are now being offered in terms of values and workplace preferences for those in the next generation of new millennials.[20] After several decades of research trying to identify the key drivers of employee turnover, it is clear that supportive relationships that build what is frequently called "relationship wealth"[21] are essential, and are becoming increasingly important to new generations of employees (for example, Generation Xers and new millennials). What this suggests to companies like IBM is that organizations must not simply look to attract and retain talent, but must focus on employee development and ultimately engagement of talented knowledge workers.

The third challenge is that the particular issues faced by the IT industry may require a somewhat unique approach to workforce development and utilization. The vital role that knowledge and intellectual capital play within the IT industry has been recognized by a number of industry leaders. For example, Microsoft CEO Bill Gates noted in his speech before the Joint Economic Committee of Congress that, "The lifeblood of our industry is not capital equipment but human capital." Similarly, Intel CEO Andy Grove commented that today's global economy "is all about human resources." In a speech at INSEAD, IBM CEO Sam Palmisano argued that, "We need to think seriously about issues in a global—not just a multinational context...the new skills we'll need to develop...and the new kinds of organizational culture that will be required." Each of these leaders within the IT industry points to the demands for knowledge workers, the challenges faced within this dynamic industry, as well as potential solutions.

IT effectiveness has been clearly linked to the pool of available knowledge professionals across a wide variety of IT specializations. As demand increases yet the supply remains stagnant, those with valuable skills, knowledge, and expertise will seek out the best options.[22] In one research study of human capital within the IT industry, the profile of the typical IT worker was found to be distinctly different than that in other industries. IT professionals were found to typically be younger workers who have less of an investment in a firm-specific employment relationship compared to older and more long-term employees.[23] This means that they utilize a different cost-benefit perspective to determine whether to join, stay, or leave any organization or employer.

In addition, change within the IT industry happens at a rapid pace, which has a significant impact on career opportunities and mobility for people within the field. The issue of "knowledge obsolescence" or having expertise that is no longer in use or that has been replaced by newer knowledge and technology is a challenge for these workers. Career stagnation, or what is called "career plateauing" which creates a feeling of being trapped in one position with little opportunities for growth and change, is also a key concern.[24] What this means for IT and IT-related organizations is that the need to develop an approach to recruiting, training, and developing employees must be done in a manner that is flexible enough to meet the challenging demands for these talented knowledge workers.[25] Employees within the IT industry require access to rapidly changing information,[26] broad information sharing within the workplace, and flexible opportunities for competency development. Interestingly, a number of studies also focus on the need to go beyond traditional monetary bonuses and rewards to effectively drive performance and retention among IT professionals.[27]

Clearly this array of challenges highlights the need for an innovative set of solutions for companies like IBM. To outline a response, IBM examined the market trends, but then focused on internal analysis and benchmarking to determine the specific issues within the IBM culture. Several key questions were raised. What is the nature of recruitment, retention, and development across the business enterprise? How was the climate and culture of IBM viewed by current and potential employees? Did people see the existing employee support system, including mentoring, as useful? The response and revitalization of mentoring came as part of IBM's response to these critical questions.

IBM's Response

In the early stages of this effort, IBM conducted a series of benchmarks and internal research (interviews, surveys, focus groups, and so on). Analyses of these data revealed a number of shortcomings regarding employee recruitment and development at IBM. One of the key factors that emerged was a need and desire to revitalize and expand mentoring throughout IBM. Employees and managers perceived mentoring as an opportunity targeted more toward executives and high-potential employees rather than something that was accessible across broad and diverse segments of the organization. Research results indicated there was confusion about how development techniques such as mentoring could help employees grow their skills and careers, and that information about key resources such as mentoring was not available from one easy-to-access central location. Across IBM, individual business units developed a number of homegrown programs such as "mentoring matching" tools that added to the information confusion. Further, the human resources department found that employees were challenged to find the time to engage in mentoring relationships in the company's complex and demanding business environment.

Mentoring was also not generally viewed as critical to transferring knowledge or fostering innovation. Rather, it was seen as just a "morale-booster," and not a vital tool that helps to drive core business-related outcomes. Further, there was a lack of clarity about the roles of mentors and mentees, as well as the different types of mentoring relationships that could be valuable, including peer-to-peer mentoring, group mentoring, junior-to-senior (or "reverse") mentoring, and mentoring relationships in virtual environments (or e-mentoring).

While there was an interest in mentoring and career development within IBM, the solution that needed to be identified and then implemented was far more complex. One of the key challenges IBM faced was how to create a mentoring initiative that would meet the needs of more than 356,000 employees working with clients across 170 different countries. The mentoring effort had to meet the diverse needs of employees across generational and other diversity dimensions. In addition, the program had to take into account evolving work arrangements where close to 49% of IBM's employees worked outside of a traditional office environment. This array of challenges meant that the answer to IBM's mentoring questions could not be found in a one-size-fits-all type of mentoring program with a traditional design. For example, four distinct generations coexist in the IBM global workforce. Each has a different style, preference, and approach to acquiring and disseminating crucial knowledge. To blend within and across generations in the learning process and address the different styles, IBM's approach to mentoring had to be flexible, sensitive to different learning styles, and take into account diversity across generation, culture, and other important dimensions (for example, race, age, and gender).

After an extensive internal and external analysis, IBM began revitalizing mentoring through a corporatewide initiative. To meet the challenges and opportunities its internal and external audit identified, a new mentoring program took shape as an innovative, multipronged approach. However, the first step was to raise the visibility of mentoring as a potential tool for meeting some of the challenges and opportunities within IBM. The early stages of the mentoring revitalization efforts directly targeted some of the key feedback gained within the internal benchmark and included:

- Developing a *single Web site* as a "trusted source" for all corporate mentoring information
- Creating a series of streamlined and easy-to-access *mentoring resources,* such as mentoring podcasts, success stories, mentoring guides, and mentoring best practices that focus on the mentor and mentee relationship, and how to make it work
- Leveraging *search capabilities* of the corporate "telephone" directory to find a mentor for any level of expertise, career advisement, or social networking
- Establishing *international and cross-geography mentoring programs* whereby employees from other countries and cultures could learn from one another
- Forming *group speed mentoring cafes,* whereby an experienced mentor meets with numerous mentees in a group setting for topical mentor moments

- Changing the *Individual Development Planning* tool so that mentoring relationships can be recorded and included as part of the annual employee development plan

- Providing managers guidance on ways to include mentoring as a form of recognition in the performance evaluation process

- Building a *"Dear Mentor" chat capability,* where employees can electronically ask questions of a team of mentoring experts

- Designing an extensive Mentoring Promotional Campaign across the enterprise

- Securing executive backing through creating *executive champions* who act as advocates for the mentoring program

This initial array of IBM mentoring initiatives was used to launch its multilevel deployment approach. In a top-down phase, the human resources department, together with an executive leadership team, provided the charge and mandate for mentoring through a series of promotional activities across the business units. Executives were involved in speaking engagements at global organization meetings, panel discussions, webcasts and podcasts, and mentoring jam sessions. Parallel to engaging executives, a bottom-up phase was simultaneously launched through many grassroots efforts to touch numerous employees in a short period of time. This included engagement of diverse employee networks such as the Global Women's Council, which includes several thousand women who developed a resource guide for mentoring; the Asian Diversity Network Groups, which conducted a webcast focusing on mentoring; and the Global Black Executive Network team that helped to develop an electronic book that outlines important mentoring and career development resources available throughout IBM. These efforts involved peer, group, expert, and reverse mentoring activities throughout the organization. In addition, the revitalization initiative engaged a mentoring team that included "volunteers" from within the business to help drive the development and deployment of various grassroots activities. While organizations usually address only one or two types of mentoring, the IBM approach generated a diverse portfolio of mentoring activities, thus yielding an innovative strategy not widely seen in literature or in practice.

The approach that has emerged from IBM represents an innovative use of mentoring for several reasons. First, the use and revitalization of mentoring has taken place as a "grassroots" effort, that is, within various department and segments of the organization. At the same time, the leadership of the organization has been fully committed to the use of mentoring as a strategic tool. The synergy created by this dual approach was critical for signaling the importance of mentoring throughout IBM and for building support among the sponsors and participants of the revitalization effort.

Second, IBM has taken the unique approach of creating a **strategic mentoring portfolio** or series of formal and informal efforts to infuse mentoring within the culture of the organization. This portfolio approach means that there is not one type of mentoring program or structure that can be the solution for any challenge or opportunity facing the organization. Instead, managers, business units, and HR professionals select from a wide variety of mentoring tools and techniques to find the mentoring solution, rather than simply implementing a traditional mentoring program. Third, the use of mentoring was placed within the overall strategic objectives of the organization. As illustrated by Figure 1-2, core features of IBM's mentoring portfolio are linked to the key components of its global business strategy. In this way, mentoring is not seen as a special or extra activity. Rather, mentoring is seen as a central and integrated aspect of how business is accomplished and executed throughout IBM worldwide.

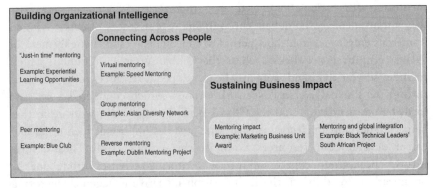

Figure 1-2 IBM's mentoring portfolio.

IBM's methodology reflects a strategic approach to mentoring that moves away from the traditional single role or person as "mentor" paired with one or more junior "protégés" and toward an understanding of the various benefits that a diverse portfolio of mentoring tools and techniques can offer. Building a mentoring portfolio means that the right mentoring solution can be applied to meet the specific needs or opportunities of the organization, employees, and other key stakeholders. IBM's portfolio approach also links its diverse array of formal and informal mentoring programs to key strategic objectives of the firm, as depicted in Figure 1-2. The synergy created by matching mentoring solutions to strategic objectives of the firm is both essential and innovative. Thus, throughout the chapters of this book, we highlight various examples of IBM's approach to mentoring and discuss how it supports critical components of the company's global business strategy. While each example has been developed out of a series of trial-and-error efforts for IBM, they all represent a unique approach to mentoring that can help any organization attract, retain, and develop its most important asset—people.

Creating a Mentoring Portfolio

While IBM has built a portfolio of mentoring activities, traditional forms of mentoring are still part of this innovative mixture. There is some disagreement on the effectiveness of most formal mentoring programs.[28] Key issues of debate include clarity of mentoring goals and objectives, access to mentoring relationships across different functional and expertise areas, and employee input into the matching process. Based on IBM's internal benchmarking, similar issues were also identified. Access to information in a "just-in-time" manner, employees being able to gain critical knowledge, and support to develop important competencies that are transferrable across business units also emerged. Early on, one of the ways IBM intended to reach its strategic objective of creating organizational intelligence was to capitalize on its Experiential Learning Opportunities Portfolio described in Chapter 2, "Organizational Intelligence: Using Just-in-Time Mentoring Solutions." The Experiential Learning Portfolio uses a web-based and cross-functional approach to traditional mentoring, yet provides employees with global experiential developmental opportunities, such as stretch assignments, cross-unit projects, job shadowing activities, and a host of other features that are typically found in traditional mentoring programs. However, the access to and sharing of knowledge about mentoring activities was vastly increased because of the Experiential Learning Opportunities initiative. It provides a mechanism for employees to develop critical and transferable skills because they can access existing and emerging developmental opportunities and mentoring on a global basis.

The ways in which mentoring is developed within IBM is evidence of the importance the organization places on developing communities of knowledge worldwide to support and sustain organizational intelligence. For example,

IBM's Latin American team developed the Blue Club Mentoring program, which was born out of frustration, feelings of isolation, and workplace stress articulated by new and less experienced managers within this region. Chapter 3, "Organizational Intelligence: Fostering Communities of Knowledge," focuses on how Blue Club involves a "high-touch" approach to mentoring that provides support, information, and resources to up-line managers for use in mentoring sessions with new and less experienced managers. Especially within cultures that do not acknowledge a separation of professional and personal lives,[29] the need to provide career and social support within a community or via group mentoring is important as people try to balance the demands of a highly competitive and rapidly changing work environment with the dual demands of their family and nonwork lives. As you will see from the Blue Club example, these types of "high-touch" mentoring relationships may take longer to develop but can help to support a company's strategic objectives, such as IBM's focus on building trust within its global business enterprise.

An imperative for IBM's mentoring portfolio is to focus on how to build connections across people and across geographies. As a cutting-edge technology company, the use of virtual solutions to solve critical organizational challenges was part of the normal business process. As a result, IBM launched several virtual mentoring efforts to provide broad access to knowledge on a just-in-time basis. One example is the unique approach called "speed mentoring" discussed in Chapter 4, "Connecting People: Creating Meaningful Engagement." This concept was developed within one unit and then expanded across the organization as a way of providing broad access to people, ideas, and solutions. Speed mentoring utilizes virtual group mentoring for problem-specific assistance, socialization of relatively new employees, or the sharing of vital information on current or emergent topics. As you will see, speed mentoring allows many people to gain access to information, connect with organizational experts, and develop their expertise by linking to these knowledge resources within a fast-paced, technology-enhanced environment.

Helping to strengthen and build connections across people involves mentoring activities that provide a wide variety of career as well as social and emotional support. In Chapter 5, "Connecting People: Mentoring as a Tool for Diversity and Inclusion," we highlight the work of the Asian Diversity Network Group (ADNG), located at IBM Austin, Texas, that began mentoring employees in the United States and then expanded to mentoring new employees in the China Development and Research Labs. The ADNG is one of various Diversity Network Groups (DNG) within IBM that provides support for the expanding and diverse employee segments throughout the organization. Ron Glover, VP Global Workforce Diversity, described these networks as IBM's "Diversity Army"; the network also includes the Women's Subnet, where women of all levels and functions mentor each other and provide support. These various networks or affinity groups provide critical support for employees who may otherwise feel disconnected from the overall organization, or who work in remote or developing locations that may produce feelings of isolation.

In addition to the affinity group mentoring efforts, reverse mentoring is also part of IBM's mentoring portfolio. As discussed in Chapter 6, "Connecting People: Using Mentoring to Signal Value in People," most people think of mentoring only as a more "experienced" or senior-level person providing advice or expert knowledge to a more junior or younger person. The reverse mentoring effort within IBM involves a type of role reversal, whereby a senior-level person is actually mentored by a junior-level employee, usually one who is new to IBM—somewhere between a recent graduate and an employee with two years' tenure or less. This example provides IBM with a better understanding of how mentoring not only helps to build relationships, but is also a powerful tool for knowledge transfer across generations throughout the organization. To build a culture of collaboration and innovation, knowledge must be shared across traditional boundaries such as functional unit, as well as location and demographic categories, such as generational diversity. The reverse mentoring effort within IBM provides a useful example of one approach for cutting across the boundaries that block the development and transfer of critical knowledge, and for supporting employee as well as organizational outcomes.

While mentoring can be successful in helping to address specific needs of the organization, a critical part of its success is sustaining the business impact of these efforts. While most organizations have broad reward and recognition programs, the marketing business unit within IBM combined mentoring and employee recognition to help support the exposure and visibility of employees within the group and provide critical metrics on its impact. In conjunction with its more traditional formal mentoring program, the marketing group developed a mentoring award and recognition program. Not only do individuals receive recognition for their functional knowledge or job-specific performance, but also the mentoring award helps to provide visible reinforcement and endorsement of these mentoring efforts as a valuable part of the business unit. As we discuss in Chapter 7, "Business Impact: Using Mentoring to Deliver Value for Competitive Advantage," this effort has led to some innovative approaches for sustaining the mentoring effort within the marketing group.

In Chapter 8, "Business Impact: Using Mentoring Solutions to Solve 'Wicked Problems,'" we discuss an initial pilot program that matched high-potential employees in South Africa with technical leaders and business executives in the United States for one-on-one mentoring relationships, along with monthly modules that covered global leadership competencies and critical business topics. The concept of this cross-geography program has been expanded to include the pairing of employees in different parts of China and India to technical leaders in mature organizations in the United Kingdom, United States, and Canada. In addition, the Black Technical Leaders Forum (BTLF) was created out of a need for technical leaders to support the socialization, development, and connection of new and less experienced black technical employees throughout the organization. While initial concerns focused on retention of this diverse talent segment, the BTLF initiative developed a model that has been leveraged by other diverse constituencies within IBM's global business enterprise. We use both of these innovative examples to discuss how mentoring can be integrated across the entire value chain of the organization. The activities of the BTLF and the use of mentoring as part of IBM's South African expansion are powerful examples of how effective mentoring can help to address current issues faced by the organization and can also be integrated into emerging opportunities worldwide.

Each of these examples is provided within the context of the mentoring tools, techniques, and strategies that make them a good fit for the overall business model within IBM. Together with new and emerging research on mentoring, we focus each chapter on how mentoring can provide solutions to critical business challenges and help leverage emerging business opportunities. Sharing the knowledge gained by the IBM mentoring experience yields a wide range of potential contributions detailed throughout the chapters of this book.

Contributions of *Intelligent Mentoring*

As we discuss in more detail throughout the book, the contribution of this diverse portfolio of mentoring initiatives is that it taps into different approaches and forms of mentoring in a way that helps to sustain the business impact. Early success is shown by worldwide requests to assist and guide in the development of local mentoring programs. Data was also collected from evaluations of mentoring panel discussions, webcasts, speaking engagements, and "jam sessions" and shows that high satisfaction levels are being sustained. Participant evaluations show that IBM's mentoring initiative also has measurable human capital results. Employee feedback indicates that employees are expanding their search for mentoring outside of their business units and geographies to gain diverse skills, experience, perspectives, and knowledge. Mentoring is helping employees find new ways to connect and build their abilities and productivity. The mentoring program continues to receive unsolicited positive feedback. Hits to the Mentoring Web site are up 12% over last year, and the Explore Mentoring Web site has had nearly 132,000 discrete hits since its launch. Mentoring contributed to a 5% increase in 2006 over 2005 on favorable responses to an internal employee survey data question, "Do you have the opportunity to improve skills?" Lastly, a companywide formative evaluation survey was developed to determine the broader range of the mentoring initiative's ongoing impact. All of these are positive early signs of the potential long-term impact that this mentoring portfolio will have on IBM's global business enterprise.

However, as we discuss later, the most significant impact of the mentoring initiative is yet to be realized, as mentoring is helping employees practice and adopt their IBM Values through Collaboration by making learning a strategic priority. The long-term goal is for mentoring activities to instill a sense of value among employees that supports positive morale and excitement around learning and innovation. In addition, the goal of the mentoring initiatives throughout IBM is to develop and share what is known as **deep smarts**.[30] Deep smarts are all about tacit qualities such as culture competence, emotional intelligence, and organizational competence, which are vital for leadership and innovation within the twenty-first century. One long-term goal of the mentoring relationships across IBM is to demonstrate that these types of deep smarts require that employees stay with a company to fully develop their expertise. The commitment to mentoring at IBM must be sustained over time to see the true benefits of this strategic approach in developing this type of knowledge. For IBM, mentoring is not a "quick fix." It is part of an overall strategy to reshape and revitalize the organization for not only short-term recruitment and retention goals, but also for long-term learning and innovation priorities. Thus, we will see that an important long-term aspiration for IBM's mentoring initiatives is to build organizational intelligence and a culture of collaboration.

In addition to developing the learning capacity and deep smarts throughout the organization, another critical long-term goal is to reshape the culture at IBM. In *Why Innovation Matters to IBM*, the "management and culture of innovation" is identified as necessary for creativity. "Advanced technology plus collaboration make it possible," as it is stated in the document. The goal is to build a collaborative culture that helps employees and business partners to co-produce innovation. However, what must come first is an environment that actively promotes collaboration. And that's exactly what knowledge management experts recommend to reverse the loss of deep smarts. They suggest that work must become a dual-purpose project that includes the opportunity for new employees to absorb the tacit knowledge and explicit skills that could easily exit a company forever, as well as for experienced employees to develop, utilize, and share their knowledge in diverse collaborations throughout the organization. As you will see from the best practice examples provided throughout the book, mentoring at IBM is being strategically used to assist the transfer of business skills, support ongoing leadership development, and create a collaborative culture. While traditional mentoring still holds enormous value, an essential end goal for IBM is the creation of this collaborative *culture,* which is being facilitated by a wide variety of different mentoring activities. The hope is that in the future IBM environment, the sentiment by a majority of employees will be that "I am responsible for your—and my—learning" as one indicator of this culture of collaboration.

When writing this book, we wanted to understand more about the complex nature of mentoring relationships and to strike a balance between mentoring research and real-world application. As Kathy Kram and Belle Ragins write, "Mentoring research needs to inform and be informed by mentoring practice."[31] Unfortunately, there is often a disconnection between the research on mentoring and the practice of mentoring. Frequently, books are published that offer a "practical guide" for mentoring without being informed by the state-of-the-art research that provides the evidence of how mentoring activities can be effectively designed, implemented, and evaluated. On the other hand, research on mentoring is often conducted outside of the industry, organizational, or cultural context that is known to have a profound impact on these types of efforts. Our goal and contribution of this book is to accomplish both without sacrifice to either research or practice.

Thus, the chapters within this book seek to address this critical gap. Research on mentoring must be shaped by the reality of mentoring practice, and practice must be grounded in rigorous research. Thus, we explore the various ways that IBM is leveraging existing knowledge and research on mentoring to shape and sustain its strategic efforts toward organizational intelligence, connecting people, and having a business impact. Our attempt is to focus on the interface between research and practice on mentoring, using the successes and challenges faced by IBM's mentoring initiatives as one piece to solving its long-term strategic puzzle. By sharing the IBM experience, we provide an in-depth look into one organization's journey from a large global enterprise trying to better connect "virtually dispersed" people who once felt isolated and disconnected and, at the same time, keep pace with a rapidly changing technology industry. We attempt to capture how IBM used mentoring to transform its organization from a place where employees referred to IBM as meaning "I'm By Myself" into IBM as meaning "I'm Being *Mentored.*" Our hope is that the story of the successes and challenges of IBM as outlined in the following chapters will provide a catalyst for all types of organizations to revitalize and expand their use of mentoring as a strategic tool for the recruitment, retention, and engagement of a diverse and talented workforce that continually adds value to the organization across its worldwide enterprise.

References

[1] Allen, T.D., Eby, L.T., Poteet. M.L., Lentz, E. and Lima, L. (2004). Career benefits associated with mentoring for protégés: A meta-analysis. *Journal of Applied Psychology, 89,* 127–136.

[2] CCH HR Management Web site: http://hr.cch.com.

[3] Clutterbuck, D. and Ragins, B.R. 2002. *Mentoring and Diversity: An International Perspective.* Oxford: Butterworth-Heinemann.

[4] Ragins, B.R. and Cotton, J.L. (1999). Mentor functions and outcomes: A comparison of men and women in formal and informal mentoring relationships. *Journal of Applied Psychology, 84,* 529–550.

[5] Palmisano, Samuel J. (2006, October). Leadership, Trust and the Globally Integrated Enterprise. Text from speech given at INSEAD.

[6] Kram, K.E. (1985). *Mentoring at Work: Developmental Relationships in Organizational Life.* Glenview, IL: Scott-Foresman and Company.

[7] Rousseau, D.M. and Schalk, R. (2000). *Psychological Contract in Employment: Cross-national Perspectives.* Newbury Park: Sage.

[8] DiMaggio, P. (2001). *The Twenty-first Century Firm: Changing Economic Organization in International Perspective.* Princeton, NJ: Princeton University Press.

[9] Friedman, Thomas L. (2004). *The World Is Flat: A Brief History of the Twenty-First Century* Farrar, Straus and Giroux; Sommer, R.D. (2000). Retaining intellectual capital in the 21st Century; Arthur, M.B. and Rousseau, D.M. (1996). *The Boundaryless Career: A New Employment Principle for a New Organizational Era.* New York: Oxford University Press.

10 Aiman-Smith, Lynda, Paul Bergey, et al. (2006, July/August). The Coming Knowledge and Capability Shortage. *Research Technology Management.*

11 Arthur, M.B., and Rousseau, D.M. (1996). Introduction: The boundaryless career as a new employment principle. In M.B. Arthur and D.M. Rousseau (Eds.), *The Boundaryless Career* (pp. 3–20). New York: Oxford.

12 Higgins, M.C., and Kram, K.E. (2001). Reconceptualizing mentoring at work: A developmental network perspective. *Academy of Management Review, 26,* 264–298.

13 Ragins, B.R. and Kram, K.E. (2007). *Handbook of Mentoring at Work.* Thousand Oaks, CA: Sage Publications.

14 Fishman, C. (1998). The war for talent. *Fast Company, 18,* 104–105.

15 *BusinessWeek,* April 2007.

16 Kiger, Patrick (2002, June). How Deloitte builds global expertise: How to redesign and market a global professional development program. *Workforce Magazine.*

17 Corporate Leavers Survey. (2007). Retrieved from www.lpfi.org/docs/cl-executive-summary.pdf.

18 Tulgan, Bruce. (1997). Managing Generation X. *Employment Management Today,* Winter, 22–26.

19 Deal, J.J. (2007). *Retiring the Generation Gap: How Employees Young and Old Can Find Common Ground.* San Francisco, CA: John Wiley & Sons.

20 Howe, N. and Strauss, W. (2000). *Millennials Rising.* New York: Vintage Books.

21 Rousseau, D.M. (1995). *Psychological Contracts in Organizations: Understanding Written and Unwritten Agreements.* Newbury Park, CA: Sage.

22 Santosus, M. (2003, August). Here in body only. *CIO Magazine.* Retrieved from www.cio.com/archive/081503/reality.html; Earls, A. R. (1998, February 9). Retention deficit lessons. *ComputerWorld.* Retrieved from www.computerworld.com/news/1998/story/ 0,11280,29775,00.html.

23 Interpersonal Technology Group, Inc. (2003). Managing for the retention of IT professionals (Workshop description). Retrieved from www.InterpersonalTechnology Group.com.

24 Josefek, R., Jr., and Kauffman, R. (2000, June). IT human capital at work: The information systems professional's decision to leave the firm. Retrieved from http://misrc.umn.edu/ workingpapers/fullPapers/2002/0218_010103.pdf.

25 Thibodeau, P. (2001, January 15). Survey: Above all else, IT workers need challenge. *ComputerWorld.* Retrieved from www.computerworld.com/printthis/2001/ 0,4814,56335,00.html; Wingreen, S. (2000, December). *Theoretical Model of Training Factors for IT Professionals.* Unpublished thesis, University of South Florida, Tampa, Florida.

26 Paré, G. and Tremblay, M. (2000, September). The measurement and antecedents of turnover intentions among IT professionals. In *Cirano Scientific Series* (pp. 1–5). Montreal, Canada: Ecole des Hautes Etudes Commerciales.

[27] Agarwal, R., and Ferratt, T. (2002, September). Enduring practices for managing IT professionals. Communications of the ACM, 45, 73; Agarwal, R., and Ferratt, T. (1999). Coping with labor scarcity in information technology. Cincinnati, Ohio: Pinnaflex Educational Resources; Watson, S. (2001, June 11). Building careers, not just jobs. *ComputerWorld*. Retrieved from www.computerworld.com/printthis/2001/0,4814,61217,00.html.

[28] Allen, T.D., Eby, L.T., and Lentz, E. (2006). Mentorship behaviors and mentorship quality associated with formal mentoring programs: Closing the gap between research and practices. *Journal of Applied Psychology*, 91(3), 567–578.

[29] Lynnes, K.S. and Thompson, D.E. (2000). Climbing the corporate ladder: Do female and male executives follow the same route? *Journal of Applied Psychology*, 85(1), 86–101.

[30] Fisher, Anne. (2005). How to Battle the Coming Brain Drain. *Fortune*, 151(6), 121–128; Gary, Loren. (2005, August). Build Your Company's Deep Smarts. *Harvard Management Update*, pp. 3–5; Leonard, Dorothy, and Walter Swap. (2005). Ten Years to Deep Smarts, *Across the Board*, 42(4), 12–13.

[31] Ragins, B.R. and Kram, K.E. (2007). *Handbook of Mentoring at Work*. Thousand Oaks, CA: Sage Publications.

2

Organizational Intelligence: Using Just-in-Time Mentoring Solutions

Chapter Contents

Overview: Revitalizing Mentoring

Within IBM and similar global organizations, a key priority must be to build organizational intelligence and abilities. Organizational intelligence is characterized as the ability to cultivate an arsenal of skills and competencies that can address current needs and at the same time engage in continuous development of new skills. Strategic forecasting and projections help to foster a climate of readiness to solve business problems quickly and deliver solutions to clients. As future needs are determined, actions must be undertaken to continually develop all members of the organization, especially those who demonstrate the ability to acquire new competencies quickly. An intelligent organization must recognize that skills may become obsolete much more quickly than new ones can be built, and efforts must be made to employ multiple means of rapidly cultivating new knowledge and skills among all employee segments.

To develop and sustain organizational intelligence, IBM was challenged to rethink its existing formal or organization-sponsored activities and efforts. Looking at its existing mentoring efforts revealed several challenges in terms of enhancing and supporting organizational intelligence abilities throughout the organization. Internal benchmark and focus group data indicated that some employees were not aware of how mentoring was structured or supported within their own unit or across the global business enterprise. Thus, many of the efforts to offer formal support for the development of mentoring relationships were underutilized and thus formal mentoring across the organization was seen as ineffective or unavailable. A key question that remained is what role should IBM play in developing and supporting formal mentoring to help cultivate and sustain organizational intelligence throughout the organization?

Within the existing research, there is little consensus on the overall effectiveness of formal mentoring, especially when directly compared to informal mentoring. Some researchers argue that while formal mentoring is better than no mentoring at all, informal mentoring is most effective.[1] Others point to key dimensions of effective mentoring relationships that are important across both formal and informal efforts. Despite lingering questions, issues of quality of relationships, accessibility of information, frequency of interaction, and clarity of purpose are a few of the factors that have been acknowledged as being important for effective formal, as well as informal, mentoring relationships.[2] Thus, the key issue for IBM was how to address the need to develop

organizational intelligence, yet avoid the potential limitations of organization-sponsored formal mentoring programs.

To address broad issues of employee development, IBM uses a blended and
distributed approach to help employees develop new skills and build organizational intelligence. The IBM Global Business Service's Human Capital
Study noted that "Given how quickly new skills need to be acquired, companies relying on resource-intensive learning strategies, such as classroom
instruction and on-the-job training, may find themselves struggling to keep
up with demand. Blended learning programs that balance the strengths of
distributed learning technologies with opportunities for face-to-face engagement will play an increasingly important role in building the workforce of
the future."[3] Ranging from a combination of traditional classroom training,
to e-learning, rotational assignments, shadow experiences, and so on, the idea
quickly emerged to attempt the same blended learning approach to define
IBM's mentoring solutions. In addition to addressing some of the limitations
of formal mentoring, this approach fit well within the existing toolbox that
IBM uses for supporting employee development and building organizational
intelligence.

In this chapter, we describe how IBM's revitalization of mentoring supported the Experiential Learning Opportunities Portfolio approach through
tacit learning options such as job shadowing, as well as temporary, rotational,
and stretch assignments. The Experiential Learning Portfolio is an employee-
driven, technology-based, and multi-usage platform that allows managers to
post mentoring opportunities to increase access to and visibility for the IBM
initiative. With the revitalization effort and its launch of the Experiential
Learning initiative, IBM emphasized the importance of practical learning
throughout the organization and signaled to its employees that the firm
placed a high premium on employees sharing their knowledge as a means of
developing new skills and capabilities.

An important component of revitalizing mentoring throughout IBM
includes initiatives that provide a hybrid between formal and informal mentoring that is geared toward overcoming some of the limitations of either type
of mentoring effort. This hybrid approach to mentoring is conducted through
a range of tools that enhance access to mentoring relationships, provide critical information, and support the ongoing cultivation of formal and informal
mentoring relationships within a "just-in-time" delivery system. The key lesson from this revitalization effort is that the need for organizational intelligence required that IBM take a unique approach to mentoring that could

leverage the benefits of both formal and informal mentoring relationships within a system that provides broad access and high visibility. Its hybrid approach, as discussed in this chapter, provides an interesting illustration for how innovative mentoring techniques can be used to support and develop organizational intelligence abilities within global companies like IBM.

Creating a Mentoring Hybrid

The existing research on the advantages and disadvantages of formal versus informal mentoring programs is inconsistent and incomplete. Much of the knowledge on the differences between these two structures focuses only on the needs and outcomes for the mentees, or protégés, and does not include measures for the mentors or assess key organizational outcomes.[4] Some argue that while formal mentoring is better than no mentoring at all, informal mentoring relationships are superior to those sponsored and structured by formal organizational efforts.[5] This sentiment was reflected in an assessment of why "mentoring doesn't work." Anderson argues that, "For mentoring to deliver real value, it has to take place regularly and have clearly defined expectations" (p. 3).[6] However, she also notes that, "obtaining support throughout the organization for a mentoring program is crucial" (p. 5). Thus, a critical question for IBM became how to structure a revitalized mentoring effort that showed support for mentoring, allowed employees to participate and share ownership in the effort, but still had structure and clearly defined goals. Its efforts must overcome the limitations that existing research pointed to as the flaws in traditional one-on-one formal mentoring, such as mentor-protégé mismatch, lack of resources/support, interpersonal conflict, and barriers to relationship separation.[7] On the other hand, there were some noted benefits of formal mentoring, such as socialization of new employees, early identification of talent, support for leadership development, improved organizational communication, and enhancement of diversity.[8]

Based on the existing research, several factors emerged that influenced the choice made by IBM in its mentoring revitalization efforts. For example, recent research by Allen and her colleagues examined key design features of formal mentoring programs across a number of different organizations that sponsored various initiatives. Their findings point to the importance of employee input into the mentoring process, along with high quality and easily accessible training as two significant factors for the impact of these formal mentoring programs.[9] Thus, to ensure overall effectiveness, enhance clarity of purpose, and signal organizational support, aspects of formal mentoring had to be included in any revitalization effort. However, flexibility in connecting with various mentoring relationships, particularly outside of the employee's own unit, together with allowing the employee to have input and drive the efforts were also key factors identified by prior research. Interestingly, these latter characteristics are typically associated with informal mentoring relationships. Lastly, the need to have access to information about mentoring effectiveness, tools for solving problems, and techniques to address negative mentoring experiences when they arose were also important features. to include.

For IBM, it seemed that neither a traditional formal mentoring approach nor a standard informal mentoring structure would accomplish all of these critical goals. Thus, a blended, or hybrid, approach to mentoring was created that allowed for a balance between a formal support structure and fluid employee involvement, together with an open and accessible technology-driven infrastructure. This blended approach not only fit well within the overall culture and design of employee development activities at IBM, but also provided just-in-time mentoring solutions for employees and managers that could be linked to the overall goal of strengthening organizational intelligence.

IBM Revitalizes Mentoring

Based in part on the company's own experience as well as lessons learned from research, efforts were undertaken to revitalize and re-energize mentoring activities within IBM. Involving employees early in the revitalization process was a key strategy that IBM used to garner support and enlist employee involvement in the mentoring program. A principal rule that IBM used as its guide in the mentoring revitalization process was to get input from employees on what would make mentoring work for them in their development and growth, ways to simplify the mentoring process, and what the business needs to do to create tools to facilitate mentoring connections across the company. To a great extent, the mentoring revitalization process was constructed with employee input, which appears to be the platform upon which this effort gained traction. It allowed IBM to construct a formal mentoring program that had many of the key benefits or advantages of informal mentoring efforts, such as being accessible and employee-driven.

Using feedback and input from employees also allowed the revitalization effort to be developed in a way that signaled the importance of mentoring within the organization. While many programs view mentoring from a theoretical position, IBM's approach is a very practical one. In response to the findings from various employee focus groups, the decision was made to make mentoring a principal component within the activities of employee career development. A primary goal of mentoring in IBM is to transfer knowledge and build organizational intelligence. As IBM started its efforts to reinvent its mentoring program, some people got distracted by the use of varying terminologies to describe the complexity of organizational intelligence. It was, therefore, determined that time would be better spent helping employees realize the power of mentoring in gaining new knowledge, rather than trying to define complex terminologies that may not be visibly tied to immediate work outcomes. Specifying the goals and the process also addressed one of the key limitations noted with formal mentoring efforts. Furthermore, it provided the catalyst for employees to focus their attention on how to make mentoring work for them in building their abilities and ultimately, the capability of the organization.

Prior to the creation of IBM's hybrid mentoring program, the company discovered that it lacked a formal way to structure experiential learning systematically and consistently across its global business, or incorporate it into employee development plans. For example, past attempts to provide a framework for experiential learning activities happened in silos and inconsistently across the business. During one of IBM's regular Global Pulse Surveys, issues related to mentoring and employee development were identified as one of the top focus areas for the organization. However, IBM's size, complexity, and global scale created several challenges. First, it had a history of prior attempts at corporatewide programs like job rotation and exchange programs that had been less than successful based on employee feedback. Second, there was a need to pull limited resources from the HR unit, but at the same time access untapped resources, such as the availability of enterprisewide IT solutions. Third, there was a need to reduce the perceived incapability of short-term business unit goals (for example, billable utilization) with long-term employee development. Lastly, the need for employees to perceive executive and line management support for mentoring and employee development was significant.

Thus, IBM embarked on a three-year project to revitalize its mentoring and employee development processes. Many initiatives were launched to address the issues that were identified through the focus groups, thus making mentoring at IBM a practical and more viable tool for knowledge transfer and career development. As a cornerstone of these efforts, the Experiential Learning Portfolio evolved into a solution that is perfectly aligned with the objectives of the business to move in the direction of increased practical and tacit learning. As IBM revitalizes its mentoring program, one of the goals has been to align these efforts with its overall Global Business Model (as discussed in Chapter 1, "Introducing IBM's Mentoring Portfolio"). As part of this revitalization, expert mentors from mature organizations are linked with employees across various business units and around the globe, especially those employees who are in emerging countries. To expand these efforts, mentoring programs have now been developed between China and the United States; employees in India have been connected with mentors in the United States, United Kingdom, and Canada; and employees in South Africa have been matched with executive leaders in the United States. These are just a few examples of using mentoring to link people who are located throughout IBM's global business enterprise with the purpose of providing them with ongoing learning opportunities. We discuss these efforts toward global integration in more detail in Chapters 7, "Business Impact: Using Mentoring to Deliver Value for Competitive Advantage," and 8, "Business Impact: Using Mentoring Solutions to Solve 'Wicked Problems.'"

Because IBM is particularly sensitive to the fact that high-performing employees thrive on constant intellectual stimulation and assignments that stretch their imagination, the mentoring revitalization efforts also had to be a key driver of organizational intelligence. In the absence of challenging assignments and mental growth opportunities, high-performing employees run the risk of experiencing career derailment, developing a feeling of being underutilized, and becoming unmotivated or disengaged.[10] A major contributor to organizational intelligence is the use of mentoring to support talent retention and at the same time address the learning needs of the employees within the business unit. It has been determined that the unmet needs and perceived lack of opportunities among high-performing employees is a recipe for talent flight. Thus, a principal arsenal in the retention of talent is to give employees the assurance that they are supported and that their development is critical to business success.

To emphasize the need for this systematic approach, Sam Palmisano, Chairman and CEO of IBM, declared that "We have to unleash our people's creative energy, trust them and empower them to get everyone working together in a way that is consistent to IBM's brand promise." What this means is that as the company provides tools and resources to enable the acquisition of new skills to bridge expertise gaps, employees must work together in a collaborative and meaningful manner. Bridging skills gaps cannot be done in isolation or in a vacuum. Further, employees are expected to demonstrate professional responsibility and accountability to use the resources and support that are available to them. As an illustration, IBM has multiple tools to help employees to self-select mentors who have the right set of skills to address their specific needs. Employees are trusted to define what benefits they want to gain personally and professionally from these mentoring relationships. Thus, a core objective of the revitalization effort was to strengthen the link between mentoring and organizational intelligence throughout the organization.

Linking Mentoring to Organizational Intelligence

Developing organizational intelligence is not just a matter of mere business survival; it is about having the capacity and capability to develop a portfolio of skills that is relevant, always current, and diverse. Striving toward this goal helps any business to compete effectively within the global marketplace.[11] As a company designs its plan to manage its human capital and knowledge base, it has to be diligent in defining the skills needed both for the present time and for the future. If the company is multinational, it has to be mindful of the varying skills needed across different countries and cultures.[12] For example, the "hot" skills in the United States may not be the hot skills in Asia at a given moment, based on product, service mission, competition, and local market needs. This underscores the point that organizational intelligence can be attained through the proper forecasting of skills needs, based on mission, product set, and service delivery, as well as changing and diverse client needs. So the key question within IBM's mentoring revitalization efforts is how does this approach help to support and enhance building organizational intelligence and capacity?

The meaning of organizational intelligence can be easily left up to differing interpretations and as a result, it is necessary to offer a definition of what it means within the current context. We define organizational intelligence as an assessment and forecasting of skills and competencies that an organization requires to do both current and future work effectively.[13] All members of the organization are given adequate tools, resources, support, guidance, and opportunities to acquire these requisite skills. As employees gain new skills, they must be given the latitude to creatively apply them. As employees build new knowledge and expertise, leaders must encourage calculated risk-taking.[14] Allowing employees to flex their intellectual muscles is a way to create enthusiasm about learning and the development of new ideas but requires allowing some element of risk-taking in applying these ideas. Leaders in this environment must expect that, from time to time, some of these untested but creative ideas may not yield the desired or short-term outcomes. Should this happen, managers must refrain from creating a punitive environment, which often results in a risk-aversion culture and which can depress creativity and innovation, both building blocks of organizational intelligence. Instead, the leaders and managers in the organization should leverage suboptimal outcomes as an opportunity to learn, examine the reasons the approach did not yield the desired outcome, and outline strategies for change in the future.

Thus, building organizational intelligence requires what Capelli calls a "market-driven approach" to talent management.[15] This means that companies must make a concerted effort to foster a culture of knowledge sharing and collaboration and design a practical approach to make this happen, from recruitment to socialization to retention.[16] There are certain behaviors that must be discouraged as the organization sets the stage to develop its knowledge base. For example, employees must be discouraged from relying solely on the set of current skills that they possess. Instead, they should be encouraged to constantly seek opportunities to grasp new knowledge that has importance to the organization. As employees acquire new knowledge, it is important to hold them accountable to not only apply their knowledge in practical and creative ways on the job but also to share their experiences and make it a priority to document these experiences.[17] Building a knowledge repository is an essential method for capturing and preserving important information. Documentation is critical in building knowledge repositories and should become part of the knowledge management process.[18] Each of these factors points to an essential component in IBM's just-in-time mentoring solution. Thus, we identified four essential areas where mentoring solutions were used to develop and support organizational intelligence throughout the IBM organization: attracting and recruiting new talent, socializing of new hires, accessing knowledge and expertise, and supporting knowledge retention.

Attracting and Recruiting Talent

Attracting the right skills into a business is a major component of the knowledge management strategy and the efforts to create organizational intelligence. Because the war for talent is so different today from what we have seen in the past, having a workforce goal that makes continuous learning a priority can provide a competitive advantage.[19] There has been a dramatic shift in how companies look at the recruitment of talent. Clearly, recruitment plays an extremely important role in the talent management process of an organization. The trend today is that recruits are interviewing companies just as companies are interviewing them, making this a competitive environment for individuals with skills and talents within the global marketplace. Some data suggest that companies with the most opportunities for growth and development, along with flexibility programs, strong diversity initiatives, and ample reward and recognition systems, are competitive within the demand for talented employees.[20] Thus, recruitment is a dynamic process such that companies must not become complacent after a person accepts their job offer; they must deliver on their promise to offer continuous learning opportunities and ongoing support for employee-driven growth and development options.

Some existing research has documented the importance of having an organization-sponsored mentoring effort in place as part of the successful recruitment of new talent.[21] As organizations engage in attracting talent, prospective employees are interested to know that the organization will be able to stimulate them intellectually and that there are ample opportunities to learn from others through a strong mentoring program. As new employees enter the business, they are encouraged to learn and quickly adjust because of the support that they are offered by their colleagues. As discussed later, having an organization-sponsored mentoring effort in place also assists in the successful socialization of new employees.

As part of using mentoring as a strategic resource for recruitment, firms like IBM are paying attention to the changing demographics of the workforce and how these trends impact its capability to attract the next generations of talent. Organizations must develop initiatives and processes to attract different employee populations that exist and are increasingly mobile in the workforce. Those organizations that can develop a diverse array of recruitment strategies for the purpose of learning in a collaborative environment should be more successful in recruiting this diverse talent. Through the use of both formal and informal mentoring activities, the energy and insights of the new entrants in the workforce can be matched with the skills and knowledge of the experienced worker. These early relationships help to strengthen recruiting efforts and can be a key factor in the successful socialization of these employees once they are hired.[22]

Thus, within its just-in-time approach, IBM's mentoring revitalization efforts were designed to be used across the entire talent development process and do not end when new employees have been identified and successfully recruited into the organization. A complementary focus was to define mentoring activities that not only help to attract potential new hires but also help new hires quickly become adept at operating within the IBM culture. When a person joins a company, the recruiting process does not end but rather transitions into ongoing socialization and the development of commitment and engagement. If companies fail to deliver on their recruiting promises, this may have an early impact on socialization and, later on, retention. A company's retention issues can begin as early as the hiring and selection process if assurance is not given that the company will truly follow through on its commitments.[23] If new hires observe that the culture does not promote continuous learning and provide opportunities for growth, it is likely that they will begin to question their decision about joining the company. Through its hybrid approach to mentoring that is linked to building organizational intelligence, IBM attempts to create a seamless array of mentoring solutions that begins with talent recruitment and continues with the socialization of new hires.

Socializing of Employees

The socialization of new employees, whether they are new to full-time work or experienced workers, is a critical endeavor for any organization. One study reported that 35% of employees who do not receive mentoring opportunities seek other employers within 12 months of their initial hiring, compared to 16% for those who were provided with early mentoring.[24] Within IBM, the early socialization of new hires, also known as on-boarding is the process of integrating and orienting new hires into the workplace. This process includes traditional activities such as exposure to career development tools and resources, policies and practices, strategy of the department and how they are linked to the overall IBM strategy. New hires also learn about the business in a formal educational experience called Your IBM. As part of the mentoring revitalization effort, information and mentoring opportunities were integrated into the on-boarding process. Along with the dedicated Your IBM classes, business units began to offer new hires mentoring opportunities to help them become orientated to the business operations and organizational culture. The data on recruitment and retention of new hires made it clear that IBM and firms like it should use mentoring solutions to give new hires immediate support, critical information, and access to resources that enable them to be successful.

By developing connections with senior and peer members of the organization on a formal and informal basis, efforts such as the connection coach, buddy pairings, and group mentoring programs were implemented to provide support to new hires. This mentoring practice is not limited to the new hires that come to IBM through the normal recruiting process, it is also applied to those employees who join IBM by way of mergers and acquisitions. The goal of integrating mentoring within the on-boarding process was to facilitate socialization as employees learn how to navigate within the IBM workplace culture. These types of mentoring practices help new employees understand both the spoken and unspoken rules and protocols of the organization. These mentoring activities also help employees develop key relationships that can be the source of support, advice, and important knowledge throughout their time in the organization. Clearly, understanding the protocols, culture, and the acceptable code of conduct helps to shorten the adjustment period for any new employee. The more rapidly people become socialized into the culture and process within an organization, the more likely they will stay within the organization, and some suggest this early socialization also has a positive impact on overall performance.[25]

While an organization may be successful in recruitment and early socialization, efforts to attract talented employees must also be connected to efforts to equip and retain these employees. Companies have to understand and appropriately respond to the ongoing needs of all their employees, regardless of tenure in the business. Because many dimensions of diversity co-exist in today's workforce, a one-size-fits-all approach is ineffective in addressing the developmental needs of employees. Thus, IBM has taken steps to design a menu approach to mentoring that fits together with its ongoing career development efforts. In essence, key developmental programs such as mentoring can be tailored to meet the unique needs of the different segments of the employees within its global workforce. In addition, these mentoring efforts are designed to pick up where recruitment and early socialization efforts leave off—by helping employees gain access to the knowledge and expertise that is available throughout its organization.

Accessing Knowledge and Expertise

Organizations must be proactive and strategic in their efforts to capture, harness, and transfer knowledge and experience from all segments of employees, thus developing its learning capacity as a core component to sustaining organizational intelligence.[26] Intelligent organizations are always looking for ways to identify and support experts throughout their organization and then share this knowledge across the broader organization.[27] Connecting employees with expert knowledge, especially early in the socialization process, is important for retention as well as enhancing role clarity and commitment.[28] However, the pertinent question to ask is this: After the experts have been identified, what can the organization do to support the transfer of knowledge to others that also helps to develop new experts?

As part of its revitalization efforts, IBM designed a core focus on employees being able to access expert knowledge that was identified through the company. Its launch of the Expert Mentoring program as part of the revitalization process is a concrete example of how mentoring was used as a means to bridge skills and knowledge gaps. It identified and recruited various employees to act as "expert mentors" who were seen as having a specialized and unique body of expertise, skills, and knowledge acquired over a period of time. This idea was based in part on existing information about the role of expertise in knowledge transfer and innovation.[29] These experts gain their knowledge through many years of specialized formal, structured, and guided learning, coupled with many years of tacit, practical, and experiential learning. Employees who fit this description were invited to be mentors to the new and existing generations of IBM employees and used as key resources to transfer their knowledge through the various units within the organization.

One example of these efforts is provided by Dr. Mark Dean, an IBM Fellow who earned his Ph.D. from Stanford University. As a leading African American expert, Dr. Dean has been inducted into the National Hall of Inventors because of his work as an architect of the modern-day personal computer, and he currently holds a number of patents, with 30 more pending. Dr. Dean is considered an expert in the field of technology and is well known through the organization for his knowledge and innovation. As part of the expert mentoring effort, Dr. Dean is actively engaged in ways to pass on his knowledge to his fellow IBM colleagues and is recognized by the organization because of his commitment to mentoring others. Not only is he leaving a rich legacy of knowledge behind, he is helping to develop the new technologists and future experts through this collaborative mentoring process.

While this is part of IBM's overall effort to protect and maintain its leadership status in the field of technology, it is also a critical component for sustaining organizational intelligence using expert mentoring. One of the lessons learned from IBM's use of expert mentoring as part of the revitalization effort is the importance of leveraging existing knowledge and unique skills within the organization. If a company does not identify and engage experts such as Dr. Mark Dean in meaningful ways throughout the business enterprise, it is likely that the company will be less successful in its talent management efforts and thus become stagnant and unable to maintain its position in the global marketplace. Companies like IBM should consider techniques such as expert mentoring as strategic tools for accessing knowledge and expertise to help support and sustain organizational intelligence in meeting both short-term objectives as well as long-term goals. In addition, the connecting of people with existing expertise can also help with another core aspect of ongoing talent development, which is the retention of this critical knowledge throughout the firm.

Supporting Knowledge Retention

If companies are slow in capturing expertise, they run the risk of losing key knowledge, widening the skill and leadership gaps, and ultimately eroding the company's organizational intelligence. For example, DeLong argues in the book, *Lost Knowledge: Confronting the Threat of an Aging Workforce,* that "In the future, organizations serious about improving performance are not going to have a choice. Leaders will have to address the challenges of knowledge retention if they hope to avoid the unacceptable costs of lost knowledge." What is interesting about this perspective within the current context is that it reminds us that retention is not just about keeping people or employee numbers stable within the organization. Retention as a part of talent management must also be about the retention of critical knowledge within the organization. A significant aspect of using mentoring to support organizational intelligence points to the value of developing and retaining expertise inside of the organization for current needs and future challenges. To support this idea, Leonard and Swap, authors of *Deep Smarts,* assert that "Throughout your organization there are people whose intuition, judgment, and knowledge, both explicit and tacit, are stored in their heads and— depending on their task—in their hands. These are people with deep smarts, and it is not an exaggeration to say that they form the basis of your organizational viability."[30] Thus, another component of IBM's mentoring revitalization focused on supporting and retaining the key sources of "deep smarts" that exist throughout the organization.

One critical factor to the development and retention of "deep smarts" focuses on removing barriers for expert mentors to evolve into organizational thought leaders. These are individuals who move from sharing task-specific or problem-focused knowledge to thinking and acting strategically as they dissect complex problems and render creative solutions.[31] In addition, thought leaders are highly visible throughout the organization and can model important knowledge processes, such as gathering relevant and accurate information to make decisions. Thought leaders typically use a collaborative process, engage colleagues, and exercise deep thought in the decision-making process. This also means that they generally refrain from making judgments or decisions in a vacuum or in isolation. Inherent in this line of thinking is that organizational thought leaders are experts who are well read, well known, and frequently well respected. They must also demonstrate a hunger to fully understand the mission and strategy of the company and know how their immediate organization or business unit is interlocked into the big picture. Thus, thought leaders can be seen as content experts who take on a strategic and informal mentoring role within the organization as facilitators of knowledge transfer and retention. The organizations that are tapping into the collective knowledge base of these thought leaders stand a good chance of stemming the imminent knowledge drain that is expected to occur when the generation of baby boomers (a term that describes those born between 1946 and 1964) begin to exit the U.S. workforce in great numbers over the next two decades.

An essential activity that thought leaders may provide that facilitates knowledge retention involves the process of documentation. This practice prevents the tendency to repeat past mistakes and possibly spend countless hours re-creating major processes. An advantage of documentation is that it allows continuity of activities when someone moves to another business unit or organization.[32] When employees with crucial skills share their knowledge, the organization naturally benefits, but many people fail to see that the employee who is sharing the knowledge also derives benefits.[33] As thought leaders rely on documentation to share collective knowledge throughout the organization, they can also gain new skills (for example, collaboration and consensus-building) and get exposed to a broad or strategic view of the organization. As employees build personal ability and then pass on their knowledge, they are contributing to improving the company's capability and strengthening their own skills as leaders in the organization.[34]

For example, recorded After-Action Reviews are important tools for documentation and can facilitate knowledge retention. After a major deployment or product release, thought leaders are strongly encouraged to conduct a recorded After-Action Review with all individuals who worked on major projects, ensuring that less-experienced employees are included in these discussions. This allows a full examination of what worked well, pinpoints mistakes that may have occurred along the way, reviews methods of correction, and identifies process dependencies that are internal and external to the organization. The involvement of thought leaders as key resources in the process of After-Action Reviews ensures that documentation takes place that allows for ongoing connections and informal knowledge sharing facilitated by these well-known experts.

Sharing information during these reviews also allows all involved to critically reflect upon and analyze the important business processes in a forum that promotes learning, knowledge transfer, and skill development. The presence of thought leaders helps to retain and transfer critical "lessons learned" into other areas throughout the organization. While explicit learning is supported through formal methods, the transfer of knowledge is also greatly facilitated via informal relationships and networks. For example, it has been observed that a great deal of learning in the workplace occurs in informal settings through practical application and fluid collaboration among peers.[35] This, of course, supports the importance of formal expert mentoring along with informal thought leaders who help to develop communities of practice and retain knowledge through the process of documentation. While the development and use of thought leaders is proving to be a valuable activity within IBM, it alone does not ensure that knowledge will be retained throughout the organization. A significant aspect of knowledge retention must involve a change not only to a select group of experts or thought leaders, but also a transformation to the overall culture of the organization.

Sustaining a Knowledge-Resilient Culture

Towers and Perrin, in their report titled, "Winning Strategies for a Global Workforce," make the point that "People place a huge premium on having opportunities to learn and build skills. The ability to acquire skills is the single most important element in creating higher levels of engagement in the workforce."[36] Effective use of both formal and informal mentoring may help shape the culture of the organization into one where employees feel supported, valued, and ultimately engaged in the work being done.[37] The Towers and Perrin report brings out an essential point that developing organization intelligence through the use of mentoring and other employee development tools is a continual and ongoing process of organizational transformation. While key individuals play vital roles within this effort, the capability of the organization to sustain these efforts rests on how its approach can impact and, in some sense, change the overall culture of the organization. Through its various efforts, IBM made a commitment to developing a mentoring culture so that individuals can share knowledge, gain access to others with important expertise, and contribute significantly to the development and retention of talented employees. However, sustaining these efforts means that mentoring activities must go beyond a specific program or effort, such as After-Action Reviews, and toward a culture where knowledge sharing among experts and thought leaders is visible, valued, and rewarded. Thus, the long-term goal of the mentoring efforts such as those developed within IBM is to produce a workplace that is energized and focused on sustaining knowledge and high performance.

High-performing and knowledge-resilient workplaces are ones in which highly skilled people are committed to and passionate about exceeding expectations.[38] Creating and sustaining this type of work environment requires a long-term perspective that includes an array of ongoing mentoring activities. But to be sustainable, mentoring must be connected and integrated into the overall culture of the organization. An essential strategy for beginning this process within IBM has been to link a menu of mentoring activities across the entire talent management process from recruitment to socialization through ongoing employee development. Any one tool or mentoring program in isolation may prove to be insufficient to change and sustain a culture that is "knowledge resilient" or can adapt and change given the dynamics of the business. Thus, creating a culture that is knowledge resilient requires a healthy preoccupation with building and rebuilding, tooling and retooling, inventing and reinventing the skills and competencies within the organization's portfolio in response to a competitive and dynamic work environment.[39] Based on the early results of IBM's revitalization efforts, mentoring can be a valuable and strategic tool for use in this type of ongoing transformation process.

Given that employee development is a critical business investment, IBM's intent is to support its employees in making use of the learning opportunities by fully applying their knowledge in sustainable ways. This is the reason mentoring is so important in the overall learning process, and if done properly, few employees should be left out of this critical effort. Creating opportunities for skills development while encouraging and rewarding knowledge sharing are key to developing a knowledge-resilient enterprise that is always poised to respond to the changing needs of its global clients.[40] However, in today's business—particularly in large corporations—decision making can be an arduous and lengthy process. Clearly it takes time, resources, and people throughout all levels of the organization who are committed to making this a success.

In light of this, many companies are grappling with the challenge of finding ways to integrate and infuse knowledge-based decision making throughout their culture, as outlined in an approach known as evidence-based management.[41] Within IBM, this approach is referred to as "lowering the center of gravity." Lowering the center of gravity means that decision making is formed around existing knowledge and expertise and is pushed down to the employee level, which inevitably allows employees who are closer to the work, closer to related issues, and closer to the clients to make decisions. When an organization can lower the center of gravity, it means that employees take ownership in the knowledge process and also have access to resources as needed or "just-in-time" to address the critical problem or opportunity. Lowering the center of gravity can be effective if employees are provided with the key knowledge and support within the fluid process that supports making sound decisions. While this may sound relatively straightforward, lowering the center of gravity can be a challenge to the organization if the leaders do not offer the tools and support so that their employees are empowered to make these decisions. One of the ways that IBM supports the notion of lowering the center of gravity is to give employees access to formal and informal mentoring relationships that involves sharing technical information, tacit knowledge, and unique expertise. As one of IBM's best practice examples of how this was accomplished, IBM created a global infrastructure that uses both formal and informal mentoring to support experiential and tacit learning[42] through its innovative approach branded as the Experiential Learning Opportunities Portfolio program.

Developing a Portfolio of Experiential Learning Opportunities

IBM's Experiential Learning Opportunities Program is a Society of Human Resources Management award-winning initiative that provides employees with several options through the use of mentoring relationships to acquire new skills and develop tacit knowledge. The efforts by IBM to create Experiential Learning Opportunities were based on the emerging knowledge of mentoring as not merely a social support tool, but also a powerful mechanism for organizational learning, knowledge transfer, and the building of critical intelligence across the organization.[43] As an example of how this hybrid approach to mentoring has been designed and implemented within IBM, we will discuss the details of IBM's Experiential Learning Opportunities program.

IBM examined several key pieces of data that served as the catalyst for the creation of the Experiential Learning Opportunities Portfolio. First, the global and virtual nature of the workplace requires that IBM employees acquire and maintain key technical and professional skills, knowledge, and expertise. To do this, employees need a climate in which they can learn and develop effectively. Yet as mentioned earlier, in the annual Global Pulse Survey, an assessment given to a random employee population, employees registered a marked drop in perception regarding the opportunity to grow their skills, which was considered a contributor to rising levels of attrition. Second, data emerged from "World Jam" (an online, collaborative event where thousands of IBM employees, managers, and executives give feedback on business problems) showing that employees wanted greater access to experiential opportunities and expertise development as they grew their careers. A similar need was highlighted by the "technology team assessment," an executive-sponsored program that focused on ways to improve professional development for IBM employees. In response to this information, the Experiential Learning Opportunities Portfolio was piloted as a solution to provide a systematic approach for employees with the following key objectives:

- Support employees' acquisition of new skills or enhancement of current skills by participating in global experiential developmental opportunities (for example, stretch assignments, cross-unit projects, job-shadowing activities, and so on)
- Expand employees' knowledge and professional development without limitations of geographical borders and physical classroom constraints
- Develop a just-in-time resource that makes mentoring and other employee development tools accessible through the use of an "Opportunity Bank" that outlines various experiential developmental opportunities available on a global basis
- Provide visible and accessible support for employees to find the best alternatives for personal career growth and development and to take ownership in the cultivation of ongoing formal and informal mentoring relationships based on individual needs

The IBM Learning Business Unit obtained support for the Experiential Learning Opportunities Program by creating a strong business case that more structured experiential learning was needed. By starting with small targeted populations to pilot the program and demonstrating to the business that opportunities could be customized to accommodate flexibility in time for employee participation, business units were more receptive to making it a part of their career development offerings. The HR department was then able to build on successes of the program, gain valuable feedback for continuous improvement, and multiply the number of opportunities to be offered.

During the initial pilot, the planning team provided access to the Experiential Learning Opportunities for more than 35,000 global employees. At that point, the initiative focused on enabling stretch assignments, job rotations, and job shadowing activities across organizations as a way to build expertise outside of the more traditional forms of training. The program included a comprehensive business process model, guidelines, a Web site, as well as an opportunity bank that offers the functionality to post and search for short-term learning activities. By the end of the initial pilot, the program transitioned to a phased, targeted deployment that included a global mix of employees. In the version implemented across IBM, the Experiential Learning Opportunities Portfolio consists of three components:

- **Career development and mentoring component**—The component defined experiential developmental opportunities to include stretch assignments, cross-unit projects, job rotations, and so on. This involved defining "experiential learning" as a career development concept within HR policy, and developing a process to enable managers to create opportunities and employees to discover them.

- **Information and training component**—Managers and employees were trained on the learning opportunities through a Web site that defined the program and the processes for opportunity creation and engagement.

- Resource and knowledge-sharing component—The component is an "Opportunities Bank," where managers can post their opportunities and employees can apply for them. The Bank leveraged code from an existing "job bank" tool as an interim IT solution that significantly reduced development cost and time—a record five weeks for the pilot.

The ongoing deployment strategy is based on the needs of the business and the timeline in which business units and geographies can commit. This approach has had a positive impact on the business units, geographies, and communities throughout IBM. It encouraged employees to align the Experiential Learning Opportunities with their business objectives and make it a part of their long-term career development and individual development plan (IDP) goals. The current objectives have been to continuously expand the program to become operational and more pervasive across the organization.

To overcome the complexity involved in building the Experiential Learning Opportunities Portfolio and communicating its objectives, a grass-roots approach was used to design the program, using direct employee and manager input on an on-going basis. Collaboration with extended team members across multiple business units and geographies helped in gathering the requirements to create a global solution and expand the program across the firm. A key theme that continued to surface regarding employee partici-pation in Experiential Learning Opportunities was the lack of time to engage in these types of experiential learning activities. While IBM clearly saw the value in the program, the continued pressures of deadlines, sales quotas, and increased workload acted as a countervailing presence. As a result, the amount of time available for employees to participate in career development activities was somewhat limited.

Overall, the Experiential Learning Opportunities Mentoring effort helped IBM refocus on-the-job learning activities by creating a self-directed and employee-driven program that supported the overall employee development strategy. This hybrid mix of formal mentoring activities and informal men-toring experiences is intended to help IBM worldwide employees grow their skills through a blend of formal and informal mentoring activities and access critical information without regard to location, function, or situation. This aspect of IBM's mentoring approach has proven to be vital given that an increasing number of IBM employees work outside a traditional office and in non-U.S. locations. Additionally, the sharing of knowledge and learning from others through the mentoring platform embedded in Experiential Learning Opportunities is providing access to a resource that had previously been provided only to those designated as "top talent" within the organiza-tion. This technology-driven tool helped to address a key issue raised during IBM's early benchmarking and also identified by previous work on formal mentoring programs—accessibility. The need to provide an easily accessible, integrated, enterprisewide tool that created opportunities for relationship building, knowledge sharing, and other aspects of mentoring has been another key factor in the successful implementation of IBM's Experiential Learning Opportunities tool.

Experiential Learning Opportunities in the Future

The Experiential Learning Opportunities Portfolio is showing measurable impact in a number of areas. For example, access and utilization of Experiential Learning Opportunities by employees worldwide has increased substantially each year since its implementation. The experiential, self-directed learning is proving to be more cost-effective than traditional class-room training and e-learning. There have been an increased number of opportunities in the bank—more than five times what it was since the program launched, as more employees utilize the program for their career development needs. In addition, the Experiential Learning Opportunities Portfolio has been successful in its goal of encouraging exposure to cross-business unit and global career development opportunities.

In addition to providing just-in-time mentoring solutions, the Experiential Learning Opportunities Portfolio has also integrated mentoring into the overall fabric of employee development activities across IBM. In our exploration of the impact of this initiative, employees and managers shared several poignant examples of this integration. For example, an employee from India filled a short-term customer-facing opportunity in Italy, using his acquired skills to train less experienced engineers. A manager who was initially hesitant about using the Experiential Learning Opportunities Program, fearing it would have a negative impact on retention, found just the opposite to be true. His feedback was that employees who have become stagnant in their roles were able to gain advice from others and try new positions via the job shadowing option without having to change jobs. In addition, shadowing employees in other departments and sharing their learning with the rest of the team had a very positive impact on transfer of knowledge as well as employee morale. Lastly, in Dublin, Ireland, a manager whose team lacked the appropriate programming skills to complete a project posted an Experiential Learning Opportunity for someone who met a specific skill profile. In return, the Dublin manager agreed to act as a mentor to the programmer. It turned out that a programmer in Brazil who had those exact skills was looking for a mentor, and the ensuing virtual relationship was most beneficial on both sides.

Personal interviews with both managers and employees showed more than 90% agreement that the Experiential Learning Opportunities Program had value and that the investment in it should continue. The Experiential Learning Opportunities Portfolio has had an impact on employee morale and retention. It has opened employees' eyes to the breadth of opportunities available to them at IBM. Employees frequently comment that it has helped them appreciate their current positions, changed the perception that "there's nothing here for me" and showed them that IBM is committed to their development. Each of these examples of employee feedback has shown the positive impact that the Experiential Learning Opportunities Portfolio effort has produced on employees' attitudes and utilization of mentoring resources. In fact, based on its initial success, one business unit executive made the strategic decision to deploy the Experiential Learning Opportunities Portfolio worldwide as part of a major career development initiative, reaching an additional 27,000 employees. This success has added more credibility and value to the program, opened up new job possibilities, and created a demand for the program from other business units.

While the initial success of IBM's just-in-time mentoring solution has been quite positive, continuous improvement to the Experiential Learning Opportunities Program is an ongoing activity. Within these ongoing efforts, there are several lessons learned from the IBM experience that are beneficial to other organizations considering a mentoring effort or revitalizing their current activities. A key challenge within the formal mentoring activities was visibility or access across all segments of the employee population. Thus, a lesson learned from the IBM experience is that creating access and visibility for organization-sponsored mentoring efforts is an ongoing activity. Getting people to understand the concept of posting the opportunities as well as overcoming managers' resistance to employees accessing these opportunities requires continuous education and communication. Employees need to see access to mentoring and other activities as a tool for developing their competencies and not as a guarantee for promotion or salary increase. Managers need to support employees accessing Experiential Learning Opportunities as important for their overall effectiveness and not as a threat to retention, distraction from regular work activities, or competition to their role as supervisor. All of these require ongoing information sharing and communication about the mentoring program and its objectives and fit within the overall IBM employee development strategy.

The Experiential Learning Opportunities Portfolio provided a great deal of information and resources to employees as part of the mentoring revitalization campaign, yet the one resource that is still in short supply is time. Employees still frequently comment that while they are more aware of the resources provided by the organization, they don't have enough time to access all that is provided within the Experiential Learning Opportunities Portfolio. Resources are always a challenge, and because a large portion of IBM's business is services-oriented, the need to balance work-related responsibilities and personal development opportunities is an ongoing challenge for many organizations, including IBM.

These issues pose important challenges for providing just-in-time mentoring solutions such as the Experiential Learning Opportunities Portfolio;

therefore, the potential drawbacks of moving forward without such an effort are substantial. Equipping employees with the right skills and empowering them to use the skills and knowledge in making decisions for the company demonstrates the highest level of respect, confidence, and trust in the employees' judgment and ability. High-performing employees thrive on being able to think and act on their intuition, yet they also need to have access to the key resources from mentors, advisors, peers, and managers. Availability of and access to these resources is crucial in the process of strengthening the arsenal of existing skills, as well as building the capacity of future capabilities—both cornerstones of organizational intelligence. The long-term result of this focused effort sends a strong message to employees that they are valued members of the organization and cultivates a strong sense of individual accountability for excellence throughout the workplace.

Organizational intelligence must be created through an integrated solution, and the key lesson learned from IBM's experience is the development of the Experiential Learning Opportunities Portfolio which includes mentoring as a valuable tool. While there are well-noted benefits and limitations to formal mentoring initiatives, the hybrid approach taken by IBM provides a useful example of how organizations can move beyond the constraints of traditional one-on-one mentoring toward an integrated, technology-enhanced, and employee-driven solution. This just-in-time mentoring approach means employees are encouraged to build cross-organizational and cross-geography skills through diverse mentoring relationships.[44]

A key challenge for the future of this effort is expanding the global reach of the Experiential Learning Opportunities Portfolio. The main focus for the future is building collegiality and cultivating an atmosphere where individuals take pride in becoming responsible for their growth as well as the growth of their colleagues across the global business enterprise. The designers and sponsors of the Experiential Learning Opportunities Portfolio are hopeful that it can support the dynamic challenges that arise in a globally integrated company such as IBM by seamlessly linking all parts of the business together. The hope is that the Experiential Learning Opportunities Portfolio will become contagious across business units and worldwide operations. While this is a long-term goal, it is based on the core premise that "When everything is connected, work flows." This not only speaks to processes but is also germane to people as well. Because IBM functions in a work environment where a great number of its employees are dispersed, a just-in-time and technology-support mentoring approach is one way of connecting knowledge and people across IBM. Hopefully, the success created by the Experiential

Learning Opportunities Portfolio effort can be replicated by other organizations that are faced with similar challenges for developing and sustaining organizational intelligence. From the work done at IBM, efforts should be focused on enhancing access, awareness, and participation in both formal and informal mentoring relationships in a way that can cut across function, location, and demographic group. The sponsors and global users of the Experiential Learning Opportunities Portfolio remain energized at the long-term potential impact of this use of mentoring as a strategic tool for building and sustaining organizational intelligence.

References

[1] Allen, T.D. and Eby, L.T. (2003). Relationship effectiveness for mentor: Factors associated with learning and quality. *Journal of Management, 29*, 469–486.

[2] Ragins, B.R., Cotton, J.L., and Milles, J.S. (2000). Marginal mentoring: The effects of type of mentor, quality of relationship and program design on work and career attitudes. *Academy of Management Journal, 43*, 1177–1194.

[3] Unlocking the DNA of the Adaptable Workforce: The Global Human Capital Study 2008. (2008). IBM Global Services at http://www.ibm.org.

[4] Wanberg, C.R., Welsh, E.T., and Hezlett, S.A. (2003). Mentoring research: A review and dynamic process model. In G.R. Ferris and J.J. Martocchio (Eds.), *Research in Personnel and Human Resource Management* (Vol. 22, pp. 39–124). Oxford, England: Elsevier.

[5] Allen, T.D. and Eby, L.T. (2003). Relationship effectiveness for mentors: Factors associated with learning and quality. *Journal of Management, 29*, 469–486; Chao, G.T., Walz, P.M., and Gardner, P.D. (1992). Formal and informal mentorships: A comparison on mentoring functions and contract with non-mentored counterparts. *Personnel Psychology, 45*, 619–636; Fagenson-Eland, E.A., Marks, M.A. and Amendola, K.L. (1997). Perceptions of mentoring relationships. *Journal of Vocational Behavior, 51*, 29–42.

[6] Anderson, H. (2003). Why mentoring doesn't work. *Harvard Management Communication Letter*, C0306B.

[7] Baugh, S.G. and Fagenson-Eland, E.A. (2007). Formal mentoring programs: A "poor cousin" to informal relationships? In, B.R. Ragins and K. E. Kram (Eds.), *The Handbook on Mentoring at Work* (pp. 249–271). Thousand Oaks, CA: Sage Publications.

[8] Ibid, Baugh and Fagenson-Eland (2007).

[9] Allen, T.D., Eby, L.T., and Lentz, E. (2006). Mentorship behavior and mentorship quality associated with formal mentoring programs: Closing the gap between research and practice. *Journal of Applied Psychology, 91*(3), 567–578.

[10] Arthur, M.B., Claman, P.H., and DeFillippi, R.J. (1995). Intelligent enterprise, intelligent careers. *Academy of Management Executive, 9*(4), 7–22.

[11] Knight, G.A. and Cavusgil, S.T. (2004). Innovation, organizational capabilities and the born-global firm. *Journal of International Business Studies*, 35(2), 124–141.

[12] Ghoshal, S. and Bartlett, C.A. (1990). The multinational corporation as an inter-organizational network. *Academy of Management Review*, 15(4), 603–625.

[13] Ibid, Argote, 1999; Levitt, B. (1988). Organizational learning. *Annual Review of Sociology*, 4, 319–340.

[14] Brown, J.S. and Duguid, P. (1991). Organizational learning and communities of practice: Toward a unified view of working, learning and innovation. *Organization Science*, 2(1), 40–57.

[15] Capelli, P. (2000). A market approach to retaining talent. *Harvard Business Review*, 78(1), 102–113.

[16] Salk, J.E. and Simonin, B.L. (2003). Beyond alliances: towards a meta-theory of collaborative learning. In M. Easterby-Smith and M.A. Lyles (Eds.), *The Blackwell Handbook of Organizational Learning and Knowledge Management* (pp. 252–277). Malden, Blackwell.

[17] Orlikowski, W. (2002). Knowing in practice: Enacting a collective capability in distributed organizing. *Organization Science*, 13(3), 249–73.

[18] Hansen, M.T., Nohira, N., and Tierney, T. (1999). What's in your strategy for managing knowledge? *Harvard Business Review*, 77(2), 106–116.

[19] Jackson, S.E., DeNisi, A., and Hitt, M.A. (2003). Managing knowledge for sustained competitive advantage: Designing strategies for effective human resource management. San Francisco, CA: John Wiley & Sons.

[20] Inkson, K. and Arthur, M.B. (2001). How to be a successful career capitalist. *Organizational Dynamics*, 30(1), 48–61.

[21] Arthur, D. (2001). *The Employee Recruitment and Retention Handbook*. New York, NY: AMACOM.

[22] Ibid, Arthur (2001).

[23] Amundson, N.E. (2003). *Active Engagement*. (2nd Ed.). Richmond, CAN: Ergon Communications.

[24] Ibid, Arthur (2001).

[25] Chao, G.A., O'Leary-Kelley, S., Wolf, H., and Gardner, P. (1994). Organizational socialization: Its content and consequences. *Journal of Applied Psychology*, 79, 730–743; Baker, J.E., and Feldman, D.C. (1990). Strategies of organizational socialization and their impact on newcomer adjustment. *Journal of Management Issues*, 2, 198–212.

[26] Argote, L. (1999). *Organizational Learning: Creating, Retaining, and Transferring Knowledge*. Boston, MA: Kluwer Academic Publishers.

[27] Brown, J.S. and Duguid, P. (2001). How to capture knowledge without killing it. *Harvard Business Review on Organizational Learning* (pp.45–60). Boston, MA: Harvard Business School Publishing.

[28] Allen, N.J. and Meyer, J.P. (1990). Organizational socialization tactics: A longitudinal analysis of links to newcomers' commitment and role orientation. *Academy of Management Journal*, 33, 847–858.

[29] Leonard-Barton, D. (1985). Experts as negative opinion leaders in the diffusion of technological innovation. *Journal of Consumer Research, 11*, 914–926; Ostroff, C. and Kozlowski, S.W.J. (1992). Organizational socialization as a learning process: The role of information acquisition. *Personnel Psychology, 45*, 849–874.

[30] Fisher, Anne. (2005). How to Battle the Coming Brain Drain. *Fortune,* 151(6), 121–128; Gary, Loren. (2005, August). Build Your Company's Deep Smarts. *Harvard Management Update,* pp. 3–5; Leonard, Dorothy and Walter Swap. (2005). Ten Years to Deep Smarts. *Across the Board,* 42(4), 12–13.

[31] Quinn, J.B., Anderson, P., and Finkelstein, S. (1998). Managing professional intellect: Making the most of the best. *Harvard Business Review on Knowledge Management* (pp. 181–200). Boston, MA: Harvard Business School Publishing.

[32] Arthur, M.B., Khopova, S.N., and Wilderom, C.P.M. (2005). Career success in a boundaryless career world. *Journal of Organizational Behavior, 26*, 177–202.

[33] Lucier, C. and Torsilieri, J. (2001). Can knowledge management drive bottom-line results? In I. Nonaka and D. J. Teece (Eds.), *Managing Industrial Knowledge Creation, Transfer, and Utilization* (pp. 231–243). Sage: Thousand Oaks, CA.

[34] Garvin, D.A. (1998). Building a learning organization. *Harvard Business Review on Knowledge Management* (pp. 47–80). Boston, MA: Harvard Business School Publishing.

[35] Nonaka, I. (1994). A dynamic theory of organizational knowledge creation. *Organization Science,* 5(1), 14–37.

[36] Towers and Perrin 2007 Global Workforce Study. (2007). www.towersperrin.com.

[37] DeJanasz, S.C., Sullivan, S.E., and Whiting, V. (2003). Mentor networks and career success: Lessons for turbulent times. *Academy of Management Executive,* 17(4), 78–91.

[38] Harris, P.E. (2005). Managing the knowledge culture. Amherst, MA: HRD Press.

[39] Leonard, D. and Straus, S. (1998). Putting your company's whole brain to work. *Harvard Business Review on Knowledge Management* (pp. 109–136). Boston, MA: Harvard Business School Publishing.

[40] Hammer, M. (2004, April). Deep change: How operational innovation can transform your company. *Harvard Business Review,* pp. 85–93.

[41] Pfeffer, J. and Sutton, R.I. (2006). *Hard Facts, Dangerous Half-Truths and Total Nonsense: Profiting from Evidence-Based Management.* Boston, MA: Harvard Business School Press.

[42] Lankau, M.J. and Scandura, T.A. (2002). An investigation of personal learning in mentoring relationships: Content, antecedents and consequences. *Academy of Management Journal,* 45(4), 779–790.

[43] Higgins, M.C. and Kram, K.E. (2001). Reconceptualizing mentoring at work: A developmental network perspective. *Academy of Management Review,* 26(2), 264–288.

[44] Child, J. (2001). Learning through strategic alliances. In M. Dierkes, A.B. Antal, J. Child and I. Nonaka (Eds.), *Handbook of Organizational Learning and Knowledge* (pp. 657–680). Oxford: Oxford University Press.

3

Organizational Intelligence: Fostering Communities of Knowledge

---

Chapter Contents

Overview

One of the early lessons learned within IBM is that knowledge is a social process. Creating, cultivating, transferring, and retaining the knowledge needed to sustain a competitive advantage reside within the people of IBM. Whether in formal think tanks, face-to-face meetings, e-mail exchanges across project teams, or informal conversations in the cafeteria, the social aspects of problem solving, innovation, and creative thinking are facilitated by fostering communities at work. The notion of communities of practice is not new or unique to the IBM culture. Many firms focus on the notion of knowledge communities, a term attributed to Lave and Wegner as part of their 1991 book, *Situated Learning*.[1] They describe communities of practice as a network of people who either formally or informally share ideas, solutions, and interests for the purposes of problem-solving, collaboration, and innovation.

Clearly, these communities of practices are a way to create, facilitate, and transfer knowledge—the kind of knowledge that builds organizational intelligence. While many organizations recognize the value of these knowledge communities, few understand or have developed a deliberate process for creating and cultivating them. Mentoring at IBM has been one important tool for developing and fostering the work of knowledge communities throughout the global business enterprise. As we examine some of the specific types of mentoring efforts that help to build a sense of community around knowledge and ideas, an important message here is that organizational intelligence involves strengthening the social process of connecting people and ideas within a culture of collaboration. Mentoring is an essential tool that helps create and sustain that culture of collaboration within IBM.

Employees who are engaged in the activities of communities of practice are in essence contributing their knowledge and practical "know-how" to the members of the community. Overall, when knowledge is fluid among groups in this manner, it builds the intellectual capability and capacity of the team. In addition, the collective knowledge base improves the organization's capability to quickly respond to market volatility and the dynamic needs of global clients. Because knowledge is a core component of communities of practice, there is a tendency to use the term interchangeably with communities of knowledge. This practice of knowledge sharing is a typical characteristic of an "intelligent organization" in which employees share their complementary skills, create opportunities for teammates to acquire new skills and enhance old ones to collaborate for the purposes of innovation, solve problems, and deliver value to the organization. Inherent in communities of practice is a great opportunity for mentoring to take place; in particular, members of the community are known to mentor others to gain knowledge in certain disciplines that are important to the group and to the organization. This chapter is intended to show the many ways knowledge can be transferred through the use of approaches such as communities of practice and other forms of group mentoring.

Learning through Communities of Practice

One of the key notions within the idea of communities of practice is that organizations must understand the link between knowledge and the social context in which knowledge is created and shared. Learning seen as knowledge creation and transfer is a social process that requires participation, or what Lave and Wegner call, "social co-participation." This means that instead of just trying to figure out how to stimulate an individual's judgment and decision making, companies should focus attention on building social environments that support learning and knowledge among interrelated people. An employee does not learn or create knowledge in a vacuum; rather he must be connected to other employees within an environment that both values and supports collaboration. Thus, learning is a social enterprise that requires co-participation from communities that reside within and are supported by the organization.[2]

The original idea of communities of practices was developed from research looking at learning through the apprenticeship process. A well-known method for developing skill and expertise among newcomers, the apprenticeship approach is fundamentally about the transfer of knowledge. Inexperienced craftsmen interact with and learn from well-known experts, thus developing key skills within their trade and allowing them to put those skills to use. The apprenticeship process involves mutual engagement and a joint enterprise during which knowledge sharing and innovation frequently occur.[3] The nature of the apprenticeship process involves the sharing of knowledge that by its nature is complex, not easily replicated, and based on deep expertise.

By examining the apprenticeship process, we see that a key aspect of learning using this approach is the transfer of "tacit knowledge."[4] This category of knowledge involves nonroutine or nonexplicit types of information or ideas. Tacit knowledge is often distinguished from explicit or "codified knowledge," the latter being more straightforward and unambiguous. Being able to develop and transfer tacit types of knowledge frequently involves more complex types of learning. This is especially true for what Cross and Sproull call "knowledge-intensive work" because it requires that people continually solve complex, nonroutine problems under time pressure and with limited information.[5] They argue that when problems are complex, tasks are ill-defined, and solutions require more than a simple answer, the process of knowledge transfer is best facilitated by networks and social relationships.[6] Knowledge created and transferred by networks and social relationships involves not only finding correct answers but also constructing new ideas and developing innovative approaches. Interactions among people within networks and relationships frequently require people to approach both problems and solutions differently than they would as individuals.[7] In addition, knowledge that is created by a community of individuals is more likely to be accepted by those within the broader organization and, thus, more likely to be implemented.[8]

At IBM, the notion of building and leveraging communities that support strategic objectives of the company is also not a new idea. Establishing and maintaining a knowledge workforce that has flexibility, resilience, and agility has long been a goal at IBM. One of the ways of achieving this is through the development of expert communities, but a major challenge for IBM has been how best to retain and transfer the knowledge from these communities across the global business enterprise. In addition, IBM's core business involves knowledge-intensive work that must be actionable and yet flexible enough to adapt in response to the changing environment. Thus, IBM employees must be engaged in co-participation of knowledge, which can be transferred, replicated, and adapted to meet both current and emerging business needs.

While this challenge may appear straightforward, the solution for IBM and similar world-class organizations is extraordinarily complex. Tacit forms of knowledge are quite valuable, but they are also complex and difficult to transfer.[9] Developing employees who are capable of meeting this challenge requires a different relationship between the employer and employee. Producing this type of workforce involves developing a culture that is "dedicated to the idea of continuous learning but also stands ready to reinvent itself to keep pace with change."[10] The lessons learned from IBM as it attempts to solve this complex challenge show the important link between learning, communities of practice, and mentoring. Cultivating knowledge through communities of practice is accomplished through a broad portfolio of programs within IBM that involve a diverse array of mentoring activities. While the specialized use of mentoring has helped to strengthen learning and knowledge transfer throughout the organization, cultivating these communities is accomplished first and foremost by a fundamental emphasis on employee development within IBM.

Building Communities of Practice at IBM

The goal of producing a culture of learning and collaboration is one that has been a focal part of IBM's strategy. As a consequence, cultivating an employee's ability to seek and leverage perspectives from different sources is a vital component of its employee development activities. In 2003, IBM employees participated in what was called a "Jam Session," which helped to define the values that will take the company through the twenty-first century and beyond. IBM is a company that continuously redefines and reinvents itself while maintaining a strong connection to its core identity. For example, during the early years, Chairman T.J. Watson, Sr. crafted the company's basic beliefs which have guided IBM through many changes and challenges. Throughout these transformations, the IBM identity and brand remained intact. More recently, the core commitment that emerged from the employee jam session made a strong statement that a global company can change the way it does business based on the marketplace and needs of the clients, but at the same time maintain its core identity and values.

Thus, IBM defines and preserves its culture in a number of ways, including:

- A dedicated focus on excellence
- Adherence to a set of values that govern the actions of all employees
- Innovation that matters
- Maintenance of a high-performance culture that offers employees opportunities to develop new skills

Because employees co-participate in defining and shaping the culture, IBM can build a sense of community around its core values as they are defined, implemented, and refined. The various forms that communities of practice take across IBM encourage employees to become personally invested in acting on these core values and keeping them alive in practical ways. Using these values to drive the way employees work and partner with one another also helps to reinforce the importance of collaboration throughout the IBM culture. As employees develop their skills, they are held accountable for applying these skills in significant ways, as well as passing on their knowledge to others. In many respects, the approach IBM has taken is quite similar to the apprenticeship technique that was the focus of Lave and Wegner's early work. Thus, the IBM approach involves embedding learning within its employee development and performance management systems in a way that encourages and rewards participation, knowledge transfer, and collaboration.

As part of this effort to foster knowledge communities, the measures that IBM takes to create a knowledge-driven culture also involve a steady emphasis on skills assessment and development. This allows IBM to have an accurate reading of the company's broad skill portfolio. Because IBM has a practice of reinventing itself periodically to remain relevant to a dynamic marketplace, the firm must also be vigilant about refreshing the skills contained within its portfolio. In this way, the defining features of what ultimately drives the communities of practice throughout IBM are reviewed, updated, and refined.

This continuous improvement process is central to IBM's success and is quite similar in many ways to what is done in other global technology companies. In fact, in an article written by the Corporate Leadership Council, human resources leaders at Sun Microsystems estimated that "The skills of engineers become outdated within three years."[11] This is particularly true in the high tech industry, which is characterized by short product lifecycles and where, Cisco CEO John Chambers stated, "You have to change your company almost every two years. Skills sets must be continuously updated. Organizational ability to react quickly to market change depends on building a flexible workforce."[12] It is in this context that IBM continually revisits and redefines its communities of practice and, as a result, uses a variety of techniques to help employees upgrade and refine their skills to meet the changing needs of the organization.

Thus, the capability to seek and leverage perspectives from different sources is vital to strategic employee development. By cultivating collaborative communities, IBM employees can achieve both their organizational and professional goals through learning from one another. IBM makes significant investments in a range of career development tools and resources to help employees assess their skills needs and develop a plan to close their skills and expertise gaps. As employees develop action plans to address gaps and gain new expertise and skills, the use of both formal and informal mentoring is a vital part of how employees can address these needs by tapping into these communities of knowledge throughout IBM enterprisewide.

A Mentoring Solution

Just as with a traditional apprenticeship approach, the use of mentoring has been an essential element for IBM's efforts to develop and refine the skills, expertise, and knowledge needed to sustain its competitive advantage. As we reviewed in the earlier chapters, the traditional one-on-one mentoring is utilized throughout the organization to help provide ongoing support and development. However, the use of communities, networks, and groups to facilitate the knowledge creation and transfer is also part of IBM's approach to mentoring. For example, the traditional Individual Development Plans (IDPs) process was modified to include a section on mentoring, which allows employees to document multiple mentoring relationships across the organization. As employees document their developmental needs in preparation for career discussions with their managers, they have the ability to send their IDPs to their various mentors throughout the organization. This process links core aspects of IBM's performance management system to the network of people and mentoring relationships among its employees. Thus, mentoring relationships are connected to the existing communities that employees are engaged in throughout IBM. The inclusion of these formal and informal relationships as part of the IDP process also serves as organizational validation for employee participation (and co-participation) in these mentoring communities.

Another important aspect of IBM's use of mentoring across its knowledge communities is that it encourages employees to secure multiple mentoring relationships that represent different business units, locations, and functional areas. This sends a strong signal to employees that they should cultivate relationships with people who possess different skill sets and come from different cultures, functions, and geographies. Multiple mentors bring different perspectives and different solutions and approaches to problems along with different knowledge bases that represent the various business units across IBM. Multiple mentoring relationships also form the basis for informal and formal communities of practice that help support employee growth and development. Thus, a significant aspect of IBM's use of mentoring that helps to foster communities of practice assists employees in moving from a traditional view of a single mentor-mentee relationship, to developing a broad network of mentoring relationships that can tap into diverse knowledge, skills, and support for the individual.

Mentoring as Communities of Practice

For organizations like IBM, effective mentoring relationships help to foster a culture that hungers for knowledge and ideas. Not only is learning a pivotal part of these relationships, but mentors are also able to interpret the changes for mentees, assist them in placing the changes in their proper context, and also allow them to constructively test their assumptions. Clearly, this is the type of tacit knowledge transfer that is vital for knowledge-intensive organizations. In addition, mentors are critical in helping to relieve the anxieties that their mentees may be experiencing as a result of rapid organizational change and uncertainty. Mentoring also plays a complementary role to more formal relationships between managers and employees in the development process. Within IBM, the use of mentoring is accomplished as part of the overall fostering of communities of practice throughout the organization. The key is that partnerships and collaborations, which include various forms of mentoring, must be developed to help employees meet the needs of the organization.

The connection between communities of practice and mentoring is consistent with the original idea Kram provided, suggesting that individuals have "constellations" of mentors throughout their careers.[13] Recently, mentoring research has focused on developmental networks as a way to understand how employees rely on a collection of people for advice, support, and sponsorship. This development network consists of a group of people (peers, family, senior employees, professional contacts, community affiliations, and so on) who take an interest in an employee's career and professional advancement.[14] These networks are described based on their diversity, range of expertise that each person brings to the network, and the strength of the relationships. Clearly, this network view of mentoring is similar to the idea of communities of practice. A collection or group of individuals is formed, either formally or informally for the purpose of idea generation, knowledge sharing, advice exchange, and support.

Within IBM, an attempt to foster these constellations also reflects the view that mentoring produces communities of knowledge. In fact, some of the various forms of mentoring within IBM can be seen as their own type of knowledge community. These collaborations provide what some call IBM's "high-touch" aspect of mentoring. In contrast to the just-in-time type of mentoring (for example, speed mentoring, e-mentoring, and so on), these communities involve contact among groups across IBM who work to provide solutions and support, and to share ideas. These mentoring communities take a variety of forms that involve mentoring across geographic location, as with IBM's Blue Club in Latin America.

Developing a skilled and adaptive workforce is highly dependent on the manager's ability to engage, motivate, and retain key employees. If an organization is losing its key employees, it greatly inhibits creativity and innovation, and the onus is generally placed on the manager. It is important that managers be given adequate resources and support to position themselves for meeting the needs of employees, while remaining attentive to business objectives. For managers to be successful, the company has to find ways to continuously provide them with new learning opportunities that strengthen their leadership skills, people skills, and business acumen. The failure rate of managers can be high if a company does not invest in programs that support their development and the development of their employees, especially those employees who are in the pipeline to join the managerial ranks. Buckingham and Coffman suggest that "People leave managers, not companies. So much money has been thrown at the challenge of keeping good people—in the form of better pay, better perks, and better training—when in the end, turnover is mostly a managerial issue. If you have a turnover problem, look first to your managers."[15] Data collected through IBM's employee development and retention efforts suggested that the most vulnerable stage of the manager's career is during the first eighteen months in the organization. This data, along with the need to both attract and retain talented employees, represent two of the reasons why the Blue Club mentoring program was developed in IBM Latin America and expanded to other IBM locations.

The Blue Club mentoring program originated about five years ago and was born out of an attempt to understand what was needed to retain and motivate new high-potential managers. Employee data revealed frustration over lack of resources, coupled with having a lot of information that was pushed to the Web, which people did not have time to read, digest, and apply. Employees did not feel they had the support and resources to effectively do their jobs. They felt overloaded and disconnected from the core of the organization. For example, after new managers from Latin America attended the basic new manager's training in New York, there was no structured follow-up training upon their return to Latin America. This disconnection, isolation, and overload were seen as a contributing factor to issues with performance and retention. To solve the problem, IBM needed to provide what it called a "high-touch" approach, or one that reconnected employees in Latin America with IBM's core culture.

As a result, the Blue Club was created. It includes a set of modules designed for the up-line managers to use in mentoring sessions with new and less-experienced managers. The Blue Club uses group mentoring to foster a sense of community by actively using practical and experiential learning approaches, which help to achieve the group's overall mission. From its inception, the goals of the Blue Club have been to:

- Share success stories and challenges and use these experiences as learning tools
- Work together and build interlocking teams where new managers can learn from experienced managers
- Find future leaders and identify their strengths and developmental needs

Each of these goals as outlined by the Blue Club underscores both the importance of sharing knowledge and the value of building relationships across people within the organization. The overall goal supports the idea that formal group mentoring can produce communities of knowledge that not only build support for employees, but also provide a powerful tool for the transfer of tacit knowledge and collaborative problem solving.

While the structure and resources within the Blue Club demonstrate IBM's support for its employees in Latin America, IBM does not dictate the process and execution of this program, which is employee-driven. This effort involves fostering a mentoring community that connects employees to the core aspects of the culture both locally and globally. The program uses group mentoring on the premise that each time the group meets, a different leader presents a topic of interest. The Web is a critical tool in the process, and prior to the meeting, participants receive materials and activities to complete, which prepares them to be fully engaged during the meeting. Some of the topics that have been covered in the Blue Club sessions include:

- Managerial styles
- Organizational climate
- Time management
- Retention
- Roles of the manager
- Coaching

- Influencing others
- Decision making and speed
- Leadership competencies
- Dealing with difficult people
- How to build a high-performing team

As part of addressing these various topics, Blue Club members access the knowledge of internal human resources (HR) professionals, who play a critical partnership role with the line managers who are responsible for the program. In addition, these HR professionals provide the initial point of contact for individuals who are interested in joining the Blue Club. HR provides instructions, materials for the facilitators and the participants, and also serves as a repository for suggestions and feedback. This provides visible resources and support from the organization for the efforts needed to build and sustain this mentoring community.

The business benefits from a program such as Blue Club are numerous, especially because there is a great need for experienced employees, including managers, across IBM to make transfer of knowledge across the business enterprise a personal commitment. Also, IBM expects its managers and long-term employees to serve as role models by sharing their knowledge and expertise with others. Doing this is an opportunity for managers in the Blue Club program to contribute to making IBM a learning culture. This reinforces IBM's culture as one that expects its leaders is to be actively engaged in sharing their expertise and knowledge with others coming through the pipeline. Building this type of knowledge community utilizing group-based mentoring thus contributes to IBM's leadership development by building its bench strength and helps to close current as well as future competency gaps. An additional benefit that comes from fostering these mentoring communities is that employees can from other people's experience, which helps to minimize the repetition of past mistakes and bad decisions.

One of the participants, Marcela Leon, manager of Learning and Talent for Latin America, discussed her experience with the Blue Club. She highlighted the point that the executives and experienced managers were called upon to become role models for new managers by teaching, sharing ideas, and describing best practices. As she recalls:

"Everyone involved in the Blue Club program showed a lot of excitement about the opportunity to learn together. This approach allowed the participants to connect the theory of leadership and good management styles with the practical knowledge that they had gained from the Blue Club sessions. Because the Blue Club has seen marked success, the concept and materials were shared with others outside of Latin America."

Marcela also noted that the Blue Club continues to be refined and improved as part of is co-participation within the community. The recent focus within the Blue Club has stimulated a hybrid of the group mentoring approach into something that IBM calls **group speed mentoring**. This format involves a series of roundtable discussions to address immediate issues facing the group in Latin America that may be outside of the ongoing focus of the formal mentoring process. This new hybrid of the group mentoring approach shows that mentoring—even within formal programs such as the Blue Club—does not always have to take place in a long-term relationship. These speed group mentoring roundtable sessions are good opportunities to get quality mentoring on the spot, while reaching multiple people at the same time. Whenever executives with interesting career histories visit any of the countries in Latin America, they are asked to host speed sessions with employees and managers. Participants are exposed to the career experiences of the executives, receive career guidance, and can connect with knowledgeable people on current issues facing the organization. Executives across the business enterprise are supported and rewarded for participating in as many of these group-mentoring sessions as possible when they travel to Latin America, and similar speed group mentoring sessions have been springing up in other countries in the region and throughout IBM worldwide.

Some efforts to capture the benefits and advantages of the Blue Club program are well underway. These benefits include several key points that show the linkage between group mentoring approaches and fostering knowledge communities. They include the following:

- It is a relatively inexpensive way to transfer knowledge and practical experience in a simple fashion—a low-cost program with high impact.

- Executives and experienced managers gain personal satisfaction from developing the next generation of IBM leaders in Latin America.

- It allows new managers to learn in an informal and personal setting. IBM employees describe this as "high-touch."

- Executives can identify talent and gain first-hand knowledge of the specific needs of the people who participate in the Blue Club sessions.

- Executives are held accountable for taking an active role in developing the ability of others, and employees are encouraged and supported for participating in these mentoring communities throughout the organization.

Clearly, these benefits are quite consistent with data on the benefits and value of building strong communities of practice. Work by Defillippi, Arthur, and Lindsay[16] outlines three core benefits for creating collaborative communities around knowledge and ideas:

- First, collaborative communities help build connections between employees who are frequently dispersed across geographic location, functional perspective, and level within the organization.

- Second, knowledge communities create a joint enterprise that provides an opportunity for developing tacit knowledge and strengthening relational competencies.

- Third, researchers argue that communities of practice provide mutual engagement that helps strengthen social capital throughout the organization.[17]

Each of these factors underscores the lessons learned from IBM's use of group mentoring as a tool for fostering knowledge communities of practice as exemplified by Latin America's Blue Club.

Lessons Learned from IBM's Mentoring Communities

There are many lessons to be learned from IBM's efforts to use mentoring, particularly in the case of Latin America's Blue Club, as a tool for fostering knowledge communities within the organization. The primary benefit derived from the IBM example and other organizations that seek to foster these communities is a greater understanding of knowledge as a social process and its impact on overall organizational performance. Knowledge that is useful for the organization is rarely created by individual specialists who are detached from the company or core dimensions of its work. Rather, as von Hippel argues, useful knowledge is typically produced by those who are directly tied to the environment where a problem arises and by those who will most benefit from finding a solution to that problem.[18] This means that a key lesson learned from IBM's use of mentoring in efforts such as the Blue Club is that it groups together communities of thinkers and problem solvers who are most closely tied to and most benefit from finding a solution to the emerging issues within their organizations.

When organizations identify the knowledge base of their workforce, make the necessary assessments regarding how to improve, and use this knowledge in creative ways, they also stand to develop a knowledge-resilient enterprise. A **knowledge-resilient enterprise** is one that has the right skills to be deployed quickly to address marketplace changes.[19] Managers and other leaders must have a constant pulse reading on the skills that are currently available and what needs to be done to quickly develop new ones. This is best accomplished by supporting social connections among individuals who are close to and invested in the work that is important to the organization.

While this approach may seem straightforward, achieving it is difficult. Many companies today have people and teams that are geographically or functionally dispersed. This makes it a challenge to connect people in meaningful ways. Mentoring can be seen as one important tool for helping to connect people and ideas across the traditional boundaries that can separate thinkers from ideas and problems from the communities and thus create solutions.[20] Mentoring communities can help the organization reach across barriers and boundaries and help generate the type of knowledge-resilient enterprise that it needs to remain competitive. IBM's experience with the Blue Club and similar efforts provides important lessons about how to create communities of knowledge that span across all types of boundaries that may interfere with developing and transferring resilient knowledge.

Mentoring Across Boundaries

IBM has experienced success in launching mentoring programs that foster communities across geographies as seen with the example of the Blue Club in Latin America. In addition, high-potential employees in strong growth markets such as China, India, Russia, and South Africa have been paired with mentors in mature markets in France, the United Kingdom, Canada, and the United States. These programs typically match employees in the growth markets with IBM's technical leaders and business executives to offer mentoring connections that, similar to the Blue Club, involve a series of idea sessions and information modules. The programs have tested the power of communities to help cut across geographic distance and enable employees to collaborate despite physical distance.

Taking the lead from lessons learned at IBM, organizations should recognize that effective mentoring programs have neither borders nor boundaries, and while challenging, are not curtailed by such things as time zone differences. As IBM revitalizes its mentoring program and aligns it with its global corporate strategy, the prevalence of mentoring communities has picked up momentum. Greater use of technology can be an enabler for connecting people for the explicit purpose of collaboration and, thus, geographic lines should not be a barrier to global collaboration. Additionally, everyone in the organization should be prepared for, educated about, and held accountable for making global integration and dispersed work arrangements function successfully in the business. This requires that employees, especially managers, acquire the skills and develop the attributes to lead effectively in our highly virtual world.

The global workplace differs from anything we have experienced in the past. It is very demanding, unpredictable, and complex. While there is a misconception that mentoring can only take place when mentors and mentees are located in the same physical space in face-to-face interaction, communities of practice remind us that it is the quality and meaning of the interaction that is most important. Given the prevalence of virtual worlds, telecommuting, and cross-geography work arrangements, special effort must be given to educate mentors and mentees on how to develop meaningful relationships in a virtual workplace. For those who work across geographic borders, it is equally important to develop greater diversity and cultural awareness.[21] Although technology cannot replace direct human connection, if used properly, it has the potential to create effective collaboration, teamwork, and trust.

Technology and the many different means of communication make it possible for meaningful mentoring relationships to take place in a virtual manner. At IBM, employees are effectively using teleconference, web conference, e-meetings, instant messaging, wikis, blogs, team rooms, and regular e-mail to enable communication, as well as other virtual technology, such as Second Life, to communicate and collaborate virtually. For successful mentoring to take place, both mentors and mentees have to make the effort to build strong communities, utilize available organizational resources, and focus attention on developing the right set of skills that can sustain these relationships as they attempt to solve critical organizational challenges.

While IBM is still developing new ways to foster these communities and help them extend across boundaries, its work in this area is far from complete. Issues related to culture, demographic diversity, functional orientation, and other boundaries are still factors that can block the development of mentoring communities. Issues related to diversity are the focus in Chapter 5, "Connecting People: Mentoring as a Tool for Diversity and Inclusion"; however, one of the other lessons learned from working to develop mentoring communities across IBM is the need to strengthen the skills and competencies that can support these diverse communities. While technical skills are required to support business processes and product development activities, other competencies are vital for the development of community. Because the

Blue Club began with IBM's effort to address retention, disconnection, and frustration among employees, the need to understand and focus on relational competencies has been another lesson the organization has learned. Within organizations like IBM, managers are expected not only to deal with the operations of the department for which they are responsible, but also for their own personal development and the development of their employees. Gone are the days when managers merely managed a group of people; the current hope is for them to discontinue the practice of "managing" and begin to lead, motivate, and inspire their employees. This requires that mentoring communities not only create and transfer knowledge but also develop relational competencies for managers throughout the global organization.

Strengthening Relational Competencies

To a great extent, the attributes and behaviors required to collaborate and build communities of practice depend heavily on what many have called relational competencies. If we look at mentoring as building relationships that require the exchange of ideas, knowledge, and support, then it makes sense that one of the benefits and outcomes of mentoring communities is that they build skills that are more relational in nature. This was very much the goal IBM set forth in trying to create what it called a "high-touch" mentoring experience. Relational approaches to understanding how people interact and solve problems at work are not new.[22] This perspective on how to define important competencies at work has been a core aspect of how some define leadership competencies, especially as managers have more significant responsibility for directing and leading others.

One frequent tool that is used to help specify relationship competencies and is used in employee development work within IBM is emotional intelligence. In their work, Caruso and Salovey make the point that an "Emotionally Intelligent" manager combines passion with logic and emotions with intelligence. A manager with strong emotional intelligence, by definition, has strong relational competencies. They further elaborate that "The fundamental premise of the Emotionally Intelligent manager is that emotions are not just important but absolutely necessary for us to make good decisions, take optimal action to solve problems, cope with change, and succeed."[23] For example, Goldean's work identified 20 relational competencies that define emotional intelligence that are organized into the following four categories: self-awareness, self- management, social awareness, and relationship management.[24]

While the use of emotional intelligence (EI) has been prevalent, particularly in the context of leadership development for the past two decades, the application of emotional intelligence to the mentoring relationship is somewhat new. To put this in context, emotional intelligence is generally seen as having the mental ability and stamina to manage one's emotions even in difficult times, and in the process, creating a foundation upon which rich personal and professional interactions develop.

To achieve a high degree of EI, individuals must develop a strong sense of self-awareness, which enables them to accurately read themselves and the social landscape in which they function. Having a high level of emotional intelligence correlates to having a high degree of social intelligence, which helps individuals to make the appropriate decisions, take the appropriate actions, and make the adjustments to build and maintain meaningful relationships.

Some argue that emotional intelligence, more so than traditional cognitive intelligence, is critical for identifying strong leadership skills within the organization.[25] The connection between emotional intelligence and the quality of relationships among people is also not a new idea. However, one of the important lessons learned from the IBM effort to foster mentoring communities is how critical relational competencies like those that define emotional intelligence are both to strengthen these efforts and to signal success. New research in this area is providing strong evidence for a link between emotional intelligence and the quality and strength of mentoring relationships.[26] However, organizations like IBM must not only foster these relational competencies within mentoring communities, but also include them as critical metrics of the success of its leadership.

As these types of communities are formed and developed for the explicit purpose of collaboration and innovation, it is necessary for them to master and demonstrate strong relationship competencies, such as emotional intelligence, among its members. If members of a knowledge community fail to manage their emotions appropriately, not only will the community be ineffective, but also it potentially blocks the organization from meeting its strategic goals. Conversely, as individuals are able to do personal assessments, practice introspection, and take the required course of action to improve their emotional intelligence, they heighten their chances of a richer personal and professional experience, and the corporation stands to benefit. However, building relationship competencies requires connection among members within the community. Thus, a key lesson learned from IBM's effort to building strong mentoring communities is that competencies are developed when the interaction is meaningful. Engaging communities of knowledge in meaningful collaboration not only facilitates relationship development but also enhances the capability of the community to produce meaningful work.

Fostering Meaningful Collaboration

Meaningful collaboration requires group members to abandon homogeneous thinking—sameness in this case is dangerous, as it stifles innovative thinking. Members of a team must be open to diverse ideas and approaches and become adept at questioning assumptions. Creative thinkers have the knack of probing and investigating to gain meaning and to constructively refute the "We have always done it this way" practice. A caution: Doing the things we are accustomed to doing will yield customary results, in the same way that doing business as usual gives us business-as-usual results. This practice leads neither to innovation nor breakthrough thinking. Generally, the question of "Why are we doing this?" is met with some level of defensiveness, and colleagues must trust one another so that this question is received as a valid and constructive one. Sometimes we run the risk of doing low-value, low-impact tasks, but the question of "why" forces people to think of how a given task will improve processes and add value. Pushing back on doing low-value tasks or doing things the same way confronts the issue of limited thinking and close-mindedness to new possibilities. Employees must become skillful in asking deep, probing questions and developing a critical eye for seeing things that are not readily obvious. There is a fine line here, and the caution is that there must be a purpose to questioning things—one should question to gain meaning and understanding, not just for the sake of asking.

Also, as teams collaborate to create innovative solutions, they have to find where in the organization work is being done "business as usual" and dismantle this practice. Again, innovation never occurs doing "business as usual." On the contrary, truly creative teams find simple but unusual and novel ways to solve problems, which is one of the ways IBM employees are encouraged to approach their work. Doing things in a new way—what we might call "business unusual"—has a certain element of risk, and managers, supervisors, and teammates should refrain from creating a punitive environment when things don't work as planned. Rather, it should be used as an opportunity to critically analyze why the desired outcome was not achieved and what could have been done differently. This is an important learning experience that should be chronicled to prevent replication of the same mistakes in the future.

Mentoring Communities and the Future

Business done in an unusual manner may be considered a form of disruptive change. This idea is getting great attention from many scholars and corporate leaders. Lynda Applegate embraces the idea that "Disruptive change is a source of innovation."[27] She further states that "one of the things we know is that the interest in innovation is being spurred by radical change and disruption that is going on in business." Disruptions to doing business as usual typically give people a compelling reason to think differently, and this is consistent with what IBM employees are accustomed to. Innovative people tend to thrive on finding ways to make paradigm shifts to do things differently, and typically they have the courage and energy necessary to make change work.

The world is changing around us, and if people within an organization are not poised to accept change, they become consumed by it. To put change in context, the only thing that is constant is change, and more and more employees have to develop a propensity to creatively manage it. The global marketplace is dynamic—client needs are constantly changing; therefore, skills and knowledge must be developed or readily available to adapt to the needs of the client set. Corporations must make it a business priority to build a skilled and adaptable workforce. As employees become skilled in dealing with change, they have to accept ownership and demonstrate every effort to make the change successful for themselves and for the organization. High-performing employees generally anticipate change and take the necessary steps to prepare for it. Price Pritchett and Ron Pound, in the *Employee Handbook for Organizational Change,* explain that "One of the keys to being successful in your efforts is to anticipate. Consider what's coming, what needs to happen and how you can rise to the occasion."[28]

Additionally, Arnold H. Glasgow makes a similar point that, "The trouble with the future is that it usually arrives before we're ready for it."[29] Using innovation and collaboration to predict the future and establish a formidable state of readiness positions organizations to manage changes with minimal impact. An effective way of dealing with change is to encourage employees to form think tanks and communities to study the change and define expected implications. Mentoring communities are also a value-added tool for addressing the need to balance innovation and continual change within the environment.

Valuing Community

Communities come together to share common business and career interests, and they participate in self-organized and self-regulated activities. Members of communities share a sense of "reciprocity and commitment to each other." According to the IBM Business Impact Study, "Communities provide opportunities to increase knowledge and mastery of a subject area and through a sense of membership and common context they develop, innovate, caretake, and transfer knowledge." Communities are not constrained by geographic, business unit, or functional boundaries. They are designed to develop and maintain capabilities and build social capital as a means to providing increased value to the business and making a positive impact on market share. IBM employees have found that communities of practice are an excellent source for gaining tacit and practical knowledge. It has been noted that people tend to learn best by application, in addition to learning from the experience of others.

Communities of practice, mentoring think tank sessions, group mentoring, speed mentoring, peer mentoring, reverse mentoring, and cross-business unit and cross-geography collaboration are encouraged and supported by managers and mentors in IBM. The principal reason is to create opportunities for knowledge transfer and acquisition of new skills to occur. Different forms of collaboration and mentoring are offered to employees, which allow them to participate in learning activities based on personal preference. IBM also uses what is known as "THINK Fridays" as a means of creating learning opportunities for employees across the business. THINK Fridays is an option offered to employees in many business units within IBM as time designated for employees to use to concentrate on their learning and development. During this time, employees are empowered to take e-classes, meet with mentors, or participate in communities with which they are affiliated. THINK Fridays stimulate uninterrupted thinking, which allows the mind to become adventurous and creative. THINK Fridays have yielded increased productivity, collaboration, and skills development within IBM.

"THINK"ing at IBM

IBM has a history of encouraging its employees not just to think but also to think creatively and to apply their thinking to real business issues. In fact, "THINK" has a special historical meaning in IBM: "When T.J. Watson joined the Computer-Tabulating Recording Company—the forerunner of today's IBM—in 1914, he brought with him the 'Think' motto he coined when he managed the sales and advertising departments at the National Cash Register Company. "'Thought,'" he says, "has been the father of every advancement since time began. 'I didn't think' has cost the world millions of dollars.'" Soon, the one-word slogan 'THINK' appeared in large block-letter signs in offices and plants throughout the company.[30]

In today's environment, "think" is just a start, because employees must exhibit critical thinking and take it a step further by carefully and meticulously acting on the ideas that come from critical thinking. The question is what is the value of an idea if action is not taken? Such an idea remains a mere thought that is stored in someone's head and soon forgotten. Organizations will never reap any dividends from this great thinking if employees are not encouraged to articulate their ideas, discuss them with peers, and be open to other points of view. Being open with ideas creates a mushrooming effect of even more ideas. Critical thinking becomes tantamount as people interact in communities and other group settings. Naturally, this sets the stage for creativity and innovation, but for this to happen, organizations must foster a climate of trust and respect among colleagues. Companies and organizations must be guided by a strong set of values and ethics, which typically makes it much easier for teams to share their ideas more freely. In a trusting environment, information is fluid and collaboration becomes natural and unguarded. Managers and mentors can help to cultivate a climate that underscores the value of thinking differently and with a purpose.

Who Said an Elephant Can't Learn to Dance?

When communities of knowledge are formed to support learning and collaboration, a change takes place within the environment. Over time, this has an impact on the overall culture of the organization. As IBM attempts to promote a knowledge-driven culture, fostering mentoring communities that bring together brilliant minds to tackle critical business issues ultimately leads to positive organizational transformation. While this can be seen as disruptive, it is also necessary for success in an extremely competitive industry. Lou Gerstner expressed his views on IBM's culture in his book, *Who Says Elephants Can't Dance?* by saying, "I came to see, in my time at IBM, that culture isn't just one aspect of the game—it is the game. In the end, an organization is nothing more than the collective capacity of its people to create value."[31] Now more than ever, companies like IBM are relying on communities of knowledge to help create and strengthen their "collective capacity" to deliver value. Through collaboration and mentoring, IBM provides a strong example of how organizations can seize global market opportunities and find ways to sustain their standard of excellence and innovation. Fostering knowledge communities that offer meaningful mentoring opportunities and knowledge transfer are approaches that help IBM and other organizations achieve critical business goals today and in the future. Additionally, employees can engage in collaborative learning and skill development. Despite IBM's size, these simple but effective practices enable the company to be agile, "light on its feet," and responsive to its global clients.

References

[1] Lave, J. and Wegner, E. (1991). *Situated Learning: Legitimate Peripheral Participation.* Cambridge University Press.

[2] Wegner, E. (1998). *Communities of Practice: Learning, Meaning and Identity.* Cambridge University Press.

[3] Wegner, E., McDermott, R., and Snyder, W.M. (2002). *Cultivating Communities of Practice: A Guide to Managing Knowledge.* Harvard Business School Press.

[4] Polanyi, M. (1996). *The Tacit Dimensions.* Garden City, NY: Doubleday and Co.

[5] Cross, R. and Sproull, L. (2004). More than an answer: Information relationships for actionable knowledge. *Organizational Science,* 15(4), 446–462.

[6] Hansen, M. (1999). The search-transfer problem: The role of weak ties in sharing knowledge across organizational subunits. *Administrative Science Quarterly, 44,* 82–111.

[7] Tyre, M.J. and von Hippel, E. (1997). The situated nature of adaptive learning in organizations. *Organization Science,* 8(1), 71–83.

[8] Baker, W. (2000). *Achieving Success Through Social Capital.* Jossey Bass, San Francisco, CA.

[9] Coff, R.W., Coff, D.C., and Eastvold, R. (2006). The knowledge-leveraging paradox: How to achieve scale without making knowledge imitable. *Academy of Management Review,* 31(2), 452–465.

[10] Waterman, R. and Waterman, R. (1994). Toward a Career-Resilient Workforce. *Harvard Business Review,* July/August.

[11] Eppenheimer, J. (1997). Benchmarking Career Management. *HR Focus,* Nov.

[12] Brandt, R. L. (1998). John Chambers and the Failure of Deregulation. *Upside,* Oct.

[13] Kram, K. (1985). Improving the mentoring process. *Training and Development Journal,* 39, 40–43.

[14] Higgins, M.C. and Kram, K.E. (2001). Reconceptualizing mentoring at work: a developmental network perspective. *Academy of Management Review,* 26(2), 264-288.

[15] Buckingham, M. and Coffman, C. (1999). *First Break All The Rules: What the World's Greatest Managers Do Differently.* New York: Simon & Schuster.

[16] Defillippi, R.J., Arthur, M.B., and Lindsay, V.J. (2006). *Knowledge at Work: Creative Collaboration in the Global Economy.* Oxford, Blackwell Publishing.

[17] Lesser, E.L. and Storck, J. (2001). Communities of practice and organizational performance. *IBM Systems Journal,* 40(4), 831–841.

[18] Von Hippel, E. (1994). Sticky information and the locus of problem solving: implications for innovation. *Management Science,* 44(5), 629–644.

[19] Waterman, R.H. and Waterman, J.A. (1994). Toward a career-resilient workforce. *Harvard Business Review,* (94409).

[20] Allen T.D., Eby, L.T., Poteet. M.L., Lentz, E., and Lima, L. (2004). Career benefits associated with mentoring for protégés: A meta-analysis. *Journal of Applied Psychology,* 89, 127–136.

[21] Clutterbuck, D. and Ragins, B.R. (2002). *Mentoring and Diversity: An International Perspective.* Oxford: Butterworth-Heinemann.

[22] Jordan, J.V., Kaplan, A., Miller, J.B., Stiver, I., and Surrey, J. (1991). *Women's Growth-in-Connection.* New York: Guilford Press.

[23] Caruso, D. and Salovey, P. (2004). *The Emotionally Intelligent Manager: How to Develop and Use the Four Key Emotional Skills of Leadership.* San Francisco, CA: Jossey-Bass.

[24] Goleman, D. (2006). *Social Intelligence: The New Science of Human Relationships,* Bantam.

[25] Hay Group, (2002). Unpublished study. Boston, MA.

[26] Kram, K. and Cherniss, C. (2001). Developing Emotional Competence Through Relationships at Work. In. C. Cherniss and D. Goleman (Eds.), *The Emotionally Intelligent Workplace* (pp. 254–285). San Francisco: Jossey-Bass.

[27] Allegate, L. (2007). Jumpstarting Innovation: Using Disruption to Your Advantage. Harvard Business School, Working Knowledge Series.

[28] Pritchett, P. and Pound, R. (2006). *The Employee Handbook for Organizational Change: Facing the Problem—Finding the Opportunity.* Pritchett Publishing Company.

[29] Glasgow, A.H. (2007). "Brainy Quotes" (Google Search).

[30] Watson, T. (2008). Comments on "THINK." IBM Archives.

[31] Gerstner, L.V., Jr. (2002). *Who Says Elephants Can't Dance? Inside IBM's Historic Turnaround.* Harper Collins Publishers.

4

Connecting People: Creating Meaningful Engagement

Chapter Contents

Moving from Isolation to Engagement

Connecting people in an authentic way in today's workplace has become a challenge and organizations are grappling with suitable ways to address this issue. The challenge is due in part to the fact that employees are dispersed and are having to learn how to work across ad hoc teams, project groups, and virtual locations. In this dynamic and demanding work environment, people and their managers tend to become preoccupied with accomplishing tasks, leaving little time or room to build quality relationships within the work environment. Such a situation amplifies the disconnectedness that employees may feel, especially those who work virtually or in some other type of flexible work arrangement. In fact, some who are classified as "work-at-home employees" have joked that IBM stands for "I'm By Myself." While this is often said in jest, there is an underlying message that relates to feeling isolated that is being communicated by some employees. This is clearly an important call to action that IBM needed to address. Thus, their goal became to transform feelings of isolation and experiences of a disconnected culture to one where employees say that IBM means "I'm Being Mentored." As we discuss throughout this chapter, one tool that IBM utilized to begin the process of a cultural transformation was mentoring. The innovative use of standard group and "speed mentoring" is reviewed, as well as the lessons learned from IBM's efforts to change the perception of some emplyees from feelings of isolation to one of employee engagement.

While IBM uses a variety of approaches, including mentoring, to help reduce feelings of isolation and disconnection, the need to constantly work on strengthening employee engagement continues to be a challenge for IBM and other companies. As time goes by, the number of employees working virtually has risen steadily, which has increased the need to understand how to connect employees to their peers working in multiple locations and across diverse cultures. The idea of connecting people has a very broad meaning, and provisions must be made to provide employees with clear definitions, understanding, and guidance. As we will see, group and speed mentoring are strategically linked with other efforts that facilitate employee engagement with the ultimate goal of helping to connect people, ideas, and relationship across IBM worldwide.

The Benefits of Engaged Employees

Business experts and researchers define and discuss the notion of employee engagement in a variety of ways. By definition, an engaged employee is fully tuned into the operations of an organization and makes deliberate efforts to contribute to its overall success. As a result of this degree of involvement, employees derive a sense of value and gain excitement from their connection to the organization. Among the factors that drive the presence and level of employee engagement are compensation, quality of work, social connections, and support from supervisors.[1] While engagement is a topic receiving a great deal of attention, some contend that this idea of employee engagement is very similar to notions of employee involvement and empowerment that were popular during the 1970s and 1980s. Regardless of its origins, the idea that employees are connected to the organization and the work of the company has been argued to be in short supply across a number of organizations. In its annual survey, *Industry Week* includes employee engagement as a metric of "best plants," which they contend is related to key industry outcomes such as continuous improvement and productivity. However, results from its most recent assessment of more than 90,000 employees across 18 countries revealed that only 21% of employees indicate that they would "put forth extra effort" to help their company's success, which is often used as a key indicator of employee engagement.[2] According to a similar assessment by the American Society for Training and Development (ASTD), while most employees and management rated engagement as "highly important" to their organization, only one-third of employees meet the criterion for high engagement. In addition, nearly one-fourth of employees within this assessment reported strong feelings of disengagement.[3] Clearly, there is agreement that engagement is important for employees and the organization, but data suggests that most organizations have not been able to drive and sustain high levels of engagement.

The charge for companies like IBM is to better understand how to drive, leverage, and sustain employee engagement throughout the organization. Research links high levels of engagement to key outcomes such as voluntary turnover and organizational commitment,[4] service quality as rated by customers,[5] employee job satisfaction,[6] and prosocial behavior or willingness to go above and beyond the specific job to benefit the organization and support other employees.[7] What seems to be a critical factor in driving these outcomes is whether the company provides support and resources that are integrated within performance feedback, training, development, and opportunities for employees to apply their knowledge and skills. A team of researchers who used this broad array of indicators for employee engagement took data from a number of published research studies on more than 8,000 business units across 36 companies. Their analysis showed that the level of employee engagement was positively related to productivity, safety, turnover, and profitability.[8] Thus, while the drivers of engagement are under exploration, the research on the positive impact of employee engagement is clear.[9]

To cultivate engagement, many organizations rely on traditional human resource practices and approaches. Training of managers on topics related to engagement along with support for education, training on job-related activities such as job rotations, and special assignments are examples of these conventional tools. Interestingly, within the ASTD survey, among highly engaged employees, having access to mentoring activities was rated as a very important factor, but among disengaged employees, mentoring was seen as not an important factor. This suggests that engaged employees recognize the value that mentoring relationships play in providing meaningful connections between people and the organization. However, the utilization of innovative approaches to mentoring as a mechanism for driving employee engagement is not typically an approach that many organizations take to address this critical need. To better understand how and why IBM leverages mentoring as one tool used to strengthen employee engagement, we need to take a look at the specific challenge that this global organization faces in connecting people.

Challenges for Engaging a Globally Dispersed Workforce

The challenge of connecting people within a globally dispersed, knowledge-driven organization like IBM requires constant attention. A recent research study looked at marketing on virtual work situations and included several IBM employees as participants. This work showed how face-to-face communication opens room for personal connection and relationship building. However, as the authors said, "We find that the lack of attentiveness, misinterpretation, and the absence of contextual cues and norms resulting from a reliance on electronic communication can lead to feelings of frustration and negligible interpersonal affections in interdependent groups."[10] This finding presented quite a challenge for technology-driven organizations like IBM. It also served to reinforce the point that the degree to which companies becomes overly reliant on technology as the primary means of communication with their employees has the potential to increase the employees' sense of disconnectedness.

Working in a globally dispersed workplace becomes more complicated as employees begin to interact within work teams with peers from different functions, cultures, generations, and perspectives.[11] On the other hand, working in a virtual and global environment can also connect individuals from these diverse backgrounds in a way that often does not happen with solely face-to-face interactions. Graham's article on the global workplace asserts that the "ability to work with people we rarely see, diverse people from different regions of the globe, is increasingly required to be successful." He further states that "Global collaboration, when executed effectively, enables an energetic workplace where teamwork is enhanced through the creation of a diverse collection of ideas."[12] The problem is often that we provide technology, but don't engage people through the use of that technology. Organizations invest a great deal of resources in the selection and adoption of technology, but little time and resources in helping connect people to the technology for maximizing their investment.[13] If organizations consistently find ways to connect the intellectual capital that exists within their organizations, regardless of where they are located, a significant business benefit will be yielded. It is a known fact that when brilliant minds come together and knowledge and ideas flow, great things happen. To capitalize on this reservoir of ideas, IBM is ensuring that employees have a full grasp of how to connect with people across locations, functions, and culture using technology in creative and interesting ways.

As employees are provided with the tools that truly connect them to the organization and to each other, the fundamentals of relationship and trust-building that are the core to effective mentoring relationships are reinforced and supported using these tools. Co-located employees have an advantage in that they can do things such as going to lunch together, discussing work items, and collaborating on a personal level. This direct person-to-person contact enhances trust and creates a foundation for meaningful relationship building. However, employees who are geographically dispersed, and some employees who have flexible work arrangements, are vulnerable to the isolation and the fear of being "out of sight, out of mind." These feelings can negatively impact employees, particularly new employees who frequently find it difficult to build connections in a globally dispersed workplace with such a broad array of work arrangements. New employees do not have a corporate history of relationships that have been developed over the years, which means they will have to become creative in establishing new relationships and developing strong networking skills.

While much of how we have discussed the challenges facing IBM and companies like IBM in connecting people focuses on the nature of globally dispersed workers, the issue of disengagement and isolation are not unique to workers who are separated by physical boundaries. Employees who work in traditional offices also face the problem of feeling disconnected. In many cases, on-site employees may have opportunities for direct interaction with superiors and peers, but the pace and demands of work can serve as barriers to building connections that are as strong as the physical barriers that often inhibit engagement. In addition, the demands of their jobs can cause employees who might work in the same organization physically to connect with others who may sit down the hall using technology rather than face-to-face contact.[14] It is not unheard of for employees to use instant messaging to talk with a peer whose office is next door. Within technology-driven organizations like IBM, and within increasingly technology-savvy cultures, one key question is how can we effectively use these tools to facilitate connecting people in meaningful ways but not at the sacrifice of human connection when possible? This question is posed rhetorically because, although technology serves a very important purpose, some organizations are overly reliant on using technology to connect people at the cost of direct human interaction and contact. If a conscious effort is made to use good judgment regarding when to send an electronic mail to a peer who works virtually, compared to making a phone call, this stands the chance of mitigating the sometimes impersonal nature of electronic mail. This is, no doubt, a balancing act.

Mentoring, Technology, and Connecting People

While the topic of mentoring is not new, the issue of mentoring using technology or what some have labeled "e-mentoring" is an emerging endeavor. To address the issue of isolation and the feeling of disconnectedness, IBM has designed many mentoring tools that use technology to help build connections, support communities of practice, and help employees connect with expert knowledge that may be found anywhere within the worldwide enterprise. For example, one of the key issues facing any organization is how to connect people with the knowledge and expertise that are needed to solve specific issues or problems. Unfortunately, there is no clear agreement on whether the benefits of e-mentoring (also known as virtual mentoring or tele-mentoring) outweigh the disadvantages.

Early work on virtual teams suggests that they may reduce overall attachment to the organization, increase feelings of isolation, and block effective cross-cultural communication.[15] Others argue that e-mentoring reduces the barriers of geography and time along with equalizing the status differences that may block relationships from being formed.[16] In fact, some scholars suggest that e-mentoring can actually overcome barriers that are associated with face-to-face mentoring, particularly those barriers that are created when relationships cross diversity boundaries (for example, race, gender, ethnicity, or culture).[17] Clearly, more practice and research needs to be done to make a judgment on when e-mentoring produces a positive versus negative impact. To date, no single factor, type of technology or specific aspect of mentoring has been linked to the overall effectiveness of virtual or e-mentoring solutions. Thus, IBM's approach has been to utilize various technology forms to support a key factor that has been shown to drive effective mentoring relationships—access.[18]

Creating Access to People

IBM's, Blue Pages was created as an easy-to-use online employee directory that has many collaborative features. Not only does Blue Pages provide contact information, it also allows employees to complete a personal profile, including job roles and skill sets, experience and qualifications, projects and teams, and communities and interests. This allows employees to network and collaborate with employees/peers across the globe and to locate individuals with specific expert knowledge and skills as the need arises. Work is currently underway to expand the functionality of Blue Pages to make the tool a trusted source to facilitate mentoring relationships much like an internal social networking tool. Employees will be given the opportunity to post that they are willing to be mentors and the type of mentoring they are willing to offer. Conversely, employees can also post that they are looking for mentors who can offer advice, support, and assistance within specific areas that may include one of the following mentoring types:

- Expert mentoring, which emphasizes the transfer of a specific skill, knowledge, and expertise.
- Career mentoring, which involves coaching, succession planning, and long-term development.
- Psychosocial mentoring and socialization, which focuses on helping new hires to adjust and adapt to the IBM culture. (It can also be extended to long-term employees who are moving to a new organization within the company.)

Blue Pages has features that "encourage and simplify IBM's movement towards an expertise-based culture, which is key in the current environment of virtual and global teams."[19] IBM is constantly upgrading Blue Pages as it encourages employees to share their expertise with the world. In short, the use of technology like that involved in Blue Pages connects people in the same work environment, those who have flexible work arrangements and employees who are dispersed globally to the knowledge and relationships they need to accomplish key work tasks. The investment in developing and promoting the use of Blue Pages as an IBM internal social networking tool is much like recent work that looks at the benefits of these types of technology tools for the facilitation of employee engagement across different organizations.

In fact, human resource professionals are now paying attention to the use of social networking tools (for example, MySpace, Facebook, LinkedIn, Second Life, and more) for providing new and current employees with accessible tools for establishing and maintaining connections. Given IBM's sensitivity to the challenges that remote and virtual workers face, it has invested greatly in educating its workforce on ways to address these issues. For example, employees have access to multiple translations of a "Global Guide to Mobile Work." The company stated that the "Global Guide to Mobile Work was developed to help mobile employees and managers 'stay connected,' perform effectively in their mobile environments, and respond quickly and effectively to the changing needs of both our customers and our company."[20] Thus, IBM's investment in developing and constantly upgrading Blue Pages as a technology tool that supports the connection of people across the organization is an important business endeavor. A major effort underway is to upgrade Blue Pages as a means of cultivating and promoting mentoring relationships and to communicate to employees its purpose of enabling "collaborative networks to drive innovative thinking…it is designed to empower you, increase your opportunities and fuel the IBM engine of growth."[21]

Creating Access to Information

In addition to using social networking tools such as Blue Pages to help employees gain access to people across the business enterprise, mentoring facilitated by technology has enabled IBM to connect people and information as needed to solve problems and address challenges. When IBM launched its mentoring revitalization effort, a "Mentoring Learning Suite" was created within a designated global mentoring Web site and made available to all employees. Both of these efforts were done to help put the information and resources in the hands of employees to help them to access key information as needed. For example, the mentoring Web site is designed to be a one-stop shop for finding mentoring information, programs, tools, and a forum to communicate with peers across the globe. The Web site offers employees options for finding mentors and mentees through the "classified ad" feature. Employees anywhere in the company can post advertisements stating their qualifications and experience, as well as their availability to connect with others. Similar to Blue Pages, the Web site gives employees the ability to post key skills and resources they need and outline the specific skill gap that they are looking to close. However, unlike Blue Pages, the Web site is focused more on information and learning about effective mentoring that benefits individuals and organizations. The site includes an array of mentoring educational materials, case studies, frequently asked questions, best practices, success stories, and information on competencies that help facilitate effective mentoring. Furthermore, there is a section on the Web site that houses separate electronic mentoring education resources called "flip books" that provide practical advice and tips for managers and employees on effective mentoring and other skills related to career development.

One of the most interesting features of the mentoring Web site is that it gives employees a forum to connect on a personal level with a team of mentoring experts across the globe, most of whom are volunteers. Each person on the mentoring team has a specific area of emphasis that can be tapped into by an IBM employee for advice or information. This part of the mentoring Web site connects IBM employees with real-time mentoring information on a wide variety of topics such as mentoring approaches that work, mentoring across geographic regions, and how to form a mentoring relationship, to name a few examples. A team of mentoring experts is available to answer questions, educate employees and managers about IBM's mentoring programs, and provide information on ways to use mentoring as a tool for engaging and connecting employees.

Preliminary tracking of employees' access to the mentoring Web site has been quite strong. During the first year, the mentoring expert team recorded more than 90 mentoring speaking engagements and touched more than 30,000 employees. In addition to having access to static information (for example, help guides and frequently asked questions), employees are also able to use what IBM calls the "Dear Mentor" feature to ask career development and mentoring questions. The questions are routed to members of the expert team, and employees usually receive responses within a 20-hour timeframe. Initial measurement data during the first year of this aspect of the Web site showed that 14% of the "Dear Mentor" inquiries were from managers and

86% were from nonmanagers. From a geographic perspective, 19% were from Asia Pacific, 15% from Europe, and 66% from the Americas. Thus, access to this mentoring-focused help feature was taking place across level, geography, and functional expertise throughout IBM.

Overall, tracking numbers on access to the Web site by the end of the first 18 months yielded 237,828 hits to the site, and that number is growing. In addition, the team of mentoring volunteers themselves has experienced enhanced engagement because of the positive impact they are having on their colleagues across IBM while they sharpen their personal skills. For example, Wayne Truitt, a former member of the volunteer team, wrote a note to several senior executives expressing how grateful he is to be part of the mentoring team. Wayne stated, "I have been recognized for many accomplishments in my 22 years. I have never felt such accomplishment as I have working with this team. My hat's off to the team. Their work has empowered thousands of IBMers to reach higher goals than ever thought possible. I am one of them."

Along with the tracking data on employee use and access to the many features of the mentoring suite, this personal account provides some evidence of the impact these efforts are having within the organization. Clearly, connecting people with the right information when they need it and in a delivery format that facilitates this connection is another tool that can support the connection between mentoring and all aspects of employee engagement. While the initial idea of the mentoring experts was to connect employees with valuable information, the unexpected yet significant benefit is that it strengthens the level of engagement among the mentoring experts who themselves demonstrate one of the key metrics of employee engagement—going above and beyond to help others and the organization.

Creating Access to Virtual Communities

While IBM's Blue Pages links people together for one-on-one mentoring relationships, and the Mentoring Suite connects people to information, the importance of engaging employees within knowledge communities is critical to the overall corporate strategy. As noted in the previous chapter, these knowledge communities are important for supporting organizational intelligence, innovation, and learning agility. However, it is sometimes difficult to build communities with geographically dispersed individuals. Unlike face-to-face communities of practice, virtual communities are useful when they are focused around executing tasks, solving problems, and other structured activities.[22]

One way that IBM has attempted to build virtual mentoring communities is through the use of different approaches to group mentoring, something they call, "group speed mentoring." The goal of IBM's group speed mentoring approach is to provide employees an accessible means of quickly transferring knowledge in an informal and collaborative setting. For example, the India Lab trained a group of executives to conduct group speed mentoring for new hires. This was done to provide support for new employees who may naturally feel anxious to quickly establish connections within the organization. Similar efforts have been done across countries in the Asia Pacific, European, Canadian, and Latin American regions. In each of these locations, group speed mentoring is used as a means of passing on information at a rapid pace and connecting new employees to others within the IBM community.

The use of group speed mentoring has recently expanded to other types of virtual communities. Another example came out of one of IBM's conferences called the Technical Leadership Exchange (TLE) that involved several thousand employees from across the company. As an outgrowth of this conference, a pilot group speed mentoring program was launched using the virtual world within Second Life. Employees from Japan, Europe, and the Americas met with executives in groups of 10 within a virtual office for 30 minutes and then moved to another virtual office. There were three executive mentors for each grouping by geography, and the allotted time of one-and–a-half hours enabled participants to interact with each executive mentor. These virtual sessions allowed mentoring to take place across geographies and also served the purpose of connecting employees in a virtual space to address specific questions or simply gain exposure to key organizational leaders. To make this more personal and natural, executives are briefed on ways to personalize their virtual offices, just as they do their physical offices. This is to demonstrate how IBM uses technology-enabled means to make it possible for employees to interact and develop mentoring relationships in virtual spaces.

Amy Groves, senior engineer and learning design consultant, has been actively promoting mentoring in Second Life, and her view is that virtual mentoring can take place in many different formats. One format that is particularly effective is to divide mentees into small groups of six, allowing the groups to rotate from room to room, visiting a different mentor in each room. The suggested length of each visit is 30 minutes (although it can be longer) depending on the number of mentors available and the scope of the mentoring topics that are being addressed. The process and format work best when each mentor chooses a unique topic that is conveyed to the mentees in

advance of the event. During the event, the most effective form of communication is text chat. Text chats keep participants engaged and immersed in the
virtual environment and encourage quiet participants to "speak up."
Ongoing improvements to this process are foremost on Amy's agenda, and
here are a few options of improvements that are under consideration:

- Customize virtual office spaces reflecting interests of mentors
- Make information available on each mentor's experience and background
- Provide a question box enabling mentees to submit questions in advance
  of the event

Mentoring in virtual space has proven to be rather engaging for IBMers
who choose to participate in this manner. Amy's summary of the virtual
experience is that, "Immersion involves feeling a direct personal connection
with others in the virtual environment. When both mentor and mentee identify with their avatars and experience a feeling of personal connection with
others in the virtual space, mentoring relationship can really flourish."[23]

The long-range goal is to use mentoring via technology in innovative
ways to engage employees, regardless of where they are located.

Example of an IBM Best Practice:
Group Speed Mentoring

Group speed mentoring is an attempt to connect a diverse group of
employees in an informal setting to transfer information at a rapid pace.
Because employees work in a knowledge-driven workplace within a fast-
paced technology industry, tasks are frequently completed within an intense
and time-constrained environment. The notion of speed mentoring is a simple, yet powerful, way to connect people and manage time constraints. Some
within IBM talk about speed mentoring as a way to "expand the bandwidth"
when it comes to mentoring. Speed mentoring done at the group level allows
multiple people to form connections and get answers to frequently asked
work and career questions at the same time, allowing them to get different
perspectives on issues while building relationships and support systems.

The speed mentoring concept was introduced to IBM by Jeff Cross, vice
president, Global Integration and Communication. Jeff's vision of one-on-
one speed mentoring paired a relatively new employee with an executive for a
30-minute session. The sessions generally covered career goals, understanding the culture of IBM, learning from the career successes and challenges of

participating executives, and much more. These sessions immediately became popular, and because of this early success, they were replicated in many areas across IBM. The cornerstone of speed mentoring is that it helps employees become adept at giving and receiving relevant information and ideas at a more rapid pace than traditional advice and knowledge-sharing sessions. Unlike other more formal mentoring programs, speed mentoring gives employees the chance to interact with executives and technical leaders in a fun and casual atmosphere, while engaging in problem-specific information sharing and advice sessions. Often times employees who participate in these events proclaim that they walk away with "pearls of wisdom" that have practical application for them and assist them in solving immediate work issues.

Many executives and experienced leaders within IBM appreciate being able to connect with employees in this informal setting. Not unlike the concept of "speed dating," in speed mentoring the employee enters the session with the view that the event may or may not lead to a long-term mentoring relationship, but in fact, several employees have formed informal mentoring relationships from within these group sessions. Jeff led the first speed mentoring session at the IBM Learning Center in Armonk, New York, in 2005, coinciding with a three-day Sales and Distribution Americas Communication team meeting. The primary purpose of the event was to "maximize professional development and facilitate networking in a '30-minute mentoring session' for a communications team that is dispersed across 21 countries, and in which four languages are spoken." Prior to the gathering in Armonk, an invitation was sent to all members of the group, informing them that they would be paired with two different communications executives for 30-minute mentoring sessions. The emphasis of the sessions was to get two different points of view on career management, tools, and resources, and to learn from the experiences of these executives.

To minimize the administrative burden of the pairing process, the invitees were asked to confirm their attendance by the mere click of a button in the invitation. A database was developed to keep track of the responses, and based on this, the pairings were randomly assigned. The criteria used to do the pairings assured that each employee had the opportunity to speak with one executive whose responsibilities include external communications (for example, public relations or analyst relations) and one who handles internal communications (employee, executive, intranet, and field communication). This random pairing helps to maximize contact between people who may not have had prior experience with one another yet have valuable knowledge and resources to share. Approximately five days prior to the event, the attendees were informed of the executives with whom they were paired, along with the time and location of the event. The session was conducted in an informal manner, which was especially important to those employees who do not speak English as a first language.

Based on a formal evaluation, the "30-minute" mentoring sessions were a resounding success, not just for the employees but for the executives, as well. The session proved to be valuable for the employees in terms of the visibility and exposure they were given to the executive leaders of the communication organization, providing them with a forum for expressing their career needs and aspirations in a safe environment. For their part, the executives got the opportunity to meet first-hand the pool of talent that exists in the organization, helping the executives to set or reset goals for supporting their own employees in achieving their career aspirations. It was also an opportunity for the executives to reinforce to their employees that they are valued and vital to the organization. A few of the comments from the participants include:

> *"I found it to be tremendously helpful. Both of the mentors gave me valuable advice to work in this globally integrated company."*

> *"Speed mentoring was a great opportunity to know more colleagues who have a lot of experience and advice to offer."*

> *"I really enjoyed the experience—there was great energy in the room. Congratulations on a great event."*

In general, IBM internal conferences are excellent forums for networking, which allows many people to develop meaningful mentoring relationships. One example took place at the three-day launch of a conference called, "fast-forward" in the Boston area. Group speed mentoring was listed as an elective session on the "fast-forward" agenda, and this session was oversubscribed based on the history of its success at other events. Today, group speed mentoring is becoming pervasive across IBM. The Boston session attracted more than 35 top IBM executives and several hundred employees from various professions. Those in attendance reflect a diverse array of IBM employees, including new hires, college recruits, long-term employees, managers, administrative staff, and people who had come to IBM through mergers and acquisitions. It also gave the organization the opportunity to introduce the group speed mentoring technique within the same physical location in hopes of connecting people to an idea that would be used later in virtual locations.

Much of the feedback from the Boston event helps to explain how individual and group speed mentoring has a place in the portfolio of efforts used within IBM. Tom Fleming, vice president, HR Software Group, expressed his views as to why mentoring is a personal and business imperative and explained how the use of group speed mentoring supports this notion: "Mentoring has long been a way for senior leaders to cultivate rising stars. In a knowledge-based business that values leadership, it becomes a critical method to transfer skills, identify and nurture diverse talents, and build tomorrow's leadership. Done well, it becomes cultural. It moves from a sponsorship-based model to one of information sharing and cross-learning." Tom went on to emphasize that, "It's every leader's responsibility to give back, build organizational capability, and establish a legacy that makes a company better than the one s/he grew up in." Speaking specifically about group speed mentoring, Tom's perspective is that "At IBM, we have found that speed mentoring is a way to leverage the leaders' time and involvement to talk one-to-many and to open the door to each participant's pursuit of new informal and formal relationships. Many times the most effective, connecting relationships start with lunch and a simple question: 'Would you mind if I pick your brain?' The question is always flattering, and relationships tend to grow from there."

Group speed mentoring is a relatively easy and inexpensive process to implement, as great benefit can be derived from doing it. It is done in a large room with several round tables set up to accommodate 8–10 employees and a table host or mentor, and this session generally lasts one to two hours, depending on the objectives. A facilitator starts the session by reinforcing the importance of mentoring, what's in it for employees and what's in it for IBM. The facilitator informs the participants (including the table hosts) that they will be asked the following three questions at the end of the session:

- What did you learn at your table?
- Were there any surprises?
- What actions will you take after leaving this session?

This final portion of the group speed mentoring session is most engaging and both executives and employees are very candid about the things they learned during this exchange. The executives' feedback ranged from "I am going back to reconnect with my mentees," to "I plan to be a better role model as far as mentoring is concerned and will ensure people in my organization are using mentoring as an important career development tool," to "I have a better appreciation of what's on the minds of our employees." A sampling of the comments from employees include "I did not know IBM had such an array of tools and resources to help me in my development," "I plan to retire in a few years and this has reinforced the importance of giving back," and "I'll take more responsibility in my career development and not leave it to chance." The sessions tend to be empowering as employees express excitement about their opportunities for career development in IBM.

Where there are high expectations, there is usually also high performance, so it is no surprise that IBM employees have voluntarily come together to help the company resolve the issues of employee isolation and disengagement. Many of these employees have a sense of empowerment and realize that their contribution and commitment to their colleagues can make a difference to IBM's bottom line. There is no doubt that IBM has taken on the challenge of helping its employees feel engaged within the organization, decreasing the likelihood that people will refer to IBM as "I'm By Myself."

Engaging Employees through Mentoring– Lessons Learned

IBM's original goal was to look for innovative ways to engage employees who were geographically dispersed. The use of technology is a significant way to connect people across the business, and includes Web sites, team rooms, chat rooms, wikis, Web conferences, virtual group mentoring, and more. Other techniques used are in-person speed mentoring, group mentoring, and the IBM Mentoring suite, reflecting a portfolio of approaches whose primary goal is to make mentoring accessible to individuals who need to solve problems at a rapid pace and may be geographically separated. IBM has expanded the use of the speed group mentoring concept beyond the regular workforce to reach out to its college intern population. For example, to help retain qualified students in their student feeder programs (for example, co-op students and summer interns), IBM connected them with current employees using group speed mentoring. The sessions focused on different career opportunities that exist in IBM and were intended to serve as a relationship building and career coaching opportunity. Thus, group speed mentoring was used as a recruiting means with the goal to increase the conversion rate of graduating students who work as co-ops into members of the IBM regular workforce.

Technology as a Tool, Not a Panacea

While the use of technology-enhanced mentoring to help increase access has shown some initial promise, there are some concerns with a broad use of technology-only types of mentoring. Issues such as increased miscommunication, slower development of relationships, problems with variability in individual competency with technology, and limitations on the actual technology itself are just a few of the issues noted by organizations that have taken virtual mentoring approaches. Some argue that the use of technology actually creates an opportunity for employees to detach from the organization and coworkers, which leads to less commitment and employee engagement.[24]

Thus, organizations should take caution in seeing technology as a substitute for other aspects of community building. Recall that while the use of techniques such as virtual mentoring and speed mentoring are increasing throughout IBM, so is the focus on building knowledge communities, which are strengthened by actual face-to-face contact. These approaches are not interchangeable. Each has strengths and limitations and must be selected and implemented in ways that are consistent with the purpose, organizational culture, and objectives of the company.

Holding Managers Accountable

While mentoring may help to make connections and reduce feelings of isolation and disengagement, mentoring techniques and tools cannot replace the important role that managers must play in connecting people to the organization. There is a strong effort within IBM to hold its managers accountable for fully engaging the employees who report to them. This responsibility cannot be offloaded to even the most innovative technology tool or specialized program offered by the company. At IBM, engaging employees requires that managers appropriately challenge their direct reports to work at their fullest potential, include the employees in the decision-making process, create growth opportunities, and make sure employees know that they are valued and respected. Frankly, it makes good business sense for managers to be actively involved in preventing employee disengagement, because the resulting effect can be very costly. The negative impact of disengagement can erode the morale of an organization, and teams often fall apart if all team members are not carrying their weight. Disengaged employees tend to have low productivity and high absenteeism, both of which take up much of the manager's time. That is one of the reasons IBM has been educating managers and mentors to detect the early signals of disengagement, with the hope of salvaging these situations by re-enlisting the commitment of disengaged employees before it leads to attrition from the firm.

IBM has a history of strong investment in attracting, retaining, and engaging its employees to create an atmosphere that makes IBM a preferred place to work and to grow. To engage employees, IBM creates practical learning opportunities through shadow experience, job rotation, stretch assignments, and mentoring. As employees state their short-term and long-term growth plans, there is a joint commitment between the manager and the employee to execute the plan, check progress toward attaining the goals, and reset goals if necessary. As IBM engages its employees, the company makes it possible for them to develop broad knowledge and multidisciplinary skills. While mentoring efforts such as group speed mentoring are part of the equation, they alone cannot accomplish what a rich portfolio of employee development activities can accomplish in sustaining employee engagement.

These combined efforts are somewhat in reaction to a paradigm shift among employees who look less at job security and more toward employability and career security. Using mentoring as one of the tools that builds firm-specific knowledge but also develops employees' abilities to operate in diverse knowledge communities is one strategy that helps to support employability. Employees are expected to build skills that have value to the business today and in the future. The opportunities to learn with agility, engage in innovative solutions, and reap personal and professional rewards all help to motivate and engage IBM employees. Because IBM is a multinational business, employees are also encouraged to connect with others in different geographies as a means to develop global leadership skills and global business acumen. The variety of learning opportunities clearly has a dual benefit—helping managers to be more effective in building employees' skills and supporting employee engagement throughout the organization.

Some Final Engaging Thoughts

Interestingly, the use of technology tools to enable people connection, as in the case of speed group mentoring, has helped IBM realize that some simple, low-cost, but high-impact approaches are powerful tools for exciting and engaging employees. For IBM, engaging employees means connecting them to strategic business ventures that have meaning, purpose, and value, and at the same time, holding employees accountable to execute their roles with integrity and excellence. The company has a long history of doing business on a set of principles and values and is sensitive to the needs of its employees, clients, and the business world. These fundamental values instill pride in its employees—in being IBMers. The use of mentoring to help support employee engagement has not only revitalized mentoring throughout the organization, but also helped to engage managers and employees around these fundamental values. This is accomplished in a way that creates access to people, ideas, and communities while stimulating the creation of both formal and informal mentoring relationships. Clearly, employee engagement is a multidimensional issue that requires a multidimensional solution. The use of various forms of community-based mentoring activities discussed throughout this chapter provides some examples of IBM's efforts to connect people through meaningful engagement.

A study by Towers and Perrin titled, "Winning Strategies for a Global Workforce," parallels IBM's employee motivation and engagement approaches. The Towers and Perrin study states that "Employees now recognize that their value and employability do depend on their ability to keep their own skills fresh. They know skills have an ever shorter half-life as technology and other factors change the business model. If they have one consistent expectation of their employer, it's to help them stay relevant, valuable and employable"[25] Because of IBM's commitment to employee development and continuous learning, innovation and collaboration that matter, and a staunch focus on leveraging diversity, the company has engaged its global workforce to increase productivity and ultimately reduce employee turnover. The innovative use of mentoring has been one key to the success IBM experiences in connecting people virtually, globally, and locally.

References

[1] Paradise, A. (2008). Learning influences engagement. *Training and Development* (Jan.), 54–59.

[2] *Industry Week* (2007). Rules of Engagement, (December), p.16.

[3] Ibid, Paradise, 2008.

[4] Schaufeli, W.B. and Bakker, A.B. (2004). Job demands, job resources and their relationship with burnout and engagement: A multi-sample study. *Journal of Organizational Behavior,* 25, 293–315.

[5] Salanova, M. Agut, S., and Piero, J.M. (2005). Linking organizational resources and work engagement to employee performance and customer loyalty: The mediating role of service climate. *Journal of Applied Psychology,* 90, 1217–1227.

[6] Harrison, D.A., Newman, D.A., and Roth, P.L. (2006). How important are job attitudes: Meta-analytic comparisons of integrative behavioral outcomes and time sequences. *Academy of Management Journal,* 49, 305–325.

[7] Schaufeli, W.B., Taris, T.W., and Bakker, A.B. (2006). Dr. Jekyll and Mr. Hide: On the differences between work engagement and workaholism. In R. Burke (Ed.), *Work Hours and Work Addition* (pp. 193–252). Northhampton, UK: Edward Elgar.

[8] Harter, J.K., Schmidt, F.L., and Hayes, T.L. (2002). Business-unit-level relationship between employee satisfaction, employee engagement and business outcomes: A meta-analysis. *Journal of Applied Psychology,* 87, 268–279.

[9] Bakker, A.B. and Schaufeli, W.B. (2008). Positive organizational behavior: Engaged employees in flourishing organizations. *Journal of Organizational Behavior,* 29, 147–154.

[10] Mulki, Jay, Bardhi, Fleura, and Lassk, Ph.D., Felicia (2007). An Examination Other Than Traditional Work Situations: Personal and Professional Challenges and Coping Mechanisms.

[11] Knouse, W. and Webb, S. (2000). Unique types of mentoring for diverse groups in the military. *Review of Business,* 21(1/2), 48–51.

[12] Graham, Andrew, Collaborating in the Global Workplace: Practical Ideas to Measure Your Global Team Effectiveness. Originally published in February 2006 *Link & Learn.*

[13] O'Neill, D. and Harris, J. (2004). Bridging the perspectives and development needs of all participants in curriculum-based telementoring programs. *Journal of Research on Technology in Education,* 37, 111–128.

[14] Avolio, B.J. and Kahai, S. (2003). Placing the "E" in e-leadership: Minor tweak or fundamental change. In S. Murphy and R. Riggio (Eds.), *The Future of Leadership Development* (pp. 49–70). Mahwah, NJ: Lawrence Erlbaum.

[15] Spreitzer, G., (2003). Leadership development in the virtual workplace. In S. Murphy and R.Riggio (Eds.), *The Future of Leadership Development* (pp. 71–86). Mahwah, NJ: Lawrence Erlbaum.

[16] Ensher, E.A., Heun, C., and Blanchard, A. (2003). Online mentoring and computer-mediated communication: New directors in research. *Journal of Vocational Behavior,* 63, 264–288.

[17] Hamilton, B. and Scandura, T.A. (2003). "E-mentoring: Implications for organizational learning and development in a wired world." *Organizational Dynamics,* 31, 388–402.

[18] Blake-Beard, S., Murrell, A.J., and Thomas, D.A. (2008). Unfinished business: The impact of race on understanding mentoring relationships. In B.R. Ragins and K.E. Kram (Eds.), *The Handbook of Mentoring at Work* (pp. 223–248). Thousand Oaks, CA: Sage Publications.

[19] IBM w3 Blue Pages: Tell the World What You Know section.

[20] W3 You and IBM—Global Guide to Mobile Work—Global Workforce Diversity. Updated November 2004.

[21] IBM w3 Blue Pages: Tell the World What You Know section.

[22] Mohrman, S.A. (1998). The contexts for geographically dispersed teams and networks. In C. Cooper and D. Rousseau (Eds.), *Trends in Organizational Behavior* (pp. 63–80). New York: Wiley & Sons.

[23] Groves, A. (2008). *Virtual Group Mentoring.*

24 Bierema, L. and Merriam, S. (2002). E-mentoring: Using computer mediated communication to enhance the mentoring process. *Innovative Higher Education,* 26, 211–227.

25 Towers & Perrin Executive Report, "Winning Strategies for a Global Workforce: Attracting, Retaining and Engaging Employees for Competitive Advantage"; Towers & Perrin, "Global Workforce Study 2005, Employee Engagement As a Business Driver," *Compensation and Benefits Network of Greater St. Louis* (14 March 2006).

5

Connecting People: Mentoring as a Tool for Diversity and Inclusion

---

Chapter Contents

The Importance of Connecting Among Difference

The predicted demographic diversity of the workforce that was debated more than two decades ago has arrived. Today's pool of available employee talent is overwhelmingly represented by people from a vast array of demographics, backgrounds, cultures, and life experiences. To remain competitive, organizations need to not only place people from diverse backgrounds into the workplace, but they must also establish and strengthen connections across people and with the organization. Whether to reach emerging market segments, to strengthen corporate social responsibility, or to engage untapped talent within the global workforce, valuing diversity is critical for driving key organizational outcomes. Diversity in the workplace, whether among employees, suppliers, partners, or customers, significantly impacts all companies.

Whatever reasons drive organizations to focus on issues of diversity, it is clear that when it comes to the workforce, firms that can attract, retain, and engage diverse talent have a distinct competitive advantage over those that don't. Further, some argue that the greatest benefits of workforce diversity is experienced not by the companies that have learned to employ people in spite of their differences, but by the companies that employ people who learn because of them.[1] Within the array of tools and techniques for cultivating a diverse workforce, mentoring is at the core. Whether it's connecting people across demographic groups, or linking people separated by location and work schedule, or creating understanding across cultures and generations, mentoring is being used as a strategic tool for leveraging the positive aspects of a diverse workforce. Collaboration across difference is contingent on the acute awareness of, respect for, and acknowledgment of the varied dimensions of diversity that exist within the global workforce. Connecting people is deeply rooted in IBM's diversity commitment, and it is reinforced by IBM's core values. IBM's commitment is to encourage an open and supportive environment where all employees are welcomed, valued, and fully utilized. This type of dedication to diversity is essential within a dynamic and global organization whose primary business relies on the knowledge and innovation of its employees. Valuing diversity is also a necessary component of what firms need to be productive and function at their highest potential.[2]

In this chapter, we continue to examine the portfolio of mentoring tools that IBM uses to support its overall business model, which includes attracting, cultivating, and engaging a diverse workforce. Because much of the work throughout IBM is conducted in collaborative structures, IBM relies heavily on group-based mentoring approaches to support and drive its worldwide diversity strategy. Through initiatives such as its worldwide Diversity Network Groups, IBM uses mentoring as a means for connecting people among diverse employee segments in a way that facilitates collaboration, learning, and understanding. A key lesson learned from these efforts is how vital it is for organizations like IBM to strategically focus on ways to use mentoring to connect people who are frequently left out of the traditional informal networks within organizations. Diversity permeates every area of the workforce, and to ignore this reality is to ignore the unique experience of diverse employees and its impact on critical business outcomes. Thus, the executive leadership at IBM continually acknowledges the connection between inclusion and business results, which is reinforced through the array of employee diversity networks and organizational diversity initiatives that IBM sponsors throughout its global business enterprise.

The Workforce of the Future Is Here

Data on demographic trends within the United States demonstrates that the world predicted by Johnston and Parker's groundbreaking report on workforce diversity has been realized as organizations are now more diverse than they predicted more than two decades ago.[3] The diversity of the workforce is expected to continue that increase over the next five decades, even though some countries will experience a reduction in the overall size of their available workforce. According to the Pew Research Center,[4] the U.S. population will increase to 438 million by 2050. This reflects a slower rate of growth than the United States experienced from 1960 to 2005. However, the non-U.S. population is projected to increase at three times that rate during the same time period. As the workforce continues to be global and mobile, the influx of new workers from outside the United States will continue to increase. Thus, projections by the Pew Research Center are that immigrants will comprise 82% of the U.S. population growth, meaning that by the year 2050, about one in five Americans will be foreign born.[5]

According to U.S. census data, the nonwhite population continues to grow more rapidly than the total population. The future workforce within the United States will consist of no clear racial or ethnic majority. The largest increase is projected to be among Latinos, who will account for nearly 30% of the U.S. population by 2050. Blacks will be the second-largest population of color at 13% by 2050, and Asians (U.S.-born) will be 9% of the total U.S. population. Whites (of non-Hispanic origin), who were 67% of the U.S.

population in 2005, will drop to a minority (47%), growing only 4% from 2005 to 2050. Overall, 67 million people of Latino origin are expected to be added to the nation's population between 2000 and 2050, as their numbers are projected to increase by 188%.[6]

While national origin and racial group members will significantly change the composition of the workforce, other trends will also significantly impact diversity within global organizations, particularly the age of the workforce. Within the United States, the number of people ages 65 and older will more than double in size from 2005 to 2050, representing a 119% growth. At the same time, working-age and young age groups are expected to increase in their share of the overall U.S. workforce. This means that the ratio of children to older people, which was about 59 per 100 working-age adults in the year 2005, will change to 72 per 100 by the year 2050. With the availability of work-age and work-ready employees in the United States stable or in slight decline, the need to understand global workforce trends is clearly at hand.

While lower ranks within the organization can be used as examples of effective human resource policies and programs for enhancing diversity, there is still a lack of diversity within the leadership ranks in most organizations that has been attributed, in part, to systemic barriers facing under-represented demographic groups, including women and people of color.[7] We still see a glass ceiling that effectively keeps the top levels absent of the same diversity that may exist throughout the middle and lower levels of the organization. According to the Catalyst organization, while the number of women of color in the workforce has increased, they still represent only 1.1% of corporate officers in U.S. Fortune 500 firms.[8] Given the consistency in the Catalyst data over time, it appears that the traditional "glass ceiling" has been recast as a concrete ceiling—an impermeable barrier that keeps women and people of color effectively locked out of the corridors of power in organizations across industries and professions.[9]

These and many other demographic trends mean that the diversity in the composition of the workforce demands diversity in an organization's strategies to attract, retain, and advance its employees. While this is an important goal for some organizational leaders, many continue to grapple with how to support and enable relationships among people who are engaged in a common enterprise but, as Caproni states, "who do not share a common history or culture."[10] A traditional approach has been to link senior leadership to junior women or employees of color via one-on-one mentoring relationships as a strategy for addressing barriers to diverse talent development.[11]

However, many traditional formal mentoring programs assume that mentor-mentee matches should occur between members of the same social identity group (for example, race, gender, age, culture, and so on). The lack of available senior mentors who match important social identities of the targeted mentees has been frequently identified as one of the key barriers for gaining access to senior-level mentors, especially for women and people of color. In addition, because of stereotyping, cross-cultural communication difficulties, and lack of diversity awareness, cultivation of trust between mentors and mentees of different social identity groups can act as a barrier to effective mentoring relationships.[12] These types of barriers often leave diverse populations feeling left out of a key developmental resource, disconnected from the organization, and at risk for dissatisfaction, disengagement, and voluntary turnover.

Diversity as a Business Imperative

As we discussed previously, the need to attract and retain talent is a critical business imperative and vital for building organizational intelligence. An important factor in achieving sustainable business success is having diverse, talented employees who bring many differing ideas, knowledge, and creative approaches in executing their tasks at IBM. The more effective organizations become in operating in a diverse workforce, the better they will be at removing the barriers to knowledge, learning, and collaboration across the workplace. Issues of diversity are frequently viewed as social responsibility, a moral obligation, or an ethical imperative for the firm.[13] In addition to these perspectives; within IBM it is also viewed as a core element of its overall Global Business Model (as discussed in Chapter 1, "Introducing IBM's Mentoring Portfolio"). IBM realized that not only does lack of attention to diversity increase negative outcomes for diverse segments of the employee population, but lack of diversity and inclusion also has an impact on the overall health of the organization.

In fact, some argue that in terms of demographic diversity, people of color and women may act as a "miner's canary"—an indicator of conditions that are challenging not only for numerical minorities but also for majority groups within that same organization.[14] The presence of dissatisfaction, frustration, and high turnover among people of color and women is perhaps a precursor to future problems that will be experienced by majority group members if the issues facing these more vulnerable groups are not resolved. Thus, the need to link diversity and mentoring may not just be an outcome of shifting workforce demographics or a process for facilitating positive interpersonal dynamics in the workplace, but may also be a tool for ensuring the overall health and strength of the organization. This potential benefit means that unleashing the power of mentoring among diverse employee groups adds value to the organization and, as you will see from the experience of IBM, provides a strategic tool in addressing emerging aspects of global workforce diversity.

However, the pervasive perception that these organizations are not open, receptive, and fair to diverse employee groups poses a significant challenge to the retention of their talented employees. Issue of culture and climate with the organizations are critical in terms of shaping the connection felt among diverse employees as members of the company. Recently, there has been increased attention to the notion of "micro-inequities" defined by subtle acts (for example, public humiliation, being passed over for promotions, cultural incompetence, jokes, and so on) based on race, gender, culture, disability, or other dimensions of diversity. These micro-inequities were identified by Rowe as a way to highlight a subtle yet insidious form of discrimination that can damage the connection among people and can lead to detachment of employees, especially those who are the target of these actions.[15] This detachment over time will have a negative impact on employee retention, particularly for those who are the target of these micro-inequities at work.

According to a study of U.S. firms conducted by the Level Playing Field, people of color are three times more likely than white men to cite unfairness as the only reason for leaving their employer. In addition, gay and lesbian professionals are nearly twice as likely as white men to cite being treated unfairly as the only reason for voluntarily leaving the company. By their estimate, perceived unfairness in the workplace costs U.S. employers $64 billion a year, based on the total cost of replacing and losing professionals who leave because of micro-inequities or unwelcoming workplace culture. Interestingly, the impact of micro-inequities on key workplace outcomes doesn't just affect employee attitude and retention. According to the Level Playing Field survey, 27% of those who experience unfairness reported that they would not recommend the company to potential employees, and 13% said the same about the company's products and services.[16]

On the other hand, Diversity Inc.'s recent list of the "Top 50 Companies for Diversity" identified several key trends among the top organizations that are successful in attracting, retaining, and advancing the careers of diverse employee populations. While pay and benefits were among the top factors, more positive relationships with their supervisors, along with a more positive work environment and more respect from coworkers across the organization were also key factors. Issues such as clear opportunities for advancement were frequently cited as important factors in the success of these leading companies in diversity efforts. Clearly, issues related to culture and climate are why people in diverse segments report either staying or voluntarily leaving their companies. Thus, cultivating a workplace that allows diverse groups of employees to feel connected to the organization, supported in their personal and professional development, and free from the negative impact of micro-inequities are significant factors that define the business imperative for diversity as a competitive advantage for organizations.

Enhancing Diversity: Why Mentoring Matters

We have known for several decades that mentoring has a unique impact on the career and psychological well being of employees, especially among diverse employee segments. Work by David Thomas illustrates the power of mentoring in helping people of color (in his work, specifically African Americans) "break through" to senior levels within the organization.[17] However, a frequent finding is that women and racial/ethnic employees of color have a more challenging time gaining access to mentoring relationships than their male and white counterparts.[18] Findings from Cox and Nkomo's study of 729 black and white MBAs support this perception; they found that black MBAs reported significantly less access to mentors than white MBAs.[19] The Catalyst Organization's groundbreaking series of studies on women of color in the corporate sector highlighted the importance of access to mentoring for positive career outcomes. Lack of access to mentors was cited as one of the top four barriers to career success among the women of color surveyed.[20]

As mentioned earlier, a traditional view of mentoring relationships assumes that it is necessary to match individuals based on similar demographics, in addition to factors such as knowledge and functional expertise. Thus, the issue of access to mentoring becomes more complex when employees from diverse segments need access to mentors who not only share their knowledge or functional orientation, but also share their same culture, gender, race, or other important social identity group. Gaining access to mentors of the same identity group may be difficult for people of color because of their low numbers within higher levels in the organization.[21] Dreher and Cox posit that "a significant part of the influence differential between white men and mentors of other gender or racial groups derives from differences in legitimate power that is embedded in organizational position" (p. 298).[22] Research by Thomas showed that for women or employees from other diversity groups to gain access to similar mentors, they had to go outside of their own company and cultivate informal relationships that were not supported by the organization and thus not seen as evidence of the organization's commitment to its diverse employees.[23] Thus, gaining access to organization-sponsored mentoring within the organizations often means that people of color are thrust into interracial and cross-cultural dynamics to a greater degree than whites.[24] Access to mentors of the same race is not as available to people of color within the companies without crossing additional boundaries such as level, location, or function or seeking these relationships outside of their own organization. With little formal support or legitimacy, there is an additional burden, or what Blake-Beard and her colleagues call a "mentoring tax," placed on these developmental relationships that is a function of key dimensions of diversity.[25]

Having to address this mentoring tax may pose additional barriers to building trust and facilitating engagement that are both necessary for effective mentoring relationships. This often means that mentoring across dimensions of diversity may not involve the same type of developmental support as relationships among individuals who are similar in demographic and identity dimensions.[26] Thomas writes that the changing environment and diversity dynamics that we encounter in organizations "engenders the deeper difficulties that we face in creating a climate of authentic collaboration" (p. 280).[27] Organization-sponsored access to people who share the same race, gender, or culture may be critical for building trust and providing a signal that the organization values employees from diverse segments because of the diversity they bring, not in spite of it.

Thus, formal mentoring initiatives must not simply be about matching individuals across functional boundaries. They must also be about supporting and understanding the unique experience diverse employee segments face when confronting challenging organizational cultures that may have historically been unsupportive of diversity and inclusion. While traditional approaches to diversity focus on reducing attention to difference, contemporary approaches include an identity-conscious strategy that acknowledges the unique needs and experiences of diverse employees and openly provides support to fit these specific needs.[28] Thus, an inclusive mentoring approach means connecting people not only across dimensions of difference but also connecting people who engage in meaningful and collaborative relationships within these differences. As mentioned previously, the importance of mentoring for enhancing diversity in organizations is that mentoring provides an opportunity for learning, knowledge transfer, and psychosocial support. Being open to an identity-conscious strategy for mentoring provides opportunities for career and social support that is group-specific, inclusive, and meets the unique needs of diverse employee segments. Keep in mind that mentoring is also a powerful tool for establishing meaningful relationships both within and across dimensions of difference, as we have previously discussed. These two notions are not contradictory, but each approach provides a unique set of support and access to resources that are necessary for the development, retention, and success of a diverse workforce.[29]

Connecting within Diversity at IBM

The ability to develop and manage relationships across and within lines of difference opens the door for people to connect on a level that promotes trust and collaboration. IBM provides ongoing diversity education for employees, as well as managers and other leaders, for employees to better connect across lines of diversity. Additionally, the Business Conduct Guidelines at IBM hold all employees responsible for and accountable to help make the workforce one that is welcoming to all. That is a primary reason the diversity theme is anchored on the IBM platform that "None of us is as strong as all of us and everyone is included and no one excluded."[30]

The commitment to connect people across and within all aspects of diversity has been a focal point of IBM's strategy for several decades. Extensive measures have been taken to educate employees on the company's diversity position. It begins with the company's heritage, principles, and values and includes the clarity with which the Chairman articulates IBM diversity posture in the company's policy letter. In fact, not only are managers at IBM required to conduct an annual diversity meeting with their employees to be legally compliant, they are also expected to make it a practice to conduct ongoing conversations that reinforce IBM's position on diversity. To support managers in this effort, IBM provides them and other leaders a library of department diversity modules to use as references and guides in these conversations. Likewise, employees have access to diversity resources that they can use to build their knowledge and engage in acceptable behaviors as they interact with their peers who represent different diverse constituencies. IBM is a corporation that does business in countries across the globe, and the current strategy is to ensure that every employee has a role in transforming the business into a viable and strong enterprise that is integrated and seamless.

To meet this goal, IBM is focusing on both simple and fundamental things as well as the most sophisticated means of enabling employees to successfully function in a culturally diverse workplace. The company redesigned its portfolio of diversity course offerings with the aim of helping employees better understand the nuances of communicating across different geographies to gain strong cultural competence. As a supplement to the courses, employees have access to Web sites that house a plethora of diversity information and materials. IBM's investment in affording its employees access to a rich menu of diversity education is a strong statement of support and signals the importance of connecting people across difference. However, merely providing education and training for all employees worldwide is not sufficient for creating connections across diverse groups of employees; other measures must be adopted.

When IBM launched an extensive global revitalization of its mentoring program, one of the primary means of enabling linkages and connections was through the development of the Global Explore Mentoring Web site, as well as a mentoring learning suite. The intent of developing the Web site and learning suite was to provide employees and managers access to mentoring information, programs, tools, and resources. The Explore Mentoring Web site houses the following information:

- **Dear Mentor Feature**—Dear Mentor allows employees across the globe to pose questions to a team of mentoring experts. Since its inception, the team has been actively responding to questions related to mentoring and career development from employees not just in the United States, but also throughout the world; for example, Russia, China, India, Brazil, South Africa, Canada, Australia, UK, the Nordics, and Singapore, to name just a few. The expert mentoring team has a commitment to respond to all inquiries within a twenty-four hour timeframe.

- **The Frequently Asked Question (FAQ) section**—Questions that are of a generic nature are logged and a corporate answer is provided. Generally, these questions are related to corporate policies, practices, and employee relations. The team of mentoring experts quite often relies on the mentoring experts who reside within the different geographies to evaluate the FAQs, based on the particular country's privacy laws, customs, and cultures. In this way, the company is taking into consideration the nuances of a global workforce and the differences that exist from country to country.

- **Mentoring Blueprint for Leaders**—This section of the Web site offers managers and other leaders some guidelines and suggestions on ways of establishing a successful mentoring program. "Blueprint" defines a standard of excellence for mentoring programs and is a repository for mentoring webcasts and podcasts. For example, one successful technique in transferring knowledge through the mentoring process is using the art of storytelling. The storytelling approach tends to increase the attention span and mental retention of knowledge that is being conveyed by the mentor to the mentee. In fact, a team of experts from the IBM Center for Advanced Learning created a Quick View on Storytelling for Business results. (Quick Views are electronic modules organized in a streamlined *Reader's Digest* manner that provide IBM employees the opportunity to quickly study a particular subject.)

- **Mentoring Success Stories**—Periodically, the corporate mentoring team conducts interviews with successful mentoring pairs to learn the methods and techniques they used in their relationships. The hope is that others will learn from them and apply these techniques in their own mentoring relationships. IBM also uses the Success Story approach to spotlight executives who are role models and staunch supporters of the mentoring program.

- **Mentoring Flip Books**—Three electronic flip books are on the mentoring Web site and the content is presented in a *Reader's Digest* manner. The goal of each flip book is as follows:

  - **Flip Book for Managers**—This book targets managers and provides them with guidance on the mentoring process, ways to assist employees in participating in mentoring relationships, and various options for rewarding and recognizing employees who have made significant contributions in mentoring others. As an example, managers have been given guidance on ways to recognize employees through the performance evaluation process and other forms of rewards for making measurable impact in facilitating skill gap closures for their peers through the mentoring process. This degree of recognition serves as a positive reinforcement and support to IBMers; in addition, it reminds employees that they are valued.

  - **Flip Book for Employees**—This mentoring book is more generic and its content addresses the fact that mentoring is for every IBM employee. Its premise is built on business linkage, impact, and connections. Employees find this book particularly useful because it provides practical tips on ways to engage in meaningful mentoring relationships.

◆ **Career Must–Have Flip Book**—"The Career Must-Have," was developed as a result of a series of focus groups that were conducted separately for black managers and employees from three major IBM sites. The purpose was to determine how people are using mentoring as a critical career development tool. Although the number of participants was relatively small, IBM was still able to gather some very insightful information that was used to develop the content of "The Career Must-Have." The content of this flip book highlights IBM's historical commitment to employee learning, and it also speaks to practical ways Diversity Network Groups can use mentoring as a critical development tool. Again, based on the focus group input, the flip book provides tips on personal branding, managing up, staying engaged, relationship building, ethical leadership, derailment factors and ways to recover, using challenges as a means to learn, and how to develop the necessary foundational competencies. While this book was developed as a result of focus groups with black employees, its content and guidance is relevant to all employees as they pursue plans for career growth.

■ **Learning Suite**—The other tool that connects employees to relevant mentoring information is the Learning Suite. It is characterized as a one-stop information center, which employees can navigate by using a site index. The Learning Suite is streamlined and organized for ease of use. It has special nodes that contain information on mastering the mentoring basics, trying simulation, studying mentoring in depth, receiving messages from IBM's executives, examining best practices, using the Learn at Work tool, asking an expert for help, and assessing oneself using the prementoring engagement tool.

The Explore Mentoring Web site continues to be an invaluable tool for individuals to access information about mentoring. The mentoring Web site is linked directly to the Global Workforce Diversity Web site, which helps employees to easily gather diversity information for use in their mentoring relationships. This is deemed as an important and easy way to connect mentoring to the company's diversity practices and processes. It was significant to make this link between mentoring and diversity to amplify the point that IBM wants its employees to have the tools and resources to help them not only bridge knowledge gaps, but, equally crucial, to bridge diversity gaps. This effort is an important response to the feedback from the focus groups that were conducted with the black employees which showed that their preference is to have mentors who look like them because this gives them a sense of validation and the feeling that their needs would be better understood. From a historical perspective, this appears to be the case for many segments of the employee population that may experience a sense of isolation, micro-inequalities, and lack of access to informal sources of knowledge and information. The mentoring team seized this as a great opportunity to launch an awareness and education campaign on ways to better integrate diversity into the mentoring process with the explicit goal to establish connection across all diversity dimensions.

The Diversity Network Groups in IBM serve an essential role in providing support for their respective constituencies and, at the same time, create opportunities for meaningful collaboration and teaming across diversity lines. Thus, there appeared to be a need to connect people both across and within diversity groups to provide multiple methods of support and advice for employees. While mentoring across diversity is important, building connections based on commonalities was also a critical piece of feedback provided by IBM employees that has contributed to the company's approach to mentoring.

Mentoring Based on Affinities

The goal of connecting people across the organization is a process of social and cultural exchange. Especially within the context of mentoring relationships, this goes beyond simple acts of compliance to rules and policies by the organization. Effective mentoring relationships involve some level of compliance, but employees must cultivate the willingness to accept advice and influence from the other person involved in the relationship, a process known as identification.[31] Having reciprocal relationships that involve trust and sharing across boundaries is a critical precursor to identification and thus effective outcomes for all individuals involved within the exchange. However, it is sometimes challenging, especially within formal mentoring efforts, to facilitate these types of meaningful exchanges.

Frequently, employees from diverse backgrounds are challenged by, as Thomas and Higgins state, "The psychological instability that emanates from a work context that does not affirm salient and important aspects of one's personal identity, or provide sufficient information and guidance to sustain one's career growth and development" (p. 273).[32] Other research confirms that relational aspects of the work experience are a critical driver of career outcomes and attitudes for underrepresented minorities in the workplace.[33] Thus, while task-orientated or instrumental aspects of mentoring are important for career outcomes and success, the relational dimensions, which include issues of interpersonal trust, reciprocity, identification and feelings of connection, must not be overlooked. For example, substantial previous work on group mentoring based on demographic commonalities or what are called "affinity groups" examines the positive impact this type of mentoring structure can have on career outcomes and work attitudes for people of color.[34] Thus, there is a need to recognize and support mentoring relationships among individuals who share important dimensions of commonalities or where some affinity is created among individuals who share the same social identity (for example, culture, race, gender).

Some argue that mentoring within a social identity group is an important tool for building interpersonal support and understanding the need for connections among employee groups that are at risk for isolation within the organization.[35] Issues of identification, role modeling, value congruence, and creating a "safe zone" for difficult discussions surrounding gender, race, class, disability, and so on are frequently cited reasons why some connections among difference are as important within the organization as connections across difference.[36] The assumption is that judgments, generalization, and stereotyping may be lessened when some aspects of mentoring take place among individuals of the same identity group or what some refer to as "same image" mentoring. For example, women frequently state that having a woman as a mentor sets the stage for validation—they feel a better sense of connection, safety, and authenticity in these relationships.[37] IBM recognizes these diversity dynamics, and that is a principal reason the company provides strong support to the various Diversity Network Groups that exist within the organization; through this effort, mentoring both within and across diversity lines is a hallmark of its Network Groups.

Group Mentoring via Diversity Networks

Ibarra's work on the informal networks of white and minority managers found that minority managers had networks with significantly lower levels of diversity than those of their nonminority counterparts.[38] In addition, career advancement for minority managers was related to the configuration of their networks. Networks of low-potential minorities tended to be dominated by cross-race relationships whereas the networks of high-potential minorities were composed of a balance of same-race and cross-race relationships. Ibarra's research speaks to the importance of the pattern and composition of relationships that are developed both across and within diversity groups. People of color often must develop two complementary networks: one set of relationships with whites who may provide access to resources and opportunities, and another set of relationships with people of color who provide psychosocial and emotional support. An interesting implication of these different patterns is the suggestion that for some employee segments, same-identity-group versus inter-identity-group mentoring serve distinct and necessary purposes. The need for both types of mentoring solutions may be most relevant for employees of color and for women, because research suggests social identity (for example, gender identity, racial group identity, and so on) is not as salient for majority group members within the workplace compared to minority group members.[39] Thus, the pattern of access to developmental relationships is clearly as diverse as the people who are both engaged in these relationships and who may also stand to benefit from them. Like a number of organizations, IBM has sponsored Diversity Network Groups throughout the organization to help bring about greater understanding of diversity, not just for a particular constituency but also for all the constituencies in IBM. Unlike in most organizations, however, at IBM these networks have expanded through the support of the company and frequently work together in a supportive and inclusive manner, while supporting the development of their specific constituency. Diversity Network Groups (DNGs) at IBM foster a welcoming climate and help its members with networking opportunities, finding mentors, participating in career development initiatives, and assisting with recruiting events. The stated purpose of IBM's DNGs is to provide a place where members "voluntarily come together with the ultimate goal of enhancing the success of IBM's business objectives by helping its members become more effective in the workplace."[40]

Currently, DNGs in IBM have expanded to a global level and have been proven to be instrumental in helping the company achieve many of its core business objectives. To reinforce the importance of DNGs in IBM, Ron Glover, vice president of Global Workforce Diversity stated that, "The IBM Diversity Network Groups are the 'Diversity Army' in IBM. They are the focal point for the Diversity partnership that exists between IBM and IBMers around the world. The work they do ensures that IBMers everywhere have the ability to connect and create community with their colleagues from every part of the Human Family. These communities provide support, development, mentoring, information, and visibility to our diverse employees and are essential to building awareness and understanding across lines of difference in the workplace. They are the place and the vehicle by which what we say about our Diversity Values are made real for our people."[41]

The intent of the comments and examples is to indicate how IBM uses organizationally sponsored DNGs to help its employees flourish and enrich positive experiences at work. Diverse employees are also empowered to create networking, mentoring, and developmental opportunities with the goal of building a rewarding and satisfying career for everyone within the business. Thus, as part of IBM's global diversity approach, group mentoring or providing diverse employees access to developmental networks of peers, more senior and junior employees who are the same race, gender, culture, or other important identity group, provides a key strategic tool. While these are not the only mentoring resources made available to employees of color across IBM worldwide, they are important resources that provide a powerful source of support, advice, and access to important knowledge about how to be successful within the diverse culture at IBM.

Asian Diversity Network Group at IBM

Based on the recognition that networks among key identity groups create an important source of support along with access to mentoring relationships, IBM sponsored the Asian Diversity Network Group (ADNG). Located at IBM's Austin, Texas site, the ADNG gained the support and encouragement necessary to create the International Mentoring program that was established as a connection between the U.S.-based ADNG and IBM's Greater China Group. Its purpose was to help grow talent in the China Development Lab with the explicit goals of increasing IBM's competitiveness in Asia and exposing employees in the United States to their colleagues in the emerging countries.

The ADNG initially recruited 26 mentors from the United States who were matched with 53 mentees in the China Development and Research Labs. The program got strong support and endorsement from executives in the United States, as well as from the China labs. To put some accountability in the program, the mentees were asked to identify and document two to three areas of developmental/career needs that they intended to work on with their mentors. Progress toward closing the developmental gaps was tracked by the program coordinators. Because this mentoring relationship was done in a virtual way, it posed new and different challenges, compared to relationships that occur where both individuals are located in the same geography. As a result, the program coordinator conducted a survey to gauge how the mentoring relationships were developing and how technology could be used as an enabler in making meaningful connection in a virtual world. The results of the survey indicated that

- Telephone, e-mail, Sametime (instant message), newsletter, and wiki were used as methods of communication. The majority of the participants used e-mail and telephone as their primary means of communication.
- There was strong agreement that multiple methods of communication were necessary.
- Most mentees stated that their mentors gave them relevant and applicable advice and suggestions.
- The primary "pain points" of cross-geography mentoring relationships were directly related to things such as time zone and cultural differences.

Following the survey, the sponsoring executive in the United States conducted roundtable sessions with the mentors, while the executive in China met with the mentees. Feedback from both executive sessions was very positive and encouraging. Based on this feedback, this cross-cultural network expanded its program offerings and recently implemented some technology-based solutions to better facilitate the mentoring matching process, as well as to serve as a vehicle for communication.

To better understand the impact of the international mentoring program created and sponsored by the ADNG, we interviewed individuals who were closely connected to and were the beneficiaries of this innovative approach to group mentoring at IBM. Ray Tan, executive at Tivoli China Development Lab and past program coordinator, said the idea to launch the China mentoring program came from a Chinese-American member of the DNG whose ideas prompted the group to put together a business proposal, which was presented to a few executives. The executive team accepted the proposal and offered its support in the form of assigning a coordinator to the program; it helped to set the priorities of the initiative and, most importantly, recognized both the need to help build the technical talent in China as well as the importance of the cross-geography partnership. Further, he reflected that the program brings great value to IBM, as "Mentoring is critical to the business, and it is important for us to pass on our experiences and knowledge to the pipeline of talent to keep the business moving forward. This program also aligns with IBM's global strategy to help less experienced employees in emerging geographies gain industry and client interfacing skills." While the initial success was evident during the interview with Ray Tan, he identified some of the challenges still being addressed within the China mentoring program, including:

- Time constraints that force employees to balance volunteering their time with the demands of their regular jobs
- Connecting people across differences in time zone and work cycles
- Helping to maintain a high level of energy among global program participants

Cross-border mentoring can also be a challenge from a cultural perspective. Ray suggested that "When working with other cultures, people should be sensitive to the thought that the approach to doing business may differ from their own and not try to influence the value system of the other country." His interest in mentoring originates from not having had a mentor during his first six years at IBM. Once he was exposed to social networks and mentors, he became more aware of career choices and resources, which helped in his professional development. Because of this, he has a commitment to help new hires find mentors early on in their careers at IBM and considers the work being done by the ADNG to be an essential piece to the portfolio of programs that focus on diversity throughout IBM.

Another interview was conducted with David Chang, systems manager, master inventor, and current program coordinator in Austin, Texas. He commented that the International Mentoring Program enables "those of us in the United States to personally participate in the growth of IBM's key emerging markets. It will have a lasting impact on the building of technical skills in these markets." Over the course of time, through David's leadership and enthusiasm, the China mentoring program has attracted employees who have volunteered to serve as mentors from several sites across the United States. David and a small team of the China mentoring program leaders are in the process of launching a survey that involves all the participants in the program. The primary objectives are to use the data to improve the mentoring experience, to determine the business benefits, and to solicit information on ways to expand the program.

David Chang's comment complements our discussions with Dave Lin, a mentee from the China Software Lab, who said that the "International

Mentoring program provided [him] with much insight into the different processes and ways business is done in the United States." One of the highlights of his mentoring relationship is that his mentor, Danny Chen, makes it a practice to brainstorm patent ideas and often provides Dave with practical information that has helped him become more aware of IBM's patent process. These discussions and brainstorming mentoring sessions led Danny to present a patent workshop on a recent business trip to China. As a result of this workshop, the mentees in China were informed and energized about participating in the IBM patent program. Thus, critical knowledge about the innovation opportunities within IBM was being shared as a result of the global reach of the ADNG. Danny, as one of its senior members, offered a number of comments on his personal investment in mentoring others. His commitment is to "help [his] mentee develop skill mastery in certain technical areas such as Websphere technology, create a culture in which employees are learning the IBM business, and at the same time develop the right skills to bridge gaps and expand capabilities across geographies."[42]

As we learned from the activities and impact of the ADNG, mentoring among diverse groups provides a critical opportunity for connection, identification, and learning that can be especially important for diverse groups of employees. As we have seen in previous work on group mentoring and affinity networks, this approach provides the opportunity to learn from peers, both more experienced and newer employees within the same social identity group. The relationships being cultivated within the ADNG are based on a set of commonalities that provide a bridge for strengthening the connection that these employees feel to each other and to the organization. While some of these connections develop naturally through informal relationships, it is critical that the organization sponsor and engage in the co-creation of these invaluable connections. Employees, especially those who experience a lack of support by the organization, must see the organization as a committed partner in these efforts and that its sponsorship of diversity networks like the ADNG is part of its overall strategy for building a more inclusive workplace.

The mentoring program is successful on many levels. Both parties used this to their advantage to make the relationship more meaningful. In fact, the program coordinator was very intentional in matching mentees from China with mentors in the United States who are of Chinese heritage, which allowed the relationship to develop much faster. First of all, mentees are able to approach their career development in a more deliberate manner. Secondly, they are now able to clearly articulate their developmental needs to bridge the gaps in areas such as leadership and negotiation skills, invention disclosures, networking, and building a broad knowledge of IBM's business strategy.

Other factors that contributed to the success of this program are directly germane to the strong executive support in both countries, as well as a highly dedicated and experienced team of mentors who feel a sense of personal obligation to pass on their knowledge to others, particularly those in the emerging countries. There is no doubt that the mentees contributed to the success of the program because of their attitude and zealousness to learn and develop new skills and capabilities.

Generally, these programs are considered incubator programs until measurable success is achieved and the value is obvious; then it is expanded and replicated. The success of the China International Mentoring program has been the catalyst for the launch of a similar program in India. In short, understanding differences and mastering the ability to use diverse solutions to address business problems creates a collaborative and innovative learning climate. Clearly, employees who thrive in a diverse workforce generally demonstrate respect for differences, both theirs and others. Also, employees tend to be more engaged in a diverse and supportive workplace, which allows the company to better connect its workplace to the marketplace.

Looking Toward the Future

At IBM, diversity is core and central to every aspect of the business, not the least of which is the concept of making the workforce an inclusive one. IBM provides ongoing education for all employees, regardless of level and rank in the business, which helps to ensure that all employees understand their individual role in making the IBM workplace one that respects diversity and is welcoming to all. Through its continued spread of group mentoring and diversity networks, IBM is able to provide diverse employees with critical resources for advice, support, and connection. Previous research acknowledges the importance of relationships that cross organizational, hierarchical, and other structural boundaries as having a positive impact on an individual's work productivity.[43] As an illustration, employees have access to a robust list of diversity options, including instructor-led classes, e-classes, and internal conferences that focus on diversity and multiculturalism, and participation in external national conferences. This array of information and resources is complemented by a growing number of employee networks that provide support, work on strategic initiatives, and help to create a climate of inclusion throughout the organization. Here are several additional examples of how IBM's use of group mentoring through diversity networks is helping to build connections among and across diverse employee segments.

As a worldwide enterprise, IBM has to make a special effort to expand its diversity efforts across the globe and ensure that employees are not using culture, language, and geographic lines to inhibit the development of relationships. To this point, in March 2008, Ron Glover, VP of Global Workforce Diversity at IBM, in an interview with *HR Management Magazine* stated that, "Enabling employees to work together across those lines of difference not only fundamentally enables IBM to operate with efficiency, but also with innovation. Our job is to fundamentally enhance the ability of the people in the organization to understand those differences, to work with and across them respectfully, and actually use them to the greatest extent possible to leverage innovation and effectiveness in terms of the work we do and our ability to respond to our clients."[44] Thus, IBM's approach provides opportunities for employees to work both within, as well as across, areas of difference based on key aspects of diversity.

Within IBM, the growing use of diversity networks such as the ADNG has allowed the organization to develop multiple means and creative methods of connecting people both within and across key identity groups, and across the multiple diversity dimensions that exist in today's workplace. Because of these ongoing demographic changes, companies like IBM must find novel ways to connect employees across the variety of diversity dimensions that exist in the workforce. Employees must be educated to connect with one another and use diversity as a means of developing meaningful and rewarding mentoring relationships. At the same time, the organization must provide a supportive environment that is free from micro-inequities within the workplace and allows employees to develop relationships that connect across important dimensions of social group identity. At IBM, through efforts such as the ADNG and other networks, diversity is well-positioned as a core element of its mentoring program, further demonstrating how much the company values diversity.

For collaboration across difference to thrive, all parties involved must develop meaningful relationships that are based on respect, trust, and the genuine desire to have an open mind regarding diversity. The current workplace is made up of multiple aspects of diversity, and within technology companies, issues related to generational diversity have emerged into the forefront of new challenges for their ability to connect across people. Companies must be proactive in creating tools, resources, and diversity education to facilitate a productive coexistence among all the dimensions of diversity. This requires an intentional and deliberate effort to be ahead of changes, such as the aging of the workforce and the blending of the multiple generations that have to work together. This is important because these diverse groups must interact and collaborate to produce the next wave of innovative technologies needed to remain competitive in the market. To connect people with the specific purpose of having knowledge transfer take place, companies must understand the diverse learning styles and preferences of each generation and make provisions to cater to their different styles. The tools that worked successfully for IBM in making connections among people of different cultural, gender, ethnic and other groups are now being applied as they address the new challenge of helping to close the generational divide. As the workforce becomes more diverse, so do the needs of the employees in the workforce.

To address this, IBM designed a mentoring program that takes into consideration the different developmental needs of the generations in the IBM workforce. The company also recognizes that each generation has unique strengths, abilities, and skills. Thus, it is important for the leaders of the organization to purposefully blend the generations for maximum productivity. For example, employees from the Generation X and Millennial generations enter the workplace with new insights, new approaches, and new expectations of themselves and of their employers. Managers are expected to develop the skills necessary to effectively lead these new generations of employees, but this should not be done at the expense of the more tenured and older generations. Merging the strengths and talents of each generation makes it possible for innovative and creative approaches to occur.

This makes it even more important for the leaders of the organization to understand the full scope of diversity, including the behaviors and attitudes of an intergenerational workforce. An organization that is unable to meet the diverse needs of the multigenerational, multicultural, and heterogeneous workforce exposes itself to losing the talent that these employees possess— they are likely to exit the business. Ron Zemke, Claire Raines, and Bob Filipczak, in their book, *Generations at Work*, amplified this very point by stating that, "With employee retention at or near the top of corporate 'must meet' measures, the most generationally friendly of companies are treating their employees as customers. They are learning all they can about them, working to meet their specific needs, and serving them according to their unique preferences."[45]

Part of leading the generations effectively requires managers and supervisors not only to understand their strengths, but also to understand conflicting values and expectations of the generations and find ways to mitigate conflicts. IBM is taking specific actions to build diversity leadership skills so that its leaders have the ability to address the needs of a diverse workforce. To reinforce that point, in a February 2007, IBM Web article that was written by the Diversity team in Europe titled "You and IBM—Diversity and Inclusion: Managing a diverse workforce," it was stated that, "As a manager, you are in a strong position to influence your team environment. It may be a cliché, but when it comes to creating a culture of inclusion, lead by example is the best way to do it." This article was directed to managers and it recommended that managers "...add a commitment to diversity and inclusion in their Performance Business Commitment and here is a sample: 'I commit to actively promote and sponsor diverse inclusive leadership for all employees and to ensure that all decisions reflect this commitment.'"[46] In general, all employees—including managers—are expected to understand the reasons IBM is committed to workforce diversity and how diversity, if properly managed and articulated, results in better collaboration and business results.

In addressing the emerging opportunities and challenges for connecting people among difference, IBM continues to embrace diversity as part of its global strategy, not only because it is the right thing to do, but also because it is a business imperative. For IBM to be successful, its workplace must be reflective of all the clients that it serves. "For IBM, diversity unites different cultures, languages, perspectives and other diversity dimensions into one globally integrated body" and is anchored on the premise that "none of us is as strong as all of us."[47]

As companies give employees the skills and knowledge to build relationships across diversity lines, both employees and the company derive immeasurable benefits. Bridging the diversity gaps helps employees expand their networks and become exposed to different perspectives, ideas, and solutions. The resulting effect is that employees can build a broader skills portfolio, and learning takes place in a collaborative work environment. The organization stands to reap dividends from the mentoring culture that the Diversity Network Groups are developing in IBM. It has been noted that employees are more engaged, are learning, and are contributing more to the overall success of the business. Diversity Network Groups in IBM create programs to meet the needs of all its members but special attention is being given to the new employees who join IBM. The network groups play a significant role in helping new hires make a smooth transition into the IBM workplace. For example, the Early Career Group is a subgroup of the Black Diversity Network Group at the Research Triangle Park, North Carolina, site. The primary purpose of establishing the Early Career Group is to help employees working for IBM less than five years "matriculate easily into the IBM culture." Black new hires receive information on ways to navigate the IBM culture, and they are able to attend lunch-and-learn sessions that cover performance management, individual development and career planning, mobility, and understanding the Intellectual Patent process. Dr. Alfred Burress, co-leader of the Black Diversity Network Group at the North Carolina site, affirms that, "These sessions, in turn, benefit IBM greatly, as they assist in employee growth as well as retention."

Another example of the increased focus and attention that Diversity Network Groups are giving to the early tenured IBM employees comes from the Women's Diversity Network Group, also from Research Triangle Park. Similar to the Black Network Group, the Women's Group formed "The First Five Community" to meet the needs of women who have been with IBM for fewer than five years. The group offers networking opportunities as well as the opportunity to develop leadership, business, and technical skills. They offer "free thinking Friday Innovation sessions" where they educate and promote women inventors. The focus on women inventors is a call to action for women to play a significant role in IBM's "Innovation that Matters" strategy. The members of the Women's Diversity Network Group have been instrumental in creating learning opportunities for its constituency, and there is no doubt that they are making an impact on their community and at the same time offering great value to IBM. Lydia Do, vice president of the Women's Diversity Network Group, affirms the value of mentoring by her statement that, "People may not realize that the power of mentoring is a two-way street. Great mentors take the time to guide and counsel others while they are pursuing their professional development. Great mentees take the time to listen, reflect, and realize the opportunities to enrich and grow their knowledge-base from every exchange and interaction." These are just a few examples of the passion and purpose that Diversity Network Groups demonstrate to make the IBM climate conducive to learning and collaboration.

The lessons learned from IBM's group mentoring approach and use of Diversity Network Groups are important for any organization that wants to attract and retain employees within this global war for talent. Clearly, diversity in the workplace is a business imperative requiring companies to invest in a number of efforts for the recruitment, development, and retention of diverse employee segments. As part of IBM's global business model, valuing people and the diversity that they bring makes it a strategic priority to connect employees to the business and to their colleagues across and among all areas of difference. This underscores the idea that by making connections between employees within distinct diversity groups, IBM can foster a climate of inclusion, cultivate collaboration, and stimulate innovation. Making a commitment to connecting all groups of employees enhances its potential to retain diverse talent that can become the future leadership of the organization. As we have seen through some of the examples of employee networks within IBM, when mentoring is aligned with the tenets of diversity, a power synergy is created. The resulting impact is the achievement of organizational effectiveness, capability-building, and ongoing talent development.

We began this chapter with the reflection that the demographic diversity of the workforce predicted decades ago has arrived. Today's pool of diverse employee talent coupled with a competitive knowledge market means that organizations must establish and support mentoring relationships that don't connect people by ignoring their differences but rather connect people who learn because of these differences. Through its use of diversity networks, along with other innovative diversity solutions, IBM's business model views mentoring as an important method for connecting people and creating an atmosphere where difference is an opportunity for innovation rather than an impediment to business success. Thus, mentoring is a strategic tool for connecting people in a way that produces long-term business impact for IBM.

References

[1] Daly Thomas, D. A. and Ely, R. J. (1996). Making differences matter: A new paradigm for managing diversity. *Harvard Business Review*, September–October, 79–90.

[2] Harrison, D. A., Price, K. H., and Bell, M. P. (1998). Beyond relational demography: Time and the effects of surface- and deep-level diversity of work group cohesion. *Academy of Management Journal*, 41(1), 96–107.

[3] Johnson W.B. and Parker, A.H. (1987). *Workforce 2000: Work and Workers for the 21st Century*. Indianapolis: Hudson Institute.

[4] Pew Research Center Report, Web site: http://pewresearch.org.

[5] Ibid, Pew Report.

[6] U.S. Census Bureau (2005), Fact sheet for race, ethnic, ancestry group. http://factfinder. census.gov; U.S. Census Bureau. (2006, December 4). Looking ahead to the 2010 census. *2010 Census National Recruiting Plan*. Washington, D.C.: U.S. Census Bureau. Retrieved from the Internet http://www.census.gov/procur/www/2010communications/ rev%2012-04-06%20ext%20plan.pdf.

[7] Eagly, A. H. and Carli, L. L. (2007). Women and the labyrinth of leadership. *Harvard Business Review*, 85(9), 62–71.

[8] Catalyst. (1999). Women of color in corporate management: Opportunities and barriers. New York, NY: Catalyst; Catalyst. (2001). Women of color executives: Their voices, their journeys. New York, NY: Catalyst.

9   Murrell, A.J., Blake-Beard, S., Porter, D.M., and Perkins, Williamson A. (2008). Inter-organizational formal mentoring: Sometimes breaking the concrete ceiling requires help from the outside. *Human Resource Journal*, 47(2).

10 Caproni, P. J. (2005). Managing cultural diversity. *Management skills for everyday life: The practical coach* (2nd Edition). Upper Saddle River, NJ: Pearson Prentice Hall.

11 Hardy, L. C. (1998). Mentoring: A long-term approach to diversity. *HR Focus*, 75(7), S11.; Tyler, K. (2007). Cross-cultural connections. *HR Magazine*, 52(10), 77–82.

12 Blancero, D. M. and DelCampo, R. G. (2005). Hispanics in the workplace: Experiences with mentoring and networking. *Employment Relations Today*, 32(2), 31–38.

13 Murrell, A.J., Crosby, F. J., and Ely, R. J. (1999). *Mentoring Dilemmas: Developmental Relationships within Multicultural Organizations*. New York, NY: Lawrence Erlbaum Associates.

14 Guinier, L. and Torres, G. (2002). *The Miner's Canary: Enlisting Race, Resisting Power and Transforming Democracy*. Cambridge, MA: Harvard University Press.

15 Rowe, M. (1990). Barriers to equality: The power of subtle discrimination to maintain equal opportunity. *Employees Responsibilities and Rights Journal,* 3(2), 153–163.

16 The Corporate Leavers Survey (2007). Level Playing Field Institute, Web site: www.lpfi.org/workplace/corporateleavers.shtml.

17 Thomas, D. A. and Gabarro, J. J. (1999) *Breaking Through: The Making of Minority Executives in Corporate America*. Boston: Harvard Business School Press.

18 Hyun, J. (2005). *Breaking the Bamboo Ceiling: Career Strategies for Asians*. New York, NY: HarperCollins; O'Neill, R. M. (2002). Gender and race in mentoring relationships: A review of the literature. In D. Clutterbuck and B.R. Ragins (Eds.), *Mentoring and Diversity: An International Perspective* (pp. 1–22). Thousand Oaks, CA: Sage; Viator, R. E. (1999). An analysis of formal mentoring programs and perceived barriers to obtaining a mentor at large public accounting firms. *Accounting Horizons,* 12, 37–53; Viator, R. E. (2001). An examination of African Americans' access to public accounting mentors: Perceived barriers and intentions to leave. *Accounting, Organizations and Society*, 26, 541–561; Wanberg, C. R., Welsh, E. T., and Hezlett, S. A. (2003). Mentoring research: A review and dynamic process model. *Research in Personnel and Human Resource Management*, 22, 39–124; Wilson, J. A. and Elman, N. S. (1990). Organizational benefits of mentoring. *Academy of Management Executive*, 4, 88–94.

19 Cox, T. and Nkomo, S. (1986). Differential performance appraisal criteria: A field study of black and white managers. *Group and Organization Studies*, 11, 101–119; Cox, T. and Nkomo, S. M. (1990). Invisible men and women: A status report on race as a variable in organization behavior research. *Journal of Organizational Behavior*, 11, 419–431.

20 Ibid, Catalyst, 1999; 2001.

21 Ibid, Catalyst, 1999; 2001.

22 Dreher, G. F. and Cox, T. H. (1996). Race, gender and opportunity: A study of compensation attainment and the establishment of mentoring relationships. *Journal of Applied Psychology*, 81, 297–308.

[23] Thomas, D. A. (1990). The impact of race on managers' experiences of developmental relationships. *Journal of Organizational Behavior*, 11, 479–492; Thomas, D. A. (1993). Racial
dynamics in cross-race developmental relationships. *Administrative Science Quarterly*, 38,
169–194.

[24] Sims, A. D. (2002). *An inter-group examination of African-American executives' mentoring relationships: Traversing the invisible hurdles of corporate America.* Unpublished doctoral disserta-
tion, Rutgers, The State University of New Jersey; Thomas, D. A. (1999). Beyond simple
demography—power hypothesis: How blacks in power influence white-mentor—black-
protégé developmental relationships. In A.J. Murrell, F.J. Crosby, and R. J. Ely (Eds.),
Mentoring Dilemmas: Developmental Relationships within Multicultural Organizations. New
York, NY: Lawrence Erlbaum Associates.

[25] Blake-Beard, S., Murrell, A.J., and Thomas, D.A. (2007). Unfinished business: The impact
of race on understanding mentoring relationships. In B.R. Ragins and K.E. Kram, (Eds.),
The Handbook of Mentoring at Work (pp. 223–248). Thousand Oaks, CA: Sage Publications.

[26] Ragins, B.R. (1997). Diversified mentoring relationships in organizations: A power perspective. *Academy of Management Review*, 22, 482–521.

[27] Thomas, D. A. (1989). Mentoring and irrationality: the role of racial taboos. *Human
Resource Management*, 28, 279–290.

[28] Williamson, I.O., Slay, H.S., Shapiro, D.L., and Shivers-Blackwell, S.L. (2008). The effects
of explanations on prospective applicants' reactions to firm diversity practices. *Human
Resource Management*, 47(2), 311–330.

[29] Murrell, A.J., Blake-Beard, S.B., Porter, D.M., and Perkins-Williamson, A. (2008).
Interorganizational formal mentoring: Sometimes breaking the concrete ceiling requires
support from the outside. *Human Resource Management,* 47(2), 275–294.

[30] IBM Web site, http://www.ibm.com.

[31] Kelman, H.C. (2006). Interests, relationships, identities: Three central issues for individuals and groups in negotiating their social environment. *Annual Review of Psychology*, 57,
1–26.

[32] Thomas, D. A. and Higgins, M. (1996). Mentoring and the boundaryless career: Lessons
from the minority experience. In M.B. Arthur and D.M. Rousseau, D.M. (Eds.), *The
Boundaryless Career: A New Employment Principle for a New Organizational era.* (pp. 268–281).
New York: Oxford University Press.

[33] Cox, T. H. and Blake, S. (1991). Managing cultural diversity: Implications for organizational competitiveness. *Academy of Management Executive*, 5, 45–56.

[34] Friedman, R. (1996). Defining the scope and logic of minority and female network groups:
Does separation enhance integration? In G. Ferris (Ed.), *Research in Personnel and Human
Resource Management*, (pp. 307–349). Greenwich, CT: JAI Press; Friedman, R. Kane, M.,
and Cornfield, D. B. (1998). Social support and career optimism: Examining the effectiveness of network groups among black managers. *Human Relations*, 5, 1155–1177.

[35] Murrell, A.J., Crosby, F. J., and Ely, R. J. (1999). *Mentoring Dilemmas: Developmental
Relationships within Multicultural Organizations.* New York, NY: Lawrence Erlbaum
Associates.

[36] Murrell, A. J. (1997). To identify or not to identity: Preserving, ignoring and sometimes destroying social identity. In S. Fiske and J. Eberhardt (Eds.), *Racism: The Problem and the Response*, (pp. 18–201). Thousand Oaks, CA: Sage Publications.

[37] McKeen, C. and Bujaki, M. (2007). Gender and mentoring: Issues, Effects and Opportunities. In B.R. Ragins and K.E. Kram (Eds.), *The Handbook on Mentoring at Work* (pp. 179–196). Thousand Oaks, CA: Sage Publications.

[38] Ibarra, H. (1993). Personal networks of women and minorities in management: A conceptual framework. *Academy of Management Review*, 18, 56–87; Ibarra, H. (1995). Race, opportunity, and diversity of social circles in managerial networks. *Academy of Management Journal*, 38, 673–703.

[39] Helms, J.E. (1990). Black and white racial identity: Theory, research and practice. Westport, CT: Greenwood Press; Swan, S. and Wyer, R.S. (1997). Gender stereotypes and social identity: How being in the minority affects judgments of self and others. *Personality and Social Psychology Bulletin*, 23(12), 1265–1276.

[40] IBM Internal Web site.

[41] Knudson, Leslie. (2007, November.) Diversity on a Global Scale: an Interview with Ron Glover, IBM VP, Global Workforce Diversity. *HR Management Magazine*.

[42] Personal interview with Danny Chen.

[43] Ragins, B.R. and Kram, K.E. (2007). *The Handbook of Mentoring at Work*. Thousand Oaks, CA: Sage Publications.

[44] Ibid, Knudson, 2007.

[45] Zemke, R., Raines, C. and Filipczak, B. (2000). *Generations at Work: Managing the Clash of Veterans, Boomers, Xers, and Nexters in Your Workplace*. Broadway, NY: American Management Association.

[46] W3, You and IBM Europe. (2007). Managing a Diverse Workforce—Diversity and Inclusion/Management and Diversity.

[47] Mulki, J., Bardhi, F., and Lassk, F. (2007). An Examination of the OTTO Work Arrangement: Personal and Professional Challenges and Coping Mechanisms. Accessed at www.ociabc.org/events/NEU_Report.pdf.

6

Connecting People: Using Mentoring to Signal Value in People

Chapter Contents

The Power of Value in People

Sometimes a cliché represents the truth. Valuing people might seem like an age-old cliché but it represents a fundamental truth for firms seeking to sustain competitiveness, especially in dynamic industries such as technology. For IBM, it is imperative to give ongoing support to employees as they develop new knowledge and innovative solutions that the organization needs for its survival and success. IBM recognizes the fundamental truth that employee satisfaction and retention are the bridge to customer satisfaction and overall value to the customer. When employees feel valued by a company that makes an investment in their continued growth and development, that company is poised to reap benefits that can directly impact its performance and productivity. As the well-documented global war for talent intensifies, employees will seek out organizations that value their contribution and support their professional development. Many organizations claim to be or want to become an "employer of choice." However, few understand the meaning of that label for diverse segments of employees that makes "valuing people" more than just a slogan on the company's Web site. The challenge for leaders of organizations is to develop systems and structures that reward employee contribution and then help employees understand how their performance and contribution are valued as part of the solution for achieving both tactical, as well as strategic goals. Indeed, sometimes a cliché represents a necessary truth.

Organizations must recognize that supporting the growth and development of employees is vital to the ongoing success of the business enterprise. However, information from national employee surveys ranging from company benchmarking to individual internal assessments all reveal a disconnection between the support espoused by the firm and the support experienced by employees. On the other hand, research on the impact of employees' perceptions of support from the organization is quite clear. When employees see how their contribution makes a difference to and is valued by the firm, they feel a sense of worth and connection to the organization. It also activates the employees' desire to reciprocate the support by exhibiting effort, commitment, and citizenship behaviors that benefit the organization. In other words, providing support to employees is not simply a nice thing to do but is also a key driver of important work outcomes and performance. The critical question is how to cultivate and sustain perceptions of support that are not simply statements or slogans by the company but actually represent the ongoing experience and perception of employees.

As IBM began its mentoring revitalization process, it looked for ways that these solutions could support the overall value in people that is core to its mission and global strategy. Pairing a senior-level or experienced person with a more junior-level or less experienced employee in mentoring relationships is an important way to communicate a statement of value to the employee. This practice also allows leaders to detect how employees are perceiving their value within the organization and helps them to be proactive in addressing any issue. While the senior-to-junior relationship has certain value, this mentoring can, over time, create a somewhat paternalistic or care-taking view of mentoring where knowledge and expertise flow downward and are defined only by rank, status, and tenure in the firm.

As IBM began to expand its use of innovative mentoring approaches, it needed mentoring tools that supported a relational approach to strengthening the connection between employees and the firm. Effective mentoring relationships require partnerships with mutual engagement, participation, and shared ownership. This represents a fundamental shift in the employee/ employer relationship away from the traditional paternalistic or care-taking approach to a collegial or relational approach. It also necessitates flipping the traditional mentoring technique so that employees are not only receiving knowledge and advice but also are giving their knowledge and expertise in a way that is clearly valued within the relationship. Thus, reverse mentoring has developed in various units and global locations throughout IBM as a strategic tool for knowledge sharing and for communicating the value IBM places in people as key drivers of its business enterprise.

As you will learn throughout this chapter, reverse mentoring not only helps IBM signal to employees the value their contributions make to the organization but it also communicates IBM's commitment to ongoing learning that is required of all employees, including leaders at the most senior levels of the organization. These innovative uses of reverse mentoring support IBM's ongoing goal of building a knowledge-resilient culture that is defined by "a group of employees who not only are dedicated to the idea of continuous learning, but also stand ready to re-invent themselves to keep pace with change; who take responsibility for their own career management; and last but not least to the company's success."[1] Using reverse mentoring is helping to support and communicate the value of people and is helping IBM shape a culture of learning and support that the company hopes can produce worldwide impact. Reverse mentoring creates true collaboration between individuals, which helps to nurture the idea of bidirectional learning where both parties gain knowledge and benefit from the relationship. Bidirectional learning in a mentoring relationship is a critical element in creating an atmosphere where knowledge and information are fluid and, at the same time, dispels the myth that the mentee is the only person who is learning in the mentoring relationship.

What Employees Expect—A Relational View

There has been a great deal of attention focused on understanding the connection between employees and the firm as moving away from a traditional care-taking or provider view toward a networked or relational perspective.[2] This means that employees' expectations focus on the exchange between what they provide the organization as compared to what they need in terms of support, resources, and opportunities. Some argue that employees' expectations of organizational support emerged as people coped with changes in social and geographic mobility in the decades following the 1960s. As people became more mobile and geographically dispersed, they also became more disconnected from extended families and local communities, losing valuable sources of support and resources.

The increased demands of the workplace meant that the amount of time spent at work expanded as the demands for results and challenges to sustain competitiveness intensified. In addition, technology continued to make it possible for employees to work anytime, anyplace without limits or boundaries.[3] Thus, the demands on employees' time, knowledge, and energy have increased, while the resources and support available external to the organization have remained constant or have, in many cases, lessened. This means that as both external conditions and employees' needs changed, the expectations or rules about the dynamic exchange between employees and the firm have also changed. Because employees are spending more time working, this presents a greater demand on organizations and a greater desire from employees for the organization to provide them with accessible and more extensive support systems.

The rules governing the expectations that employees have as part of their relationship with the organization form the basis of what is referred to as a psychological or social contract. Traditional contracts are explicit and formalized in outlining the terms and conditions of a relationship or business transaction. Effective contracts are designed to be mutually beneficial and not simply a list of obligations, promises, perceived value, and so on. In a similar way, psychological contracts are one form of human contracts that guide and shape social interactions at work.[4] These psychological contracts are important for reducing uncertainty in social relations and for defining employees' roles, organizational priorities, and the nature of social exchange in the workplace. While these contracts create expectations between mutual partners, they are more than simple assumptions about a quid pro quo interaction. Rather, they involve complex issues such as obligations, promises, investment, trust, and perceived value. Thus, the notion of the psychological contract refers to employees' beliefs regarding the terms and conditions of reciprocal exchange between themselves and the organization via the actions of its agents (such as its leaders).[5] Psychological contracts both describe and shape the nature and terms of the employee-employer relationship. Unlike written or explicit contracts, psychological contracts involve expectations, perceptions, and emotions, each driving employees' desire to make sense out of the actions of the organization and understand their function or value amidst these actions. This means that psychological contracts are relational, dynamic, and thus, highly subjective.

The highly subjective nature of psychological contracts suggests that conditions, changes, and violations to the contract are in the "eye of the beholder"; that is, based on the employee's perceptions. As Rousseau and her colleagues argue, it is not actual reciprocity that creates a psychological contract but the fundamental belief (or expectation) of mutual reciprocity that creates or breaches the contract.[6] As such, these contracts provide the context for acts of either positive or negative reciprocity within employee-employer relationships. Employees make a judgment or assessment of the costs and benefits of particular work exchanges or social interactions. Exchanges that produce equal (or greater) benefits relative to cost should be continued and strengthened. On the other hand, exchanges that produce more cost than benefit to an individual must be avoided, terminated, or renegotiated. As part of this assessment, the investment of the other party involved in the exchange is constantly examined and evaluated.[7]

From the employees' side of the relationship, psychological contracts are important for shaping how they may interpret the promises, policies, actions, and commitments that come from the organization and its leaders. Relational types of psychological contracts involve exchanges that are open-ended in duration, often long term, and involve some degree of flexibility between the partners. These types of contracts involve dynamic relationships between the employer and employee but include some implicit understanding of obligations or commitments between partners connected over time. Some researchers point out that these open-ended and long-term relational contracts are shaped by good faith, perceptions of fairness, and past experiences of support that the employee has experienced within the current organization and even previous organizations.[8] Thus, a type of reciprocal interdependence develops over time within these types of relational contracts.

A wide variety of research has been conducted to examine the impact of psychological contracts, particularly relational types of contracts.[9] The majority of this work focuses on violations or breaches to the psychological contract or when employees perceive that the organization has failed to fulfill its obligations or promises. Generally, research has shown that psychological contract breach or violations are related to critical negative workplace outcomes, such as low job satisfaction, high voluntary turnover, lower performance, lack of organizational citizenship behaviors, and reduced organizational commitment.[10] Clearly, perceived breaches in the psychological contract reduce an organization's capability to engage and retain employees, as well as ensure positive outcomes that impact its overall competitive position within the market.

This idea of the psychological contract reminds us that employees' expectations are interpreted through their perceived relationship to the firm. In essence, how employees perceive the value placed on them by the organization helps shape the nature of the psychological contract that exists between them and the organization. These expectations also drive whether an employee perceives there has been a violation or a breach in this relational contract, which can elicit negative outcomes, such as dissatisfaction, lack of organizational commitment, and voluntary turnover.

For these relational contracts to develop and produce a positive impact, several factors must be kept in mind. First, there must be some opportunity for the relationship to exist and develop over time. One-shot, short-term, and limited types of exchanges do not evolve into relational contracts. In addition, it takes energy along with time for these relational contracts to develop and mature, and to build a history that can serve the purpose of creating a context, that shapes the expectations and assumptions of employees. This historical information not only defines the psychological contract, but also is interpreted through the specific lens based on the type of contract that is in place. Lastly, factors such as fairness, trust, supervisor support, and perceptions of organizational rewards and job conditions will be viewed as signals by the organization of the value it places on its employees, which can strengthen (or weaken) the psychological contract that exists between the employee and the firm. While the specific content of the psychological contract may vary across different employee-firm relationships, the dimensions that shape mutually beneficial contracts versus a perceived breach share these common factors.

Employees' Perceptions of Organizational Support

The notion of perceived support from the organization is based on the view that the employee-organization connection is a social exchange relationship in which the organization offers employees rewards and favorable job conditions in exchange for loyalty and work effort. However, an employee's relationship with the employer is not based on simple quid pro quo or one-to-one exchange. These exchanges represent the fulfillment of the organization's end of the complex psychological contract it maintains with its employees. With explicit contracts, the nature of the exchange is documented, general, and fixed. With psychological contracts, social exchange is implied, individualized, and dynamic. These distinctions point to the importance of the employee's *subjective valuation* or how employees interpret, judge, and evaluate the treatment or support the organization provides.

Robert Eisenberger and his colleagues developed the concept of "perceived organizational support," which is based on the notion that employees develop global beliefs concerning the extent to which the organization values their contributions and cares about their well-being.[11] They argue that perceptions of support develop as a result of employees' tendencies to personify the organization and attribute actions taken by its leaders to the intent of the organization itself, rather than to the individual motives of a specific leader or manager. Organizations signal to employees whether they are favored or disfavored through human resource practices, quality of supervisory relationships, fairness of treatment, and other organizational actions that impact employees. However, favorable treatment from the perspective of the leaders does not always transfer into employees' perceptions of support. Rather, employees create explanations or make inferences into the underlying reasons behind the treatment offered to them by the organization and these attributions play an important role in the development of perceived organizational support.

While employees pay attention to the fairness of organizational policies when forming perceptions of support, they also consider their relationships with organizational agents, such as supervisors, leaders, and those seen as acting on behalf of the company.[12] One of the key assumptions is that employees aggregate the treatment that they receive across all of their experiences with people who control outcomes into their general perceptions of support. The greater the extent to which an employee believes that the actions of an organizational agent (for example, supervisor, mentor, leader) is representative of the actions of the organization itself, the stronger the influence that person will have on that employee's perceived support. Therefore, a manager with high formal status or leaders who are at senior levels within the organization should have a stronger impact on an employee's perceived support than should a manager with less formal status.

Thus, having access to organizational leaders can help to shape employees' perceptions that they are valued within the organization. Actions by leaders within the organization not only send a signal about the value placed in people, but the specific connection to agents of the organization that is facilitated by mentoring can also shape and strengthen perceptions of organizational support. As employees aggregate their experiences with influential people in the organization, their contact with senior leaders who receive input and advice as part of the reverse mentoring process sends a strong signal that their input is valued and their work within the organization is supported. In addition, access to prominent organizational leaders communicates to employees that their well-being and effectiveness is important to strategic outcomes in a manner similar to how their connection with immediate supervisors signals their importance to operational outcomes. While access to significant leadership within the organization is important, these relationships are not a substitute for the critical role that the supervisorial relationship plays within the organization. Both connecting with leadership and support from one's direct manager or supervisor help to shape employees' perceptions of support by the organization.

Employees enter the workforce with a set of values and expectations of their employers that they are not hesitant to express. Managers must be proactive in getting clarification on what is of value to their employees, what keeps them excited, and what makes them feel they are having an impact on the organization. The mistake that many organizations make is to assume that money is always the prime motivator to their employees. While money is important, it is not always what gives employees a sense of value. In fact, some research suggests that only discretionary organizational actions, or actions that employees believe the organization controls rather than what it is obligated to do (for example, by law or regulatory standards) influence perceptions of organizational support.[13] This often means that what managers use as indicators of support for employees may not be tangible things such as money, but intangible things such as recognition, fair treatment, and opportunities to develop.

In essence, the actions that managers use to demonstrate support may not be the same as the actions employees use to judge whether the organization supports them and values their contributions.

How Organizational Leaders Can "Signal Support"

As the company promotes the acquisition of knowledge regarding business priorities, provides employees with resources and tools, and gives them ample opportunity to develop core skills, the next important step in the process is to hold them appropriately accountable to deliver results. Giving employees tools and information in a timely manner and then "letting them go to grow" constitutes respect for the individual. Prior to the Louis Gerstner era, employees had a different perspective as to what respect for the individual meant. Upon his arrival at IBM, Gerstner redefined respect for the individual and naturally, this redefinition elicited some employee discomfort. Gerstner explained that "Respect for the individual had devolved to mean a couple of things Watson did not have in mind. For one, it helped spawn a culture of entitlement, where the individual did not have to do anything to *earn* respect."[14] Through the Gerstner period and into the present time, employees have developed a new view of respect for the individual that involves both the value placed on their development by IBM and their responsibility to return that investment with work results. Today, some examples of the things that constitute respect for IBM employees include opportunities to develop IBM and industry-valued skills, pay for performance based on differentiation of contribution, culture of accountability, teamwork with competent colleagues, and a work environment that reflects a fun atmosphere. The act of communicating value to employees by the organization comes in myriad ways, including:

- Acknowledging the desires and career aspirations of employees is a way that shows respect for the individual.
- Giving employees room to grow and become high contributors to the business. Also, allowing employees the opportunity to broaden their skills/competency base is another way.
- Balancing collegiality and collaboration and, at the same time, preserving the uniqueness and diversity of each person on the team. Preserving the authenticity of each employee must be balanced with promoting diversity and inclusiveness as being of strategic importance to the business.

- Educating employees on ways to succeed, showing them how to avoid career derailment, and using setbacks as an appropriate teaching tool for personal and professional growth.

- Demonstrating and modeling to employees a variety of ways that show how ethical leadership and integrity are vital to career and business success.

Recognizing employees for significant contributions to the business in a timely manner is an important factor in demonstrating respect and support for the individual.

The core values used by managers and IBM's leadership signal value in people and shape the psychological contract that exists between employees and IBM. This contract is facilitated and supported by the supervisors and managers who work closely with employees. A good deal of research supports the notion that direct supervisory relationships exert an important influence on perceptions of support. Treatment that employees receive from supervisors is often interpreted as coming directly from (or as a signal from) the organization itself. That is, employees believe that the actions of their supervisors are representative of the organization's positive or negative orientation toward them. Supervisors are considered particularly important because they are responsible for directing and evaluating employees' performance, as well as conveying these evaluations to higher-level managers. Thus, research shows that employees' beliefs regarding the extent to which they are supported by supervisors are strongly and positively related to perceptions of support.[15] Perceived organizational support changes in response to specific acts of supervisor support, and research suggests that employees' relationships with high-level supervisors have a stronger influence on perceived support than relationships with low-level supervisors. These research findings remind us of two important things about how employees' perceptions of support are influenced:

- Employees' beliefs about their value in the organization are shaped by the actions of leaders and high-level supervisors who signal the value the company places in people.

- Perceptions of support are influenced by the actions of a supervisor who is closest to the work of the employees and is a key influencer of critical outcomes for the employee.

Beverly Kaye and Sharon Jordan-Evans, in their book, *Love 'Em or Lose 'Em: Getting Good People to Stay,* endorse this thinking in their statement that: "Beyond fair pay, people want challenging, meaningful work, a chance to learn and grow, great coworkers, recognition, respect and a good boss." To illustrate this point, the authors cite the story of "A.J.," an employee who documented his reasons for leaving his employer. In the exit interview memorandum that A.J wrote, he left the company with a profound point: "It is true that my new position pays a higher salary, but I am not leaving for money; I need to work in a place where I can make a contribution and people treat each other with respect. Sadly my work didn't seem to make a difference.... Please remember that thoughtful planning, honest communication, and basic human respect go a long way with your employees."[16]

One good way of valuing employees is to create learning opportunities that allow employees to apply their skills in novel ways. As you will see, one way this is accomplished within IBM is through the use of reverse mentoring within a number of global business units. Reverse mentoring options often provide lower level employees with an opportunity to get a direct glimpse of what it takes to lead a successful business operation, how and why certain decisions are made and, in general, the strategic priorities of the organization. This is one way that IBM offers support and indicates value to its employees by connecting them to organizational leaders explicitly for the purpose of developing a reverse mentoring relationship. It also reinforces the importance that all employees are required to understand the overall IBM strategy and the specific priorities of the business unit of which they are members.

IBM expects that as employees understand strategies for driving revenue and increasing client satisfaction, they will be given the chance to align their work in support of these business goals. Thus, the organization attempts to communicate its part of the psychological contract through its policies, programs, and clearly developed mission and vision. When employees have a full grasp of the strategic direction of a business and their role in the process, it gives meaning and value to their contribution. J. Bruce Herreld, senior vice president, Marketing and Strategy at IBM, underscores this point by stating that, "It is more important than ever that you understand our business strategy and how your work contributes to IBM's ability to help our customers succeed. To help, we have developed a series of strategy education modules that provide an introduction to both IBM and unit-level strategies."[17] This comment reflects the potential impact of reverse mentoring to serve as a visible indication of support from top leadership within the organization to employees looking for opportunities to grow, develop, and contribute to the overall success of the organization.

In short, as employees engage in reverse mentoring relationships with leaders of the business, they are passing on ideas, creativity, and even suggestions on ways to handle certain business issues. Conversely, employees are gaining benefits from the leaders, because they are getting a perspective of business strategies and the decision-making process.

Using Reverse Mentoring to Signal Support

While there is increased attention to the concept of reverse mentoring, we lack a good deal of research or examples of "best practice" in the use of this specific approach. The person generally credited with introducing formal reverse mentoring is General Electric's former CEO, Jack Welch.[18] In 1999, he required 500 of his top managers to find workers who were well versed in the emerging technology of the Internet and tap into their expertise. About once a month, Welch met with the 37-year-old manager of G.E.'s corporate Web site, who helped him learn how to use the technology as well as understand the opportunities of the World Wide Web. He required senior leadership of the organization to do the same. Since that time, other divisions within G.E. established reverse mentoring programs, and this trend continued to spread into other organizations as well.

Proctor & Gamble has also been cited as an early adopter of reverse mentoring, having established its first formal program in the early 1990s. To address the need to retain talented women throughout its organization, P&G launched its reverse mentoring program designed to address challenges facing women and then other areas of the organization.

Often referred to as "learning in reverse," this approach views knowledge and expertise as the key resources that are exchanged during a mentoring relationship. Thus, key components within reverse mentoring are the notion of social exchange and reciprocity. Rather than a mentor providing advice and support that is given to a mentee or protégé, reverse mentoring recognizes that there is reciprocal or mutual exchange that takes place through the sharing of knowledge and expertise. The content of what is exchanged may vary, but the assumption that both parties bring valuable knowledge and expertise to the mentoring relationship is a key factor. Whether it's technological knowledge, organizational savvy, or market expertise, reverse mentoring signals to employees that title and status alone do not determine value to the organization; rather ideas, knowledge, and expertise are valued, and employees' contributions to the organization matter.

Setting up a successful reverse mentoring program requires a good deal of planning. It's essential to create a structured program that involves meaningful interactions so that participants can develop a mutually beneficial relationship. Particularly when engaging senior leadership of the organization, it is important that the structure and design of the reverse mentoring effort not appear to employees as a mere formality. This would, unfortunately, convey a negative message and potentially damage perceptions of support. Just like with other mentoring relationships, engagement of the two parties is an essential element for success. In addition, the active participation of the more junior member of the organization playing the "reverse role" as mentor can also be seen as an important opportunity for the development of managerial and leadership skills useful for the individual in the future. This means communicating the mutual benefit of this type of mentoring relationship to both parties, which helps to provide a strong signal of support and, subsequently, develop a positive psychological contract between the mentor and mentee.

The signaling power of reverse mentoring appears to be threefold:

- **It defines the nature of mentoring relationships by expertise, not by title or status within the organization.** This change in perspective is an important practice that knowledge and the sharing of this knowledge in addition to tenure and job level is valued within the organization's culture.

- **It makes the exchange of knowledge and resources a shared enterprise and not just the responsibility of the senior person or the "mentor" in the traditional sense.** This means that through reverse mentoring efforts, organizations can capitalize on the technical knowledge base wherever it exists and transfer this knowledge throughout the enterprise in a fluid manner.

- **It transforms relationships from being primarily a tool to gain technical expertise into a vehicle for learning.** They are typically seen as a younger person sharing knowledge with an older person, but can include peer-to-peer relationships, group mentoring, and building connections across functional areas as well. This allows the flow of knowledge and information to cut across traditional boundaries in a manner that shows respect for the individual, provides support for employee development, cultivates inclusive collaboration across difference, and offsets career derailment factors from having a negative impact on employees or the organization.

In addition to the signaling power of reverse mentoring, the potential benefits of this innovative approach can help address key outcomes and needs of the organizations. Within IBM, the use of reverse mentoring has helped to support several key aspects of its desired learning culture and workforce strategy.

Respect for the Individual

IBM was founded upon a strong set of beliefs and principles that govern how the company does business and the way employees are to interact with one another. While many things have changed about IBM, certain things are considered sacred, and special effort has been made over the years to preserve these specific principles and values that have become the company's brand identity.

One of the three basic beliefs that guided IBM's actions in its early years is, "Respect for the Individual." During the 1990s, when IBM was on the verge of a historic business failure, one of the things Lou Gerstner did was to define the eight principles that would help transform IBM's workforce and reposition IBM in the marketplace. During the transformation and recovery of IBM, one of the core principles that Gerstner instilled was to be "sensitive to the needs of all employees and to the communities in which we operate." He further stated that "This isn't just warm sentiment. We want our people to have the room and the resources to grow."[19]

Clearly, the bedrock of IBM is its people; however, the relationship between the company and its employees no longer fosters a sense of entitlement; rather it is now one where employees are coached to deliver high performance with the goal of distinguishing themselves in terms of performance evaluation and compensation. In the new IBM, the paternalistic attitudes and behaviors have been dramatically reduced, and today the company gives the employees renewed respect by providing them with the tools necessary to develop skills that are of value to them and to the business. Furthermore, employees are expected to show professional responsibility to learn, grow, and contribute to the business and are rewarded according to their level of performance. Reward and recognition are commensurate with the degree to which employees contribute to the business. Should an employee fall short, mentoring, career coaching, and management guidance are all available to help improve performance. The relationship that IBM develops with its employees is one where there is mutual respect that is a defining feature of IBM's psychological contract with employees. Employees who are made to feel a sense of value tend to be engaged, and the resulting effect is higher productivity and contribution to the business. The essence of this idea is that the company reaps great dividends from clearly demonstrating that its employees are truly valued. As we will review later, tools such as reverse mentoring help IBM support its commitment to respect for the individual.

Support for Employee Development

The current mindset of employees is that they should have the opportunity to grow by developing versatile and diverse skills sets, which give them the ability to create career security. Employees today have become more aware that the notion of job (as opposed to "career") security is obsolete, and the focus is now on career longevity and resilience. Verna Allee, author of the book, *The Knowledge Evolution—Expanding Organizational Intelligence,* asserts that, "Job security is becoming a thing of the past. Today, job security lies in what you know how to do, what you can learn to do, and how well you can access knowledge through collaboration with others."[20]

In the early 1990s, IBM seized the opportunity to help its employees recognize the painful but necessary fact that the essence of job security is about building skills that are relevant to the company and that the employees themselves should play a role in articulating what they want regarding their development and also become part owners in achieving their stated goals. Employees at IBM have accepted the challenge of managing their careers, but at the same time, they hold the company accountable for providing them with the right tools and a support system.

"Letting go to let them grow" is truly a statement of employee empowerment and respect. This line of discussion shows that the new employment "contract" is binding both ways—employees expect their employers to make it possible for the employees to retool and reinvent their skills portfolio to keep up with the current and future needs of the organization. For their part, companies are responding to the need to develop their employees to have a skilled workforce and also to stem the incidents of loss and attrition. Organizations that invest in learning and development of their workforce are making the statement that they value their employees. When employees develop multiple skills and competencies, they become more valuable to the organization and at the same time develop a greater sense of worth and connectedness to the organization. As employees are given the tools and room to grow, the company expects the best from them and generally, where there is high expectation, there is usually high performance, which has been the experience at IBM.

An inhibitor to career growth is allowing employees to narrowly define advancement and opportunity, so what IBM has done is help its employees grasp the point that advancement is not always a vertical or promotional move. Lateral or horizontal moves help employees develop skills across the business. Furthermore, employees are not limited to acquiring knowledge that is relevant just for their current job or their immediate department, but they are also encouraged to build skills for the future. This practice of allowing employees to develop cross-organizational knowledge and expertise better positions IBM employees to take on greater responsibilities and remain competitive. From a practical perspective, IBM employees can gain cross-business unit and cross-geography knowledge by taking advantage of a number of options, such as shadow experience; securing multiple mentors; informational interviews; and by taking on temporary, rotational, and stretch assignments. In fact, within the IBM Experiential Learning Opportunity portfolio (see Chapter 1, "Introducing IBM's Mentoring Portfolio") mentoring and information resources gives managers the ability to post experiential openings in the Opportunity Bank that fall both within and outside of an employee's organization.

Collaboration across Difference

Collaboration in IBM is anchored on the values and principles that govern behaviors in the workplace and the marketplace. "Trust and personal responsibility in all relationships"[21] is one of IBM's stated values that all levels of IBM employees use to influence the way they do their work, the way they collaborate and innovate, and the way they interact with clients across the globe.

Collaboration today is much more than groups of people working together on projects—collaboration requires trust, respect, understanding of diversity, and the practice of inclusive leadership. A cornerstone of IBM's diversity is that "None of us is as strong as all of us."[22] Implicit in this statement is the idea that an organization gains its strength from employees working together as one team to achieve business goals. An article on the subject of how to deal with resistance to diversity, written by Gardenswartz and Rowe acknowledges that, "Employees work with and serve people from different backgrounds. Effectiveness as organizations and individuals depend on the ability to deal with those differences successfully using each person's talents and gifts to enhance performance and harmony."[23]

The differences that people bring to the table in a collaborative environment can lead to creativity and innovation. The degree of innovation is greatly enhanced when each member of the team has a voice and is fully included in the operations of the group. This approach to collaboration uses the collective experience and knowledge of the team, which validates team members, assures them of their value, and has the potential to improve morale and employee engagement. When teams function in this manner, there are many positive outcomes, not the least of which is increased productivity. IBM makes every effort to educate its workforce on the moral, ethical, and business necessity to make diversity a cornerstone of how employees interact with one another and with the clients that the company serves. However, it is necessary to build relationships that cut across traditional boundaries such as job level, demographic group, and functional area. Techniques such as reverse mentoring have provided opportunities for collaboration across all types of differences throughout IBM.

Preventing Career Derailment: A Plan for Success

An important part of career development is for employees to define career contingency and recovery plans in the event of potential career setbacks. This process requires employees to do periodic personal assessments; focus on introspection; and secure constructive feedback from managers, mentors, and peers. When employees are open to constructive feedback to determine where and how they are vulnerable, they are given the opportunity to take remedial and corrective actions to address any developmental shortcomings. Quite often career derailment hinges on factors such as negative attitudes, ineffective behaviors, poor interpersonal skills, and/or low emotional and social intelligence. It has been noted by IBM Systems and Technology Leadership Development Training that, "Leaders rarely derail because of lack of technical or functional knowledge. Instead, derailment is usually the result of blind spots, over-relying on strengths, success going to the head, or having critical areas untested."[24]

As employees do their own self-scrutiny and examination, they must be true to themselves in determining what gives them excitement, motivation, and inspiration in a job; and what gives them satisfaction and pride in their current assignment and pride in the company for which they work. A core element of this personal assessment is to determine whether their value system is aligned with that of their organization. Knowing these things about oneself will help determine whether there is a fit with the job, the company, and the individual. Employees are encouraged to discuss these topics with their managers and mentors during career development coaching sessions, rather than remaining silent on these issues. Should it happen that employees are not forthcoming with their desires and expectations, they run the risk of becoming unhappy, distracted, and disengaged, and the organization is not given the opportunity to appropriately meet their needs. Other issues that impact work performance and satisfaction, such as the balance between work and personal life, can also be topics for sharing between partners in organization-sponsored relationships such as reverse mentoring.

As employees progress in their careers, they should have a constant pulse reading of how they act during moments of crisis or in stressful situations. A recommendation is that, if undesirable behaviors surface, such as losing self-control, losing focus, and showing high levels of frustration and anger, should surface, the employee should quickly do a self-assessment of the situation and seek guidance from her managers and mentors. Generally, if these behaviors are displayed, the resulting effect is that relationships are damaged, and quite often peers and colleagues become distant and avoid contact. Crisis has a way of building character, and it also has a way of revealing the other side of a person. The strength of a leader can be determined during a crisis, and this reaction helps define a person's brand or reputation within the company. The power of reverse mentoring is in helping emerging leaders understand how to address these dynamic and unpredictable challenges, as well as stimulating thinking by current leaders on how these problems can be solved in an effective and productive way.

Other derailment factors include lack of acceptance and accountability for one's mistakes, lack of resilience, and lack of will to bounce back from setbacks. As employees manage their careers, mistakes will happen and taking responsibility for them—versus taking the easy way out—is a sign of character and leadership. What must be done in these instances is to evaluate what may have caused the error, how it could have been avoided, and what can be done to learn from it in the future. After getting an understanding of what caused the mistake, it is important that employees move on and not stay stuck. Reverse mentoring can be an opportunity for leaders to reflect on their personal lessons learned from failures and setbacks as well as their recovery and ongoing journey of resilience.

Employees who get mired in details, are unable to see the big picture, and cannot think strategically could be setting themselves up for derailment. In today's fast-paced world, leaders of an organization have to make decisions quickly. Sometimes people who are slow to make decisions get bogged down with nonessential details, insisting that everything must be just right before a decision is made, run the risk of positioning the organization for lost opportunities. We are in an age where there is an overwhelming abundance of information, so the ability to quickly filter and decipher the relevance and importance of certain information to a particular situation puts employees in a better position to make quick but thoughtful and prudent decisions. Clearly, linkages with senior leaders within the organization can help employees focus on solving the immediate issue, while keeping their perspective on broader organizational issues.

As teams work together, it is not unheard of to have disagreements and interpersonal issues. The way in which this is handled can either allow the team to prosper and become productive or to become dysfunctional and unproductive. Relationship building is a critical skill that all employees must master in today's workforce. Team issues and disagreements must be addressed, and it is important that employees use the method that attacks the issue and not the person. The goal is to confront without being confrontational and to disagree without being disagreeable. Organizations place a high premium on those employees who can inspire others and who can motivate their colleagues to action. Sharing knowledge on how to address these ongoing interpersonal challenges is an area where reverse-mentoring relationships can produce significant mutual benefit for the mentor as well as the mentee.

Managing a career successfully takes time, but it is worth the personal investment, and the payoff could be great for both the employee and the company. Most people can minimize incidences of career derailment by remaining focused and emotionally present, becoming less controlling, developing a high tolerance for ambiguity, and managing change. As employees become more responsible for their careers, they develop excitement and self-worth by seeking intellectual stimulation and curiosity—a good way to encourage continuous learning. Connecting employees with valuable knowledge matches their personal investment with company resources that support their own career development, as well as ongoing knowledge sharing throughout the organization.

As companies identify the factors that can inevitably stall or stifle career growth, they have the obligation to help their employees become aware of these factors very early in their careers. Steps must be taken to educate employees on ways to avoid career derailment and should this occur, actions must be taken to help with the recovery process. Instances such as this require management coaching, support through mentoring, and the desire from the employee to make the appropriate adjustments. Mentors can be influential in helping their mentees avoid career derailment by sharing their past areas of vulnerabilities, particularly if the mentors have experienced career setbacks. People tend to learn from the mistakes of others, so it is practical to teach based on experience. Helping employees to avoid or recover from derailment is a statement that the company values its employees and that it is willing to invest in helping them grow from this experience. However, these derailment factors can be difficult for individuals to identify, especially when they have reached a point of success within their careers. Reverse mentoring relationships can help challenge basic assumptions of success and bring to light key derailment factors that can stall or stifle growth at any career stage.

Reverse Mentoring: Signaling Value in People across IBM

As we have discussed, reverse mentoring involves a nontraditional form of mentoring whereby knowledge relationships are formed between someone with less experience in the organization or a different (and frequently lower) level within the company. In IBM's formal reverse mentoring program, a senior-level person is on the receiving end of the mentoring relationship with a junior-level employee. The junior-level person is usually one who is new to IBM—somewhere between a recent graduate and an employee with two years' tenure or less—or who recently changed organizations and is new to the IBM culture and system. Often this provides new knowledge and different views that may not carry the same history or bias that may shape the view of people who have been with the company for a number of years. Reverse mentoring is at its best when the mentor can inspire and question existing "ways of working" with new questions, thoughts, and ideas. In addition, it is also a good opportunity to learn how things are working and how strategies and priorities are interpreted from people in different levels and functions throughout the organization.

In addition to ongoing dialog and sharing of ideas, a number of the senior-level executives within IBM will even have the "reverse mentors" sit in the executive's chair, while the executive—or "mentee"—sits on the other side of the desk. While this may feel awkward to some people at first, it provides a strong signal of support and willingness by the more senior manager to receive knowledge and advice by someone who may have fewer years with the company but valuable knowledge to share. Some of the feedback from the experience of people who have participated in IBM's reverse mentoring program is that it has helped bridge critical gaps, such as functional area or generational difference and thereby facilitated the transfer of knowledge. Ultimately, this leads to the heart of effective mentoring—a mutually beneficial relationship.

Reverse mentoring is becoming pervasive across IBM. Its primary focus is to link the different generations and diversity groups that coexist in the IBM workforce in a manner that signals the support and value that the organization places on them and their professional success. In addition, it also bridges the chasm between new employees and senior leaders of the business. This allows the leaders of the business to gain an appreciation of the perspectives of new and less tenured employees and gives them the sense of how employees are viewing the business from their vantage point. To provide some evidence as to the value of reverse mentoring as a strategic tool for helping to connect and communicate value in people, we describe three areas where these efforts are having a global impact at IBM.

Reverse Mentoring in the United States

One of the pioneers of reverse mentoring in the United States is Rod Adkins, senior vice president in the Systems and Technology Group. For Rod, the importance of reverse mentoring is to determine whether the company is effectively leveraging the skills of new people and quickly getting them connected to the business. This type of experience that reverse mentoring offers employees has a direct correlation with how they develop and advance. Having meetings with his "reverse mentor" allows Rod to take appropriate action for making process changes to various important programs. Another benefit is that reverse mentoring relationships help Rod see things differently. The relationships allow him to do early identification of technical talent, and he has become more prescriptive in what he does as he looks at how to help people advance through the business.

One of the outcomes of Rod's reverse mentoring relationship was an "Early Tenure conference," which he sponsors for 100–150 technical employees who have zero to five years' tenure at IBM. The conference exposes these new employees to senior leaders of the business. The employees hear about the company and its capability and better understand their sphere of influence. His observation of these early-tenure employees is that their focus is on finding the right resources, and they tend to question whether they are working on the right things. (In contrast, the focus of those in the over-five-year tenure category tends to be on advancement, that is, how to get from here to there.)

Rod has found that one of the biggest challenges to reverse mentoring is time, and he is still grappling with this to find a workable solution. Another challenge is that the reverse mentoring relationship is sometimes slow to develop because it can be intimidating to the reverse mentor who is new to the business. You have to get them comfortable enough to open up, have a dialog, and ask questions, which may even include helping to shape their thoughts. It depends on the personality that you are dealing with because some employees are very ambitious, some are unrealistic and overly aggressive about their goals, and some are more thoughtful about issues and come in with specific things they want to do to focus on their development. Dealing with these different employee personalities and approaches requires the leader to tailor his or her coaching method to achieve the desired outcomes and attitudes.

Success for Rod comes from realizing that he made a positive impact and increased someone's confidence level. When he helps employees think things through and it helps them to engage, Rod feels that this is a productive outcome. Rod says his personal benefits from reverse mentoring are "I like people. I am always reminded that people have played a role in my development so I have the obligation to give back. We have great reasons to give back; we are developing future leaders for IBM. Granted, some may not develop and become the typical leader, but they have become better people."

Reverse Mentoring in Finland

Another of those involved in reverse mentoring is Johan Sandell, the general manager of IBM Finland. Johan has more than 20 years of experience at IBM, and his career has developed in two- to three-year steps, working in most of the company's key business areas. He feels he has been fortunate to have had many very good managers throughout his career who coached and mentored him, although before "reverse mentoring," he had never been formally assigned a specific mentor. Johan feels that in general one-on-one mentoring is exciting, interesting, and rewarding. It allows him to share some of his own experience to help others grow, develop, and be successful. It is a great investment in time, and the benefits gained from it are important to the people involved, as well as to the business. However, reverse mentoring gives him a different perspective on the organization, the business, and employees.

Over the past few years, Johan has averaged five mentees per year, some of them in other countries and all of them at more junior levels within the organization. Johan has come to the conclusion that one has to be structured to get this to work, and that it's important to schedule the sessions into both parties' calendars for the following 6–12 months to ensure a continued dialogue. The mentee might request a meeting any time it's needed, but to ensure regular meetings will happen, it's good to have them planned, so they're not forgotten or overlooked. To keep the mentoring process alive, Johan has had mentees assigned to each member of his leadership team and requested that the mentoring process be implemented throughout the management levels of each of their organizations. The benefits to the company are many. For one thing, it's a vehicle for more senior and experienced people to share their experience, business insight, management practices, and so on with others in the organization.

Johan's reverse mentor, Ville Peltola, Consultant, Strategic Innovation, Europe, noted that along with his reverse mentoring relationship with Johan, he also has a "normal" career mentor in Finland. Ville's experience was that mentoring is vital to new IBM employees. Just the sheer size of the IBM organization underlines the significance of a mentoring relationship. In Ville's opinion, the business benefits are hard to measure and quantify, but they definitely exist. One good example is the concept that mentoring helps pass on the organizational knowledge within country organizations, which needs to be captured before it disappears as people retire or leave the company.

The inception of reverse mentoring in IBM Finland arose from a trainee program assignment presented to the Nordic management team. The team liked the proposal and used the trainees as the first reverse mentors. The experience was highly successful in that Johan appreciated Ville's fresh views and ideas. As Ville already had a bit of IBM experience; he could relate his ideas to the businesses for which Johan was responsible, telling Johan how things worked "in the real world," and what could be improved. Communication and chemistry are important in these relationships, and it worked well in their case.

From Ville's point of view, he felt that communication was easy between himself and Johan. Secondly, because Johan led the business in which Ville worked, they could talk to each other about concrete cases and examples that normally would have to go through several management layers. He could tell Johan how things really were at the grassroots level. Thus, in terms of plusses and minuses, Johan said that he gained a lot of new ideas he would not have gotten otherwise, so he felt it was well worth the time invested. He felt it helped develop people at all levels and enhanced communication and discussion throughout the organization.

However, if he had it to do over again, he might not have gotten so much into specific job-related issues that almost developed into projects, which happened easily as he and Ville were both in the same business unit. Although the discussions were very important, it's possible that the two of them could have achieved even more by taking a broader view of the reverse mentorship relationship. Ville felt the program allowed him to work with problems he wouldn't have been able to do otherwise. It was also exciting and very educating to interact with an executive such as Johan.

Ville wouldn't have changed anything about the program, because he believes the nature of a relationship like this has to be very loose—each mentor-mentee pair will shape their relationship differently. Also, as a person who likes to "challenge things," this program gave Ville a unique opportunity to challenge his top executive and try to provide an alternate point of view. This was personally rewarding for him and should be one criterion for mentors in such a program. The program also gave Ville visibility within the organization. Programs such as reverse mentoring are also excellent sources of innovation and that's who IBM wants to be—the innovator's innovator.

Reverse Mentoring in Latin America

Yet another part of the world has also taken up the reverse mentoring initiative. In Latin America, the Gay, Lesbian, Bisexual, and Transgender (GLBT) community started a program of reverse mentoring, the objective of which is to have the employees of the GLBT community chat with IBM executives about the group's objectives, its initiatives, its problems, and the challenges that group members face, both within and outside of IBM.

Moises Brand, IBM Global Finance Executive at IBM Mexico is the Leader of the Organizational Climate Initiative of the GLBT Taskforce. For Moises, reverse mentoring occurs when a person who has a good level of knowledge on a topic that's relevant to the GLBT constituency shares this knowledge to promote a climate that reinforces IBM's position on diversity in the workplace. Here, the IBM executives are the mentees and the GLBT community employees are the mentors.

This mentoring program arose in 2003 during the GLBT Leadership Conference in Palisades, New York, when the Latin American participants had a meeting with Bruno Di Leo, general manager of Latin America at that time, and also one of the event's speakers, to revise the GLBT group's plans and strategies. Out of this came the idea of establishing Educational Sessions for Executives in the Region, and sharing with them knowledge of the GLBT community's problems, both within and outside of work—the difficulties that result from living as a minority. The group's desire was to become agents to educate their peers about the GLBT constituency and, at the same time, reinforce inclusiveness in the IBM Latin America workforce.

For this role, Bruno named Marcelo Lema as Executive Sponsor of the GLBT community in Latin America. Along with Alessandro Bonorino, HR executive, they designed and launched the program, in which participants received a personal invitation to initiate educational sessions. The group worked with different countries, put together an initial list of executives who would be mentees, and assigned each one a GLBT mentor. The program has been of great value for the executives who participated, giving them the opportunity to get to know members of the GLBT community, their particular needs, and the challenges they face in the corporate world and in their personal life. They also understood that diversity is really a differentiator for IBM in the marketplace—it makes IBM a vanguard company looking to reflect the marketplace in itself, and giving IBM the opportunity to grow as human beings and understand the differences among people.

Since the launch of the program, the comments have been very positive. The GLBT group is happy about the number of executives taking the opportunity to get to know and ask more questions about the constituency. Mentees in this program say that it has been a positive experience. It gives them a context in which they can ask questions and understand situations with someone who actually knows what's what. It has created an atmosphere that enabled them to talk in depth about themes that are not always easy to discuss in other forums. At times a manager may be "extra cautious" when in contact with the GLBT community and what it represents, and that constitutes a barrier that keeps them from understanding what the correct action should be. The result of the mentoring relationships was that the executives became more confident and felt that both they and their mentors were able to communicate frankly.

One executive said that participating in the GLBT reverse mentoring program was an excellent experience, both professionally and personally. Professionally, it was well organized and structured, with pertinent content. Personally, it enriched her knowledge of the GLBT community—an important point in leading a culture based on the principles of openness, diversity, and equality of opportunity for all professionals who work at IBM.

Another executive called reverse mentoring "a fantastic and true opportunity to get a better understanding of the GLBT culture, to be more involved and engaged." He said the program allowed him to evaluate how he can help improve his work atmosphere and behavior, and how he can encourage his people to eliminate all types of discrimination around the theme of diversity. He also noted that there is no better way of understanding the complexity of a diverse culture than to have the opportunity of talking with his mentor.

The existence of such a program helps create a more complete diversity culture within IBM. This shows IBM's commitment to increase awareness of differences in the workplace, which increases the manager's capacity to create an atmosphere where each person feels valued, welcomed, and able to deliver value to IBM and its clients. Such learning can expand to an understanding of the meanings, feelings, and interpretations of other diverse groups. I found it valuable hearing the other point of view about various facts and concepts. I'm sure this will contribute to creating a more inclusive and empathetic climate.

One executive noted that these initiatives help him get closer to diverse groups, allowing him to better understand their members, their needs, and their potential. It helps people put aside their prejudices and concentrate on what is really important for the business of IBM—in other words, the competencies of leadership, abilities, and professionalism. Someone else said that the GLBT reverse mentoring program motivates people to be proactive, to be change agents, to help others to better understand what diversity is, and to help build IBM. Diversity does not mean just eliminating jokes or gossip—it's much more than that. We are prepared to go forward and this program is an excellent initiative for achieving this.

An HR executive noted that because one can't always appraise or understand the differences between people—even to the point of not being able to talk about them openly and objectively—these types of activities provide that opportunity. She said, "With better understanding, a person can make better decisions on a daily basis, resulting in the creation of a more tolerant and respectful atmosphere. The knowledge of these topics is what leads us to a real consciousness. We can't act in a consistent manner without being fully aware of these topics."

One suggestion for improvement of the program going forward to a second phase might be to have those who have already been trained as mentors act as the new agents responsible for sharing their experiences with more people, to disseminate them throughout the organization. Another person suggested that all the folks who participate in this program should be prepared and ready to share their knowledge and experience with the people they are mentoring. They need to understand that there is a lack of knowledge and a different cultural charge about the subject that can be difficult to manage, but that tolerance and respect should always be present on both sides to function and evolve. IBM values its people, and to make this a reality, they have invested greatly in career development, offer strong support systems such as mentoring, and leverage differences as a personal and business imperative.

Looking Toward the Future– Multigenerational Collaboration

The success of the reverse mentoring efforts across the various global business units has led IBM to take a look at other ways this approach can help to support its strategic goal of valuing people. As Ron Glover, vice president of Global Workforce Diversity at IBM, remarked, "At IBM, we have long understood that an inclusive workplace is critical to our ability to attract the best people, serve the needs of our clients and meet the expectations of our shareholders." He continued by saying, "This new era of diversity ensures our ability to work together effectively and to constructively address a variety of emerging trends that impact IBM and our clients across the globe."[25] Although IBM has a strong history of diversity and inclusion, diversity today has become increasingly more complex and poses challenges to IBM and other corporations. One of the complexities of diversity in the workplace is the aging of the workforce, coupled with the four different generations that coexist in the same space. Adding to this is the impact of globalization, which demands that employees collaborate with people who represent different cultures, languages, and time zones. Thus, utilizing reverse mentoring is being expanded to help IBM address the challenges of collaboration across a diverse workforce that includes multiple generations around the globe.

In a multigenerational workforce, special effort must be made to understand the generational differences, and organizations are encouraged to use strong diversity techniques to help their employees develop greater awareness of the opportunities and challenges that are inherent in generational diversity. Doing so helps employees better collaborate and maximize the unique strengths of each group. A great deal of attention has been directed at research to gain understanding of age differences in the workplace, and one such study was partly funded by IBM Global Work/Life Fund. The study revealed that, "In this multigenerational workforce, you might find yourself working closely with teammates as old as your parents or grandparents or as young as your children or grandchildren. Working with people of different ages can be highly rewarding, opening the door to new approaches and ideas and to rich mentoring relationships. The more you understand the unique strengths and qualities of each generation, the more successful you will be at work."[26]

This situation is fertile ground for meaningful collaboration that leads to knowledge transfer. If we could get people to focus not so much on age but rather to turn their attention to the diverse skills that each generation has to offer, everyone could derive great benefit from age differences. In such a case, rich mentoring relationships can develop that are facilitated by a well-designed formal reverse mentoring program. In addition to this important tool, the IBM mentoring revitalization effort promotes a menu of mentoring options that offers employees the chance to select mentoring resources that best suit their unique needs. Giving people resources and tools and then connecting them to one another regardless of generation or geography is a statement of value. "Connecting this talent across generations allows organizations to provide young talent with hands-on training and give experienced workers a way to pass on their expertise, thereby keeping their knowledge in the institution."[27]

Many companies are struggling with the new issues of having four generations (traditionalists, boomers, Xers, and Yers) working together, and companies like IBM are making concerted efforts to capitalize on the benefits of effectively blending the generations. Understanding and harnessing the unique strengths and knowledge of each generation can translate into organizational impact and success in managing the talent of each generation. The challenge of connecting across generations is one being faced by most global companies and one that IBM is addressing through a number of strategic initiatives, including its innovative reverse mentoring program.

Managers and leaders of an organization play a significant role in setting the right example and the expectation of how employees should work collectively to build both their ability and also the capability of the organization. It is critical that the organization provide ongoing diversity education and hold its employees accountable to make the workplace welcoming to all. As teams form and collaboration takes place, acknowledgment and respect must be given to all dimensions of diversity that exist. Efforts must be made to uproot hidden biases and blind spots and engage in healthy dialogue on how to overcome these diversity challenges. When managers help their employees understand the business, as well as the personal benefits of collaboration and inclusion, it develops a sound foundation that helps its people and the organization as a whole to thrive. Diversity is not only a personal imperative; it is a business imperative within IBM.

Lessons Learned–Signaling Ethics and Integrity

One of the key lessons learned from IBM's experience with reverse mentoring deals with the need to cultivate mutually beneficial relationships that help to support a culture of collaboration. Issues related to fair treatment, trust, and open communication are key drivers of employees' perceptions of support and the overall effectiveness of any mentoring relationship. Many employees generally place great value on working for a company that is known for its ethical stance and one whose reputation regarding integrity can stand the test of time. Establishing a workplace that represents trust and respect is not only the right thing to do but also a business necessity. Both employees and customers want to be associated with a company that is steadfast in its values and principles. IBM holds its employees and the leaders of the company to the highest standard of integrity. In the early years of IBM, T.J. Watson, Jr. said, "No one should be entrusted to lead any business or institution unless he or she has impeccable personal integrity."[28] The experience that employees have within mentoring relationships, particularly reverse mentoring in which they are partnered with more senior leaders within the company, can serve as a strong signal of the importance of integrity within the company as these leaders provide role modeling for key values within the firm's culture.

IBM has used several methods to communicate to the workforce its position on integrity and ethics. Business conduct guidelines, the eight principles, the three values statement (which employees helped to develop), and e-classes on integrity all serve to reinforce the company's stand on integrity and ethics. Just as employees hold the company accountable to stand by its values, the company also holds employees accountable to make decisions based on the grounds of integrity. While each of these is important to signal the value that ethics and integrity has within the IBM environment, a strong message is sent to employees who are able to witness and directly experience these values in their reverse mentoring relationships with senior leaders within IBM.

Integrity comes into the picture depending on how managers and employees follow through on the commitments made during the development discussions. IBM's ongoing commitment to developing its people was reinforced back in 1974, when CEO Frank T. Cary declared, "Our investment in education is large, and the reason is plain: We cannot hope to run the IBM of tomorrow on yesterday's knowledge. It is important to keep abreast of new knowledge, whatever your job." One of the things employees value is the chance to develop personally and professionally, and it builds trust when the company delivers on such a promise. Employees gain firsthand experience with this as part of their reverse mentoring experiences. Especially for those partners where one of the activities involves shadowing, employees can witness commitment to ethics and integrity in action, not simply as a written policy of the company.

"Trust and personal responsibility in all relationships"[29] is one of the three values that employees across IBM helped to define in a worldwide "values jam." The interpretation of this value statement is that IBM employees expect their colleagues to do what's right, be accountable, and deliver on promises with a high degree of excellence. While these expectations appear fundamental, they are essential ingredients in the recipe for successful collaboration. The respect that team members show for one another helps to make IBM a fun place to work, and in this environment where people tend to freely share information, support systems are formed, and professional relationships are lasting.

Martin Luther King, Jr., said, "The time is always right to do what's right" and employees who establish and maintain a high level of integrity, respect, and fairness demonstrate the essence of a leader. To maintain integrity requires self assessment and the use of a personal moral compass to make decisions that can stand up to scrutiny. Making ethical decisions requires having accurate, current, and relevant information. Teams fall apart when they do not have the pertinent information or when decisions are made in a vacuum. IBM is on a mission to lower the center of gravity of decision making more to the employee level. For employees to make decisions that are founded on current, relevant information, leaders of the business must transmit to their employees the necessary information in a timely manner. This is reinforced within the formal mentoring process that includes reverse mentoring throughout IBM.

As employees develop their technical portfolio of skills, it is important to establish alignment with a commitment to integrity and ethics. As retired Hall of Fame basketball coach John Wooden said, "Ability may get you to the top but it is character that keeps you there." Frequently, the rise or fall of a leader can often be traced to issues of ethics and integrity. Clearly, this is why many companies, including IBM, provide tools and guidance to each employee that helps her/him develop the skills and attributes of being a successful and ethical leader. Mentors and role models are important examples of ethical decision making and integrity within the IBM culture. Thus, a positive yet unexpected benefit of IBM's reverse mentoring relationships is that they provide direct contact with how ethics and integrity are experienced and executed by key leaders across the firm. These relationships expose employees not only to ethical practices in specific customer interactions, but also to ethical behavior as demonstrated by a fundamental value in people.

As articulated by John Akers from IBM, "Respect for the individual, commitment to excellence in all that we do, providing the best service in the world—these are IBM's compass. These are the core of IBM's tradition of honesty, integrity and ethics that guided our past and that must continue to guide our business in the future. And these beliefs and values are at the heart of IBM's most enduring strengths." This message was delivered during IBM's tough times of the 1990s and reflects a commitment to the ethical standards that govern the operations of the company, reinforces the value of its people, and extends to the marketplace, business cycles, and financial metrics. Reverse mentoring has provided an opportunity to reinforce these core values that may have been initially shaped by top leadership but are brought to life by employees across all levels of the organization. The dialogue about the need for and challenges to ethics and integrity within global companies like IBM provides a rich exchange within these reverse mentoring relationships. In addition, it reinforces the value that ethical leadership and integrity are a shared responsibility of everyone within IBM. Again, standards of excellence and standards of ethics are factors that IBM has demonstrated and made clear to employees over the years that are not to be compromised regardless of how the business is doing. As we stated in the beginning of this chapter, sometimes a cliché actually represents a necessary truth.

References

[1] Simonson, Peggy, (1977). Promoting a Development Culture in Your Organization, quoting Waterman, Waterman and Collard, (1994) *Harvard Business Review*.

[2] Coyle-Shapiro, J.A.M. and Kessler, I. (2002). Exploring reciprocity through the lens of the psychological contract. *European Journal of Work and Organizational Psychology, 11,* 69–86; Coyle-Shapiro, J.A.M., and Kessler, I. (2000). Consequences of the psychological contract for the employment relationship: A large scale survey. *Journal of Management Studies, 37,* 903–930; Cropanzano, R., Howes, J.C., Grandey, A.A., and Toth, P. (1997). The relationship of organizational politics and support to work behaviors, attitudes, and stress. *Journal of Organizational Behavior, 22,* 159–180.

[3] Arthur, M.B. and Rousseau, D.M. (1996). Introduction: The boundaryless career as a new employment principle. In M.B. Arthur and D.M. Rousseau (Eds.), *The Boundaryless Career*, 3–20. New York: Oxford.

[4] Rousseau, D.M. and McLean Parks, J. (1993). The contracts of individuals and organizations. *Research in Organizational Behavior, 15,* 1–43.

[5] Rousseau, D.M. (1995). *Psychological Contracts in Organizations: Understanding Written and Unwritten Agreements*. Thousand Oaks, CA: Sage Publications.

[6] Robinson, S.L., Kraatz, M., and Rousseau, D.M. (1994). Changing obligations and the psychological contract: A longitudinal study. *Academy of Management Journal, 37,* 137–152; Rousseau, D.M. (1989). Psychological and implied contracts in organizations. *Employee Rights and Responsibilities Journal, 2,* 12–139.

[7] Coyle-Shapiro, J.A.M. and Kessler, I. (2002). Exploring reciprocity through the lens of the psychological contract. *European Journal of Work and Organizational Psychology, 11,* 69–86.

[8] MacNiel, I.R. (1985). Relational contract: What we do and what we do not know. *Wisconsin Law Review,* 483–525.

[9] Robinson, (1996). Trust and breach of the psychological contract. *Administrative Science Quarterly, 41,* 574–599; Robinson, S.L. and Wolfe Morrison, E.W. (1995). Psychological contracts and OCB: The effect of unfulfilled obligations on civic virtue behavior. *Journal of Organizational Behavior, 16,* 289–298; Robinson, S.L., Kraatz, M., and Rousseau, D.M. (1994). Changing obligations and the psychological contract: A longitudinal study. *Academy of Management Journal, 37,* 137–152.

[10] Rhoades, L. and Eisenberger, R. (2002). Perceived organizational support: A review of the literature. *Journal of Applied Psychology, 87,* 698–714; Robinson, (1996). Trust and breach of the psychological contract. *Administrative Science Quarterly, 41,* 574–599; Robinson, S.L. and Wolfe Morrison, E.W. (1995). Psychological contracts and OCB: The effect of unfulfilled obligations on civic virtue behavior. *Journal of Organizational Behavior, 16,* 289–298; Robinson, S.L., Kraatz, M.. and Rousseau, D.M. (1994). Changing obligations and the psychological contract: A longitudinal study. *Academy of Management Journal, 37,* 137–152; Rousseau, D.M. (1989). Psychological and implied contracts in organizations. *Employee Rights and Responsibilities Journal, 2,* 121–139; Rousseau, D.M. (1990). New hire perceptions of their own and their employer's obligations: A study of psychological contracts. *Journal of Organizational Behavior, 11,* 389–400; Rousseau, D.M. (2000). Psychological contracts in the United States: Associability, individualism and diversity. In D.M. Rousseau and R. Schalk (eds.), *Psychological contracts in employment: Cross-national perspectives* (pp. 250–282). Newbury Park, CA: Sage.

[11] Eisenberger, R., Fasolo, P., and Davis-LaMastro, V. (1990). Perceived organizational support and employee diligence, commitment, and innovation. *Journal of Applied Psychology, 75,* 51–59; Eisenberger, R., Huntington, R., Hutchison, S., and Sowa, D. (1986). Perceived organizational support. *Journal of Applied Psychology, 71,* 500–507.

[12] Aselage, J. and Eisenberger, R. (2003). Perceived organizational support and psychological contracts: A theoretical integration. *Journal of Organizational Behavior, 24,* 491–509.

[13] Eisenberger, R., Rhoades, L., and Cameron, J. (1999). Does pay for performance increase or decrease perceived self-determination and intrinsic motivation? *Journal of Personality and Social Psychology, 77,* 1026–1040; Eisenberger, R., Armeli, S., Rexwinkel, B., Lynch, P.D., and Rhoades, L. (2001). Reciprocation of perceived organizational support. *Journal of Applied Psychology, 86,* 42–51; Turnley, W.H., Bolino, M.C., Lester, S.W., and Bloodgood, J.M. (2003). The impact of psychological contract fulfillment on the performance of in-role and organizational citizenship behaviors. *Journal of Management, 29,* 187–206; Turnley,

W.H. and Feldman, D.C. (1999). The impact of psychological contract violations on exit, voice, loyalty and neglect. *Human Relations, 52,* 895–922; Turnley, W.H., and Feldman, D.C. (2000). Re-examining the effects of psychological contract violations: unmet expectations and job dissatisfaction as mediators. *Journal of Organizational Behavior, 21,* 25–42.

[14] Gerstner, Louis V., Jr., (2002). *Who Says Elephants Can't Dance? Inside IBM's Historic Turnaround.*

[15] Rhoades, L. and Eisenberger, R. (2002). Perceived organizational support: A review of the literature. *Journal of Applied Psychology, 87,* 698–714; Rhoades, L., Eisenberger, R., and Armeli, S. (2001). Employee commitment to the organization: The contribution of perceived organizational support. *Journal of Applied Psychology, 86,* 825–836.

[16] Kaye, Beverly and Jordan-Evans, Sharon, (2002). *Love 'Em or Lose 'Em: Getting Good People to Stay, Second Edition.*

[17] Herreld, J. B. (2007), Senior Vice President, Marketing and Strategy, IBM, IBM Strategy – Education/w3 (Web site).

[18] Greengard, S. (2002). Moving forward with reverse mentoring. *Workforce,* 81(3), 15.

[19] Ibid.

[20] Allee, V. (1997). *The Knowledge Evolution: Expanding Organizational Intelligence.*

[21] IBM, (2004). "Our Values at Work: On Being an IBMer."

[22] IBM Diversity Booklet.

[23] Gardenswartz, L. and Rowe, A. (2004). Dealing with Resistance to Diversity. *Society of Human Resource Diversity Library.* April 2004

[24] Defining and Developing Leaders in IBM, IBM System and Technology Leadership Development Training 3.1.2, Derailment Factors.

[25] Glover, Ron, VP Global Workforce Diversity at IBM, (2006). "Why IBM Works."

[26] Ceridian Corporation and IBM Corporation, (2004). "Age Differences, Work Differences: Understanding Older and Younger Co-Workers."

[27] Sowers, J. and Woody, S. (2006). "A Game Plan for Retaining Talent," *Electric Perspectives,* Vol. 31, Issue 1, p. 4652, Washington.

[28] Watson, T.J., Jr., (1962). *A Business and Its Beliefs.*

[29] IBM, (2004). "Our Values at Work: On Being an IBMer."

7

Business Impact: Using Mentoring to Deliver Value for Competitive Advantage

Chapter Contents

Adding Value through Mentoring

Understanding the impact of mentoring activities is a necessary but challenging endeavor for any organization. Similar to the way in which some human resources activities are evaluated, the emphasis is largely on costs, while less attention is paid to how these efforts help maximize productivity and impact the organization's bottom line. Thus, the notion of "adding value" versus maintaining costs must be added to any review or assessment of mentoring and other people-focused initiatives within the organization.

In the area of strategic human resource management, increased attention has been directed toward a set of value-adding activities known as **high-performance work practices** (HPWP) in an attempt to better understand their impact on organizational performance. Considerable evidence has shown that these practices increase employees' knowledge, skills, and abilities while empowering employees to leverage this knowledge, both for the benefit of the organization and for their own professional development. The impact of HPWP is more positive work attitudes (for example, job satisfaction, commitment, perceptions of support), better decision making, and enhanced creativity within work teams.

Inevitable in any discussion of business impact is the issue of the kinds of metrics to be employed. Traditionally, organizations have relied exclusively on financial or economic metrics of business impact. However, with the increased attention on ethics, corporate social responsibility, and sustainable business practices, the need for a broader array of metrics to demonstrate business impact is critical. Recently the notion of moving beyond standard metrics of business impact, such as return on investment (ROI), to a more balanced approach that has also been labeled the "triple bottom line" is receiving increased momentum.

In high-performance work environments, employees are motivated and driven to do the things that are essential to create success for them and for the organization at large. Generally, these individuals derive an intrinsic reward by participating in acts that make a difference, especially when that difference has a positive impact on others. However, the organization must respond with systems, structures, and practices that both recognize and reward such efforts by employees. Leaders in the IBM workplace strive to make their employees feel valued by providing encouragement and support, which allows them to display the desired behaviors that lead to success, especially when these efforts are "above and beyond" typical work activities and expectations.

Because of this, we examine the issue of adding value through mentoring within the broader context of HPWP. While much has been written about these systems, mentoring is typically omitted from the list of these initiatives that help to add and sustain value for the organization. We discuss the need to expand the ways in which value is measured and communicated through the organization in keeping with recent trends that involve a balanced approach for measuring and communicating the business impact of HPWP.

In addition in this chapter, we review the IBM Marketing Group mentoring program and provide an example of mentoring within the array of HPWP utilized in this business unit. We review the Americas Marketing Mentor Appreciation Award as both a method that was put in place to acknowledge the acts of employees who help advance each others' careers through mentoring and as a way to capture and communicate the value-added impact of mentoring within the marketing group. Thus, the notion of "valuating the business impact" as one of IBM's strategic objectives provides the context for our discussion of how the value-added impact of high-performance systems function to yield high contribution and results. This is not easy to achieve unless organizations invest in developing learning tools and resources that include a diverse menu of formal and informal mentoring activities.

Mentoring Solutions as High-Performance Work Practices (HPWP)

A great deal of research has been devoted to understanding the impact of HPWP on organizational performance. Unfortunately, mentoring has too often been omitted from these explorations into the HPWP-organizational performance link. Most of the HPWP research has focused on traditional HR practices, such as incentive compensation, training, flexible work arrangements, and employee participation. While these specific examples each fall under this category, a substantial amount of research shows that individual practices produce less of an overall business impact than a system of work practices that are aligned with the overall organizational strategy.[1] Huselid and Becker stated in their research on more than 2,000 firms that one standard deviation changed in HR systems was responsible for 10%–20% of the firm's market value.[2] Thus, the notion of bundles of practices having the greatest impact on key outcomes such as firm market value has received support from the research evidence.

The need to demonstrate not only the business impact of HPWP but also the specific nature of their impact is vital to organizational effectiveness. Research has shown that HPWP can produce an impact on organizational performance in one of three ways. First, HPWP operate by increasing the knowledge skills and abilities of employees.[3] Employees may perform at or sometimes below their potential because they rely on discretion over the use of their knowledge skills and abilities. Thus, learning opportunities must be consistently available to all employees, regardless of tenure and ranking in the business, geography, or work arrangements.

Multinational companies such as IBM have shown sensitivity to developing global learning programs that take into consideration the variety of workforce needs. They have adapted their mentoring program to assist employees in becoming agile learners so that the company can develop its knowledge base and at the same time meet the needs and expectations of clients. As an illustration, employees are encouraged to secure multiple mentors across business units and across geographies to get exposure to a number of learning situations. These mentoring opportunities take place in a variety of ways, including group mentoring, shadowing opportunities, and joint project activities. Employees who engage in mentoring relationships develop both new technical and functional skills, as well as personal attributes, such as how to sharpen their critical thinking, and how to be strategic and inclusive. Generally, as employees acquire new knowledge and are given the ability to use it in challenging and innovative ways, they develop excitement and are inspired to continue learning new things. This clearly helps to shape and enhance the overall business impact.

Second, HPWP have been shown to have an impact on organizational performance by empowering employees to act. A variety of research shows that talented employees may not utilize their knowledge skills and abilities unless there are organizational practices and structures in place that offer the latitude for them to act.[4] Employees must be motivated to leverage their knowledge skills and abilities through HPWP such as incentive compensation, performance appraisal, internal promotions, and reward and recognition. In addition to employee education and development, IBM has a strong recognition and awards program that rewards employees for extraordinary contributions to the business. Some of the recognition options that IBM uses to motivate and reward employees include

- Peer recognition—nonmonetary award.
- Thank Your Mentor and Thank Your Mentee cards, afford employees the ability to express their gratitude to their mentors for having a positive

impact on their development and, conversely, a mentor has the opportunity to acknowledge or congratulate a mentee for achieving milestone goals, such as closing a specific skill gap.

- Invention Achievement Award, which recognizes inventors who have achieved different invention levels.

- Innovators' Award acknowledges teams and individuals that have impacted clients through innovation. Typically, employees who are awarded in this category show true leadership in collaboration, accountability, and creativity.

- Outstanding Innovation and Outstanding Technical Achievement Awards are given to individuals who have made a technical contribution that involves deep technical skill, insight, and foresight.

- Ovation Awards are given to employees who demonstrate leadership and whose contribution results in significant value to the business.

While IBM uses various forms of recognition for motivating employees to reach their highest potential, various business units and employee groups are constantly coming up with creative ways to acknowledge their peers for significant contribution to the business. The IBM Americas Marketing Award is a unique recognition initiative that acknowledges employees for excellence in contribution, and it was designed, implemented, and measured by a group of employees.

Third, HPWP impact performance by enhancing motivation and positive work attitudes. Organizational initiatives such as compensation, incentives, promotions, and performance appraisal comprise a set of HPWP that have a direct impact on motivating employees to perform. In addition, flexible work arrangements, opportunity for advancement, and employee development activities can also increase motivation by enhancing employee work involvement and organizational commitment.

IBM's long-term commitment to employee development has been consistent, not only during financially good times, but also during times of economic challenge. An article titled, "IBM Corporate Responsibility—Our People—Learning & Opportunity," declared that "With a company investment of almost three-quarters of a billion dollars on training and development annually, IBMers have access to thousands of learning solutions, which provide just-in-time learning wherever they are, whenever they need it. Globally, employees spend an estimated 17 million hours each year engaged in formal training—either online, in a collaborative space, through experiential learning activities or in a traditional classroom. Many of our programs have a blend of learning solutions, allowing employees to take training in the way that works best for them. IBM conducts half of its employee training via e-learning, which has helped the company save over $750 million during the past two years and meet the needs of an increasingly mobile workforce at the same time."[5] IBM's staunch support for employee development is deeply embedded in its budget planning practices where dollars are earmarked for this purpose. The company sees this as a priority and proactive way to build the ability of its workforce. In essence, successful enterprise learning dictates the alignment of strategic and fiscal planning.

IBM has tracked and evaluated the impact of these efforts based not only on utilization of training, but also on the impact on employee attitudes toward work and the organization as key metrics of business impact. In consideration of these three critical areas, HPWP clearly have a link to organizational performance, which in turn has an impact on the social structures within the organization. More specifically, HPWP that link people who do not typically interact with each other or that facilitate information sharing and resource exchange have been shown to produce an impact on performance.[6]

IBM's use of expert mentoring and the technology-enhanced mentoring information available through its Experiential Learning Opportunities program (see Chapter 2, "Organizational Intelligence: Using Just-in-Time Mentoring Solutions") are examples of HPWP that facilitate knowledge and resource sharing. Similarly, HPWP that increase norms of reciprocity or that promote cooperation among different employee segments also show a positive impact on performance.[7] In addition, being able to share mental models and common problem-solving approaches such as HPWP positively impacts business outcomes. These common knowledge sets, attitudes, and approaches can facilitate cooperation and more effective decision making, which in turn produce a positive business impact.[8]

We have described several examples of how IBM uses a portfolio of mentoring practices that target building a knowledge community across the global business enterprise to reinforce the role mentoring plays in enhancing the performance of an organization. Whether using mentoring to solve "wicked problems," create innovative solutions, or enhance the overall effectiveness of the work, valuating the business impact is never a short-term endeavor. Organizations such as IBM must focus not only on short-term impact, but also on long-term, sustainable impact across HPWP that include an array of formal and informal mentoring activities.

Enduring Skills Help to Create Competitive Advantage

A description of an enduring organization is one that can withstand economic turmoil and can plan for the future by always having a portfolio of market-valued skills to address the volatile needs of its clients. The backbone of such a company is built on its strength to manage talent and the fortitude to quickly adapt to both anticipated and unforeseen industry changes. Enduring companies are guided by a core set of values and principles and are unwavering in expecting their employees to interact with their colleagues, their communities, and clients with the utmost degree of integrity and ethics.

In short, the company's brand and reputation must remain untarnished. Jim Collins, using research on companies that sustained better-than-average performance across a 15-year period, wrote in his book, *Good to Great,* "Enduring great companies preserve their core values and purpose while their business strategies and operating practices endlessly adapt to a changing world. This is the magical combination of preserve the core and stimulates the progress."[9] Collins' work clearly shows the importance of looking at enduring practices that are helping companies adapt to the challenges and opportunities that arise as they move from just being "good" to becoming "great."

IBM is a company that is enduring by nature, not just because of its principles, but also because of the value placed on its global workforce, and the uncanny manner with which it reads impending marketplace changes. This means not simply looking at short-term metrics of business impact, but also focusing on long-term outcomes of business sustainability.

An example of how IBM takes this long-term perspective in understanding its global business impact was articulated in the speech that IBM CEO Sam Palmisano made on the subject of leadership, trust, and the globally integrated enterprise. In that speech, Palmisano made the point that, "A globally integrated company looks different. This is an enterprise that shapes its strategy, management and operations in a truly global way. It locates operations and functions anywhere in the world based on the right cost, the right skills and the right business environment. And it integrates those operations horizontally and globally."[10] This renewed focus on how business is done at IBM is a strategy embodied in multinational organizations, and its intent is to enable the company to function in a seamless manner, basically ignoring geographic lines of demarcation. This approach better unifies the company and allows it to quickly respond to all clients, wherever they are located.

Having the right skills, just-in-time skills, and diverse skills enhances the company's capability to respond to the marketplace in innovative ways. To maintain this position, constant attention must be given to employee development, in the form of collaborative and blended learning practices and an array of metrics that demonstrate the overall business impact of these efforts. In addition, IBM makes it a practice to acknowledge its employees who have achieved their personal goals in attaining stellar accomplishments in their disciplines, particularly in the field of technology. Doing this leads to innovative solutions that help IBM outpace its competitors.

The Corporate Technical Recognition Event (CTRE) is an annual celebration that recognizes those technical employees who made distinguished contributions to the business through their inventions. Following the 2008 CTRE, an article written about the event highlighted the point that, "This week at the prestigious 2008 IBM CTRE, 515 technical professionals are being honored for individual and team collaborations defying limits and creating collaborative innovation. As we dedicate ourselves to more effective collaboration with clients, business partners and other leading organizations, we recognize the people that contribute to IBM's deep technical knowledge, assets and services expertise in a manner that helps our clients create differentiation in the marketplace."[11]

Through the reinvention of IBM's mentoring program, functional, technical, and leadership skill building are taking place across business units, geographies, and cultures. In addition, the approach taken within other aspects of IBM's HPWP have been integrated and infused into its approach to mentoring. The core of the mentoring program reinvention encourages global innovation, global collaboration, and global knowledge sharing. Employees in mature organizations are reaching across the globe to transfer their skills to their colleagues, with special emphasis on those in hyper-growth and emerging countries. Cross-geography mentoring programs are becoming prevalent throughout IBM with the intention of rapidly building knowledge and expertise to have an impact in the markets in which IBM chooses to do business. The cross-geography programs promote bidirectional learning where employees from emerging countries gain technical skills, global leadership strategies, and global business acumen. At the same time, mentors from the mature organizations are enhancing their awareness regarding cultural intelligence, challenges, and opportunities that exist in the emerging countries.

In addition, mentoring efforts strongly emphasize ongoing employee development and have created innovative methods of rewarding and recognizing employees who mentor others in ways that produce lasting business impact for the organization. Thus, the system of HPWP has yielded a system of high-performance mentoring practices across IBM's global business enterprise. IBM's approach is defined by a system of HPWP that includes multiple and reinforcing practices that have additive effects and produce synergies that reinforce the overall business model (see Chapter 1, "Introducing IBM's Mentoring Portfolio"). This type of coordinated system of HPWP that includes mentoring has been shown to strengthen the overall impact on organizational performance.[12] However, the challenge for IBM and similar organizations is to develop a measurement approach that reflects the multidimensional nature of its HPWP and portfolio of mentoring solutions.

Developing a Balanced View of "Value Added"

As we mentioned earlier, the challenge for any set of human resources activities is how to balance the focus of business impact on the contribution of these efforts, as well as the costs. Typically, the intent is to provide reliable and valid information on the impact. However, the result is often a disconnect between what we measure and the desired outcome of HPWP that includes mentoring. This was aptly described in the famous article by Steven Kerr on "the folly of rewarding A while hoping for B."[13]

A traditional focus on single metrics of performance such as financial ratios (for example, return on investment, return on sales) has been criticized for being backward-looking, indicating only how well the firm or business unit has done in the past. In addition, these financial metrics focus on only a single component of business impact and ignore other value-creating actions that have been shown to drive performance. However, this leaves open the critical question of how business units and organizations define and communicate the "value" of HPWP such as mentoring to key stakeholders.

Some argue that any short-term financial measure or any single criterion for impact is appropriate for defining value across different circumstances and diverse business practices. This has led to several innovations in how we discuss impact and value. One example of innovative solutions to defining value is what Kaplan and Norton called the "balanced scorecard."[14] This approach has been utilized widely across global business because it focuses attention on diverse dimensions of impact within the organization, such as customer feedback, internal business impact, innovation and learning, as well as financial performance. It also highlights the need to examine performance in ways that not only measure previous outcomes but also signal to employees the actions and behaviors that are valued by the organization to sustain its future competitive advantage.

As a result of this notion, some companies have adopted a balanced scorecard approach for the human resource function and track HR's impact across metrics of internal customer satisfaction, operational efficiency, financial performance, and strategic capability.[15] Recently, another approach to expanding how we understand, measure, and communicate value-added practices has been captured in what Savitz calls the "triple bottom line."[16] In a similar vein as the balanced scorecard, the triple bottom line has also been offered as a way to capture the diversity of dimensions needed to create an accurate picture of the value or impact of human resources practices. While both concepts offer important insight into a balanced or multidimensional approach to understanding business impact, the key question that remains is how to define and communicate the value-added impact of work practices, such as mentoring key outcomes for employees, business units, and the overall organization.

Varma and colleagues[17] conducted a survey of business organizations in terms of their use and measurement of HPWP. Their research was conducted to validate the impact of these HPWP on a variety of key organizational and human resource outcomes. While individual corporate cases of success with HPWP have been noted (for example, Xerox's recovery from downturns in the 1980s), a systematic exploration of the ways in which organizations design and measure the value of these practices was clearly needed. Varma's research team discovered a wide range of approaches used by these firms to measure and communicate the impact of HPWP. These approaches included traditional measures such as employee attitudes (satisfaction, commitment) or short-term performance (sales targets, production goals, customer service metrics) to more qualitative approaches (surveys of workplace culture, impact of key strategic objectives [for example, workplace safety]). Interestingly, one of its important findings was that using non-financial and team-based rewards was closely related to improved financial and operational performance. In addition, rewarding employees for improving their competencies and for engaging in learning activities also enhanced both operational and financial performance. Their findings highlight the link between HPWP and rewarding employees as critical for driving operational, cultural, and financial outcome.

Thus, taking a balanced approach to evaluating business impact is important for signaling the value of activities for the organization. In addition to the traditional perspective, measuring business impact also can provide additional perspectives that speak to the ways in which HPWP (including mentoring) create value and help to sustain the firm's overall competitive advantage. As we have seen from the research on firms that utilize various HPWP, using only cost measures of these efforts can introduce a control bias. That is, using only cost outcomes or short-term financial indicators of performance focuses attention on a narrow set of quantifiable actions. Taking a more balanced approach to defining and evaluating impact focuses attention on issues of learning, culture, knowledge transfer, and qualitative (as well as quantitative) dimensions. While focusing on the costs of these efforts is necessary, using this criterion alone defines value strictly as a control mechanism and does not produce information that serves as a tool to motivate and learn or celebrate and improve employee as well as firm performance.[18] Thus, a key objective of evaluating any business activity or outcome should move beyond simple questions about costs to include learning what is (or is not) working and *why*.

Ultimately, a balanced view of the value of any HPWP such as mentoring is essential in bridging what Pfeffer and Sutton call the "knowledge-doing gap."[19] Traditional short-term financial or cost metrics answer the question of the impact of what is done but leaves managers ill-equipped to answer the question of *why* certain practices succeed or fail. They argue that measures and the measurement process can be one of the largest barriers to an organization's capability to turn knowledge into action. Focus on short-term metrics such as sales per quarter can produce pressures that are inconsistent with the organization's culture and long-term business objectives. In fact, Pfeffer and Sutton, in examining the situation facing HP, argue that, "The focus on making the budget numbers not only produces behavior that is inimical to developing long-term capabilities and contrary to the history and culture of the company, but also some behavior that is almost unethical."[20] This shows that using multiple ways to measure and communicate the business impact helps to unlock the "black box" that often exists between measurement of outcomes versus understanding the drivers of (and barriers to) performance.

Opening this black box means understanding how the people management process is linked to and helps support the overall strategic objectives of the organization. It also means communicating this value to key internal and external stakeholders. As we learned earlier from some of the research in this area, rewards for employee performance and learning are key management tools for bringing people together to understand the collective relevance of strong performance across the organization or within a specific business unit. In addition, the use of employee rewards and recognition provides acknowledgment of goals and accomplishments and helps to strengthen individuals' sense of personal achievement and self-efficacy.[21] While using rewards or recognition has been a standard management tool, it is often not seen as important, or it is disconnected from the overall approach to measuring business impact. Recognition and reward is not simply compensation for past efforts by employees. Celebration helps others recognize common objectives that are operational as well as strategic for the organization. The use of rewards and recognition helps to promote collaborative communities throughout the company, as well as competence that is valued by the organization. In addition, research indicates that celebration may also attract potential collaboration from other organizations that seek out "best practice" and successful approaches that have been developed through the organization.[22] Thus, expanding the array of measures of business impact is critical for understanding and closing the knowledge-doing gap, and for cultivating an organization that values excellence and shares innovative practices across function, location, and other organization boundaries.

Therefore, defining the value of mentoring as an HPWP must not only measure outcomes, but also must direct future actions that sustain desired outcomes. Important elements of the impact of mentoring cannot be overlooked by one-shot measures such as satisfaction with the mentoring experiences. To substantiate this point, an illustration of the impact of mentoring can be seen through an important mentoring initiative between the United States Software Group Client Support team and Greater China Support team. Late in 2005, Mike Hervey, a technical support professional, and his colleague, Paul Lee, were given the responsibility to transfer knowledge to the team in China through the mentoring process. While there is great potential in this emerging market, it presents such challenges as lack of a few specific product skills, and communication and cultural barriers between the two countries.

Taking this into consideration, Mike and Paul defined a goal to leverage native language and cultural skills as a conduit for assisting the sales, services, and support teams in China. Through regular communication, skills transfer sessions, product education classes, and cultural lessons both in the United States and China, the team achieved a significant increase in productivity. The team expanded this mentoring initiative to include the identification of mentors in India who possess strong product skills. These Indian employees partnered with mentors from the United States to transfer product skills to the employees in China. Including mentors from India expedited the learning process and helped ease the challenge of time zone differences. Significant business impact has been achieved through this mentoring program by helping IBM win sales contracts through support-assisted proof of concepts, and improving China's call center's self-sufficiency rating on one particular product from a low of 20% to a high of 80% in 18 months.

As a result of this mentoring initiative, best practices have been created, a strong working relationship has been developed, and the foundation has been laid to deliver high customer satisfaction. Mike and Paul were recognized for their efforts, and their manager summed up their contribution to the business with the following comment, "This team has done an excellent work where no previous efforts had been employed and with no model to copy. I applaud you, not only for the results you have achieved with this project; but also for the continuous creativity and tenacious work effort you have displayed throughout the life of the project." Mike and Paul, along with the mentoring team in India, demonstrated the power of mentoring in building essential product skills, which allows IBM to deliver solutions to the client.

In addition, assessment of the impact of mentoring cannot become so complex that it blocks the adoption of successful practice by other units and locations throughout the organization. While there are many aspects to understanding the value added by mentoring activities throughout the organization, the idea of using rewards and recognition to validate mentoring and communicate the important outcomes that are supported by mentoring relationships helps to broaden how we define and communicate the value of this approach to HPWP. As one concrete illustration, we examine IBM's Americas Marketing group as an example of how reward and recognition can be key components to defining business impact and communicating the important outcomes of successful mentoring relationships. The IBM marketing group effort takes a traditional human resource practice (rewards and recognition) and use it in an innovative way to evaluate and communicate the value of mentoring within this business unit. Thus, not only do rewards provide a tool for capturing the business impact of mentoring, but innovative uses of rewards provide an opportunity to celebrate and define a culture of collaboration and excellence surrounding the actions of successful mentors in a way that motivates others and provides learning opportunities throughout the organization.

Dangle the Carrot–IBM's Marketing Group Mentoring Award

As part of IBM's mentoring revitalization, business units were charged with creating their own sustainable efforts to develop employees and cultivate knowledge transfer through formal and informal mentoring. Because these mentoring efforts were integrated into the overall global business model, the need to understand and measure their impact was critical. In addition, the use of various forms of reward and recognition as tools for motivation and driving performance has been a cornerstone of IBM's employee development activities.

The IBM Americas Marketing Award provides a unique example of how metrics of business impact can be integrated within ongoing HPWP, such as employee reward and recognition. This award is a unique recognition initiative that not only acknowledges excellence in mentoring, but also measures the impact of mentoring efforts and services as a communication vehicle for the importance of these efforts within the marketing business unit. It underscores the point that reward and recognition are not simply about past performance of the individual being acknowledged, but are also an important measure of business impact that shapes the expectations and efforts of other employees who observe this celebration of mentoring excellence. In this light, the marketing group's mentoring recognition effort does not suffer from the backward-looking problem (measuring outcomes based on past performance) of pure financial metrics; rather it focuses employees' attention on forward-looking examples of value-creating actions through mentoring in recognizing effort, learning, and successful mentoring relationships.

The Mentor Appreciation Award was implemented in the fall of 2006 and covers an organization of approximately 700 people. Employees have the chance to nominate their mentors twice yearly for this recognition. Typically, every year the mentor pool is refreshed, and managers and employees alike are encouraged to participate in the mentoring program. Communication within the organization is fluid and varied—employees are provided with mentoring information in a quarterly newsletter, and they have access to a mentoring database as well as a corporate mentoring Web site. To keep the mentoring program viable and exciting, mentoring surveys and focus groups are conducted periodically to gauge the success of the program and also to better understand how the organization can improve the mentoring process to meet the needs of the employees.

Nominating a mentor for the award requires only the completion of a simple nomination form that asks the following:

- Mentor's name
- Length of time this person has been your mentor
- Why this person makes a great mentor
- Examples of how your mentor has helped you with a situation or issue
- Why you think the relationship has been successful

Winners of the award are informed by e-mail, along with a small thank-you gift, and the submission write-ups are featured on the Americas Marketing Web site. Giving this visibility to a wider audience serves the purpose of promoting mentoring, sharing best practices, and offering relevant tips and hints about mentoring.

Marion Atwater, senior marketing specialist, and Mary O'Donnell, program manager, Marketing Communications, have both been instrumental in the growth and success of mentoring within the Americas Marketing team. They noted that the appreciation award was implemented as a promotional tactic to bring greater visibility to mentoring and also to provide employees with the ability to say "thank you" to their mentors in a simple way.

The mentoring program is part of a broader career development initiative, and the approach to learning and development is a holistic one. While mentoring is critical in the development process, it is not sufficient to help employees learn the requisite skills and competencies they need to attain their full potential in the business. To this end, it is common practice for the organization to sponsor informal career chats that mimic a talk-show format.

Marion and Mary designed the learning experience intentionally without the typical PowerPoint charts. Instead, they capitalized on the power of human factors, a high personal-touch approach to delivering learning, and the transfer of knowledge and experience.

This approach is also done in a targeted manner, whereby mentoring and coaching sessions are offered to the managers in the organization. The up-line and experienced managers offer guidance and support to the less-experienced managers in these chats. The premise behind the manager-only chats is to continue to place emphasis on building leadership and people management skills, and to better equip them with the necessary information to help their employees.

It is well known that first-line managers are on the front line to their employees. Because of this, employees go directly to them for guidance and coaching. IBM expects its managers to respond to the needs of their employees with accuracy and speed, which is one of the primary reasons it makes good business sense to have a knowledgeable and competent management team, starting with the first-line manager.

A "heartbeat" survey conducted by the organization outlined the benefits of these mentoring and career development initiatives to the Americas Marketing organization and eventually to IBM. Survey results revealed that these initiatives have a direct positive impact on the morale and climate of the organization. Additionally, employees feel cared for and believe that the content and information to which they have access aid in their development. This is an affirmation to the leaders of the organization that employees are satisfied with the career progression process and that the right people are being placed in the right jobs based on career interests and skills. These grassroots activities also play a significant role in complementing and supporting the role of the manager.

To substantiate the value of mentoring and other career development grassroots initiatives, an interview was conducted with Gail Walker Jarrett, one of the award recipients. Gail indicated that mentoring keeps her grounded, and while she is helping others to grow, she is gaining a lot from the people she mentors—mentoring is a reciprocal learning process where both parties learn from each other.

Gail has held several management positions in IBM and recalled a remarkable situation that occurred during her first management assignment. An experienced manager in the area approached her and offered to have lunch with her for the explicit purpose of passing on to Gail the manager's many years of management experience. During lunch, the manager gave Gail a stack of handwritten notes on the essential and practical things Gail needed to do during the first 30, 60, and 90 days in her new management assignment. Gail asserted that "Those notes were invaluable and got me off to a positive start."

This underscores the point that passing on practical and relevant information at the right time has the power to help others develop the right set of skills. This experienced manager exemplified what we expect others to do to cultivate a workplace that thrives on knowledge sharing. The impact that mentoring has on individuals can be lasting. Not only do mentoring relationships help develop skills and expertise, but they also have the potential to shape the attitude, behaviors, and future of others in positive ways.

The impact this experienced manager had on Gail was a memorable one. Here is an excerpt of a letter Gail wrote to her role model and mentor upon her retirement from IBM. Gail stated, "Let me take this opportunity to express my sincere thanks to you for the impact you have made on my IBM career. You were instrumental in the development of my people management style. You gave me some great advice when I accepted my first management position in Indianapolis. You sat down with me and gave me your handwritten notes on what to do during the first 30, 60, and 90 days. Those notes were invaluable and got me off to a wonderful start. Thanks so much for being a wonderful role model." Even today, when you talk to Gail, she speaks with such gratitude for the positive start she got in her role as a new manager.

Gail claims she is a naturally giving person, but the mentoring she has received over the years strengthened her zeal to mentor others and pass on her knowledge to them. The person who nominated Gail for the Americas Mentoring Appreciation Award had this to say about Gail, "She is a terrific mentor—she is willing to offer her time to meet with me in person or by phone. She is a great listener and offers sound advice from her own experience. Gail is an expert in coping with change."

It is clear that the elements of the Americas Marketing Award help IBM in many ways. Employees who manage the program designed a process that is easily tracked, measured, and replicated. This awards program produces role models and mentors and allows skills to be transferred at a rapid pace. One of the unique features of this awards program is that all employees are full participants, which creates learning opportunities for employees as well as managers. This underscores the fact that both mentoring and learning are for everyone at IBM. What this group of employees did when they created the mentoring awards program was to foster a climate where people learn together, build the skills of the organization, and prepare IBM to meet the needs of its clients.

In short, for a company to sustain its competitive advantage, it must have a constant and current reading of its talent profile, ensuring that it has the right skills for the moment and for the longer term, and also that it has enough people with these skills to deploy at a moment's notice across the organization. Talent management is a critical aspect of establishing a dominant presence in a competitive marketplace. The talent that the company amasses has to show results by high performance, creativity, innovation, and an unparalleled standard of excellence. The company has the obligation to develop an environment that encourages knowledge sharing and a thirst for continuous learning. Positive reinforcement and rewards are essential in employee engagement and in keeping morale high. These practices help to characterize the organization as adaptable and ready, and show that it possesses a workplace arsenal capable of delivering impact and sustaining competitive advantage. According to IBM employees Randy MacDonald and Tim Ringo, "The global economy is transforming into an integrated market, full of opportunity, competition and swirling change... There can be no doubt that winning in competitive and quickly shifting markets requires responsive organizations."[23]

Lessons Learned—Adding Value and Sustaining Business Impact

Being competitive in a knowledge-based economy that values innovation means that organizations must identify the methods they will use to capture, understand, and communicate the value of their work practices in new and different ways. This is the critical point of development and attention within today's practice of mentoring in organizations. Together with the ongoing question of how to sustain business impact is also how to measure the impact of business practices. While many organizations utilize various forms of mentoring solutions, few understand its impact above one-shot employee surveys of satisfaction with a specific program or single mentoring relationship. Even fewer efforts provide reward and recognition for the work of mentoring, which sends a strong signal throughout the business unit that these efforts are not simply nice to do, but rather are both valued and essential to sustaining the business impact of these high-performance work practices.

Within IBM, business units such as the Americas Marketing Group are developing new ways to understand and communicate the value of mentoring that is not separate from its core business activities, but rather integrated within the core of its business. While these efforts are ongoing and constantly evolving, they represent merely one example of the need for organizations to develop ways to understand the business impact at a pace consistent with the need to innovate in meeting the demands of the dynamic global market. As IBM employees continue to develop innovative mentoring programs and raise the bar to accomplish new levels of excellence, there is continuous focus to reward and reinforce these desired employee behaviors and attributes.

The nature of how business is done today is dictated by the rapid pace at which clients require solutions and services, which has a ripple effect on how quickly organizations can develop the requisite skills to respond. The utilization of employees' knowledge, skills, and abilities must be stimulated through a defined set of high-performance work practices that includes a portfolio of mentoring activities. In addition, the metrics of these efforts must be as diverse as the HPWP being evaluated. As Verna Allee, author of the book, *The Knowledge Evolution: Expanding Organizational Intelligence*, quoting Laurence Prusak, argues, "The only thing that gives an organization a competitive edge—the only thing that is sustainable—is what it knows, how it uses what it knows, and how fast it can know something new!"[24] This point of view underscores how important it is for corporations to manage their array of HPWP and integrate mentoring solutions into these efforts in a way that maximizes the long-term business impact. Previous research clearly shows that a single metric or one-shot assessment will not give an accurate or useful picture of the business impact. Furthermore, any HPWP is more likely to produce sustainable business impact when it's integrated into the overall business strategy.

The key lessons learned from IBM's attempt to understand the overall business impact of its mentoring revitalization efforts are clear. Organizations that make mentoring and employee development a strategic business priority are better positioned to experience employee retention, engagement, trust, and motivation. Global organizations cannot afford to ignore the impact of these efforts as they attempt to influence the triple bottom line. Clearly, meeting a dynamic and diverse list of business challenges requires a system of HPWP that includes a portfolio of mentoring activities measured by an approach that is balanced in capturing the range of different outcomes of these value-creating efforts.

References

[1] Delery, J.R. (1998). Issues of Fit in Strategic Human Resource Management: Implications for Research, *Human Resource Management Review, 8,* pp. 289–309. Youndt; M.A., Snell, S.A., Dean, J.W., and Lepak, D.T. (1996). Human Resource Management Manufacturing Strategy and Firm Performance *Academy of Management Journal, 39,* pp. 836–886.

[2] Huselid, M.A. and Becker, B.E. (2000). Comments on Measurement Error in Research on Human Resources and Firm Performance: How Much Error is There and How Does Its Influence Effect Size Estimates? *Personnel Psychology,* 53, pp. 835–854.

[3] Becker, B.E., Gerhart, B. (1996). The Impact of Human Resource Management on Organizational Performance: Progress and Prospects, *Academy of Management Journal,* 39, pp. 779–810. Becker, B.E. and Huselid, M.A. (1998). High-Performance Work Systems and Firm Performance: A Synthesis of Research and Managerial Implications. In G.R.

Ferris (Ed.) *Research in Personnel and Human Resources Management,* Volume 16, pp. 53–101, JAI Press, Stamford, CT.

4 Delvery, J.E. and Shaw, J.D. (2001). The Strategic Management of People in Work Organizations: Review Synthesis and Extension, In G. R. Ferrid (Ed.), *Research in Personnel and Human Resources Management,* Volume 20, pp. 165–197, JAP Press, Stamford, CT.

5 "IBM Responsibility—Our People—Learning & Opportunity," w3 (IBM Web site) article.

6 Evans, W.R. and Davis, W.D. (2006). "High-Performance Work Systems and Organizational Performance: The Medicating Role of Internal Social Structure," *Journal of Management,* 31, pp. 758–775.

7 Tsai, W. and Ghoshal, S. (1998). Social Capital and Value Creation: The Role of Intrafirm Networks, *Academy of management Journal, 41,* pp.464–476.

8 Gelade, G.A. and Ivery, M. (2003). The Impact of Human Resource Management and Work Climate on Organizational Performance, *Personnel Psychology, 56,* pp. 383–404.

9 Collins, J. *Good to Great: Why Some Companies Make the Leap and Others Don't,* Harper Collins, New York, NY, 2001.

10 Palmisano, S., "Leadership, Trust and the Globally-Integrated Enterprise," Final remarks at INSEAD on October 2006.

11 Ibid.

12 Huselid, M.A. (1995). The Impact of Human Resource Management Practices on Turnover, Productivity and Corporate Financial Performance, *Academy of Management Journal, 38,* pp. 635–672. MacDuffie, J.P. (1995). Human Resource Bundles and Manufacturing Performance: Organizational Logic and Flexible Production Systems in the Work Auto Industry, *Industrial and Labor Relations Review, 48,* pp. 197–221.

13 Kerr, S. (1976). On the Folly of Rewarding A, While Hoping for B, *Academy of Management Journal,* 18(4), pp. 769–783.

14 Kaplan, R.S. and Norton, D.P. (1992). The Balanced Scorecard—Measures that Drive Performance, *Harvard Business Review,* 70(1), pp. 71–91.

15 Walker, J.W. (2002). Are We Using the Right Human Resource Measures? *Human Resource Planning,* pp. 7–8.

16 Savitz, A.W. and Weber, K. (2006). *The Triple Bottom Line: How Today's Best Run Companies Are Achieving Economic, Social, and Environmental Success*, Jossey-Bass, San Francisco, CA.

17 Varma, A., Beatty, R.W., Schneier, C.E., and Ulrich, D.O. (1999). *Human Resource Planning,* 22(1), pp. 25–37.

18 Behn, R.D. (2003). Why Measure Performance: Different Purposes Require Different Measures, *Public Administration Review,* 63(5), pp. 586–606.

19 Pfeffer, J. and Sutton, R.I. (2000). *The Knowing-Doing Gap: How Smart Companies Turn Knowledge Into Action,* Harvard University Press, Boston, MA.

20 Ibid, pp. 145–146.

21 Locke, E.A. and Latham, G.P. (1984). *Goal Setting: A Motivational Technique That Works,* Prentice Hall, Englewood Cliffs, NY.

[22] Behn, R.D. (2001). *Leadership Counts: Lessons for Public Managers,* Harvard University Press, Cambridge, MA.

[23] MacDonald, R. and Ringo, T. (2001). Unlocking the DNA of the Adaptable Workforce, *The Global Human Capital Study.*

[24] Allee, V. (1997). *The Knowledge Evolution: Expanding Organizational Intelligence*, Butterworth Publishing, Woborn, MA.

8

Business Impact: Using Mentoring Solutions to Solve "Wicked Problems"

Chapter Contents

Mentoring as a Strategic Solution

Using the case of IBM's mentoring revitalization efforts, we discussed how a well-designed and diverse portfolio of mentoring programs and activities can provide a powerful strategic tool for organizations facing the rapidly changing demands of developing talent and transferring knowledge across a global business enterprise. We've described how IBM uses a broad portfolio of both formal and informal mentoring solutions that includes traditional one-on-one mentoring, group mentoring, peer mentoring, reverse mentoring, speed mentoring, and other innovative approaches. All of these efforts are designed to support three core components of IBM's global mentoring strategy:

- Building organizational intelligence
- Connecting across people
- Sustaining business impact

In the previous chapter, we focused on sustaining business impact by examining the various ways in which mentoring serves as high-performance work practices (HPWP) that impact many aspects of organizational performance. Although this is a critical part of understanding the business impact of mentoring solutions, it is not the entire story. While mentoring as an HPWP can produce short-term effects on important outcomes, the overall business impact of mentoring as a tool for driving global strategy cannot always be captured in simple and easily quantifiable ways. Business impact also encompasses the capability to integrate mentoring within the company's overall strategy that extends beyond one-shot solutions and involves continued growth, improvement, and innovation over time. While much has been written about environmental sustainability, a key challenge for organizations today is achieving *strategic sustainability*. This aspect of sustainability is contingent on how well a company aligns people, process, and outcomes to achieve its overall business success. In today's dynamic and sometimes volatile business environment, it also means defining strategies quickly, often for problems that may not have easy, obvious, or even attainable solutions.

Some argue that companies are ill-equipped to address most types of complex problems using traditional approaches, planning techniques, or contemporary analytic tools. Companies that want to sustain their competitive advantage must respond to both expected and unexpected shifts in customer needs and market opportunities. Staying abreast of paradigm shifts and emerging needs requires the development of a sustainable business strategy with built-in flexibility and contingency plans for rapid adjustment to a dynamic and global business environment. Ironically, it is becoming harder and harder for companies to sustain their marketplace impact and position without developing some capacity for addressing problems that may have no clear solution. However, the payoff for companies that build capacity to address dynamic challenges is that they can reinvent and reposition themselves, thus keeping up with marketplace volatility and thriving among fierce global competition.

Mentoring in IBM has been defined as a critical learning and talent management tool that has been linked to important aspects of the overall business strategy. For example, IBM has invested heavily in developing a blended learning approach through the tools and resources that are available to its global workforce. Together with its portfolio approach to mentoring, it is developing an internal capacity to create and sustain business impact whereby organizational systems and communities of people can address complex problems for which there is no clear solution. As we discuss in this chapter, mentoring communities like the Black Technical Leaders Forum leverage the knowledge and skills that already exist within IBM in a way that doesn't avoid challenges and complex situations, but rather uses them to engage people, reinvent processes, and develop innovative solutions that have real business impact. Thus, sustaining business impact is facilitated by IBM's use of these emerging mentoring communities and as such, mentoring is being transformed from an isolated set of programs into a portfolio of solutions that complement its global business strategy.

As we discuss in this chapter, a key lesson learned from IBM's use of mentoring to solve ongoing challenges and leverage emerging opportunities is the need to transform mentoring from being viewed as strictly an operational tool to being viewed as a strategic solution. As such, concepts such as "learning agility" and "speed to competence" are foremost on the minds of IBM's organizational leaders and central to their mentoring revitalization efforts. Clearly, the pace at which employees acquire new and critical knowledge and then apply this knowledge in significant and meaningful ways will create sustainable business impact in the marketplace. We suggest that as employees develop and transfer knowledge within mentoring communities throughout the global organization, they are better equipped to help companies like IBM sustain business impact by solving what are called "wicked problems."

Using Mentoring to Solve "Wicked Problems"

In a recent *Harvard Business Review* article, John Camillus applied principles taken from engineering and political sciences to address the ongoing challenges faced by companies and their global strategy.[1] He argues that in today's dynamic and global economy, most organizations face "wicked problems" for which they are ill-prepared. Based on principles first identified by Rittel and Webber,[2] organizations must cope with and address a number of properties of problems that are more complex and challenging than traditional approaches can address. Several properties differentiate what can be labeled as wicked problems from traditional ones that are difficult and challenging but can be ultimately solved using traditional approaches. While we discuss only a few of the features of these wicked problems, our goal is to link mentoring solutions and discuss specific examples within IBM's approach as a model for how companies attempt to cope with these complex issues.

First, within dynamic and complex environments, companies often face problems that can be characterized as "wicked"; that is, unprecedented challenges that occur in a complex social, political, and economic context. As Camillus writes, "It's the social complexity of wicked problems as much as their technical difficulties that make them tough to manage."[3] Thus, problems become "wicked" when their roots are complex and tangled. Often opportunities turn into challenges, and the organization's advantages turn into disadvantages across time or global markets. As a result, classic approaches to define, analyze, and diagnose these types of problems are often insufficient.

Another significant feature is that the social complexity of wicked problems means not only that they are complex and difficult to define, but also that there is no clear formula for solving such problems. Every wicked problem is unique in its complexity, its root causes, and ultimately its solutions for coping and adjusting to its impact. While these three features alone provide a tremendous challenge for most organizations, the unique nature of wicked problems also means that they are difficult to address simply because of their dynamic nature. As companies study wicked problems and attempt various solutions, their efforts are often greeted with additional issues not clearly revealed by the initial analysis or forecast. Wicked problems change as companies attempt to address or solve them, making the process of finding a solution even more challenging for the firm. Thus, the tools, capabilities, and approaches needed to address them must be innovative and adaptable to change.

Using the perspective on wicked problems outlined by Camillus, the dynamic, unpredictable, and complex nature of these types of challenges also lends itself to a characteristic that makes mentoring solutions a useful tool for addressing these types of problems. Along with being dynamic, complex and unique, wicked problems also involve multiple stakeholders (or those who effect or can be affected by an organization's actions) each with distinct values, knowledge, and priorities. In fact, according to Camillus, "the greater the disagreement among stakeholders, the more wicked the problem."[4] Problems quickly transform from difficult to wicked ones when organizations navigate across global boundaries, demographic segments, as well as into emerging markets in which key stakeholders include employees, customers, shareholders, government, and various nongovernmental organizations (NGOs). Together with differences in values, knowledge, and culture, the interaction across these various stakeholders frequently poses both a challenge as well as an opportunity for global firms like IBM.

While exact solutions may not always be possible, our observation of IBM's approach is that mentoring can be an important tool for tackling complex issues, including myriad wicked problems. There are several reasons why. First of all, managing wicked problems requires input and communication among multiple stakeholders. The need for knowledge sharing and problem solving across groups with different perspectives, expertise, and priorities is an important part of addressing traditional complex problems.[5] For addressing wicked problems, however, the need for diverse, multistakeholder involvement is essential. A core aspect of this involvement is the opportunity for enhanced communication that not only addresses the problem, but also yields greater clarification and agreement on the problem to be addressed. Unfortunately, this type of solution-focused dialogue frequently involves only the top echelons of the organization.

However, through the use of a range of mentoring solutions, the communication about strategies to address wicked problems can be extended to the employee in the lab, to the product manager, to the sales team, and to the senior leadership of the company. We presented one example of this approach through IBM's use of reverse mentoring in which important knowledge flows up and across traditional power distinctions and levels within the organization (see Chapter 6, "Connecting People: Using Mentoring to Signal Value in People"). Providing a forum for discussing, diagnosing, and dissecting the problems facing the organization is at the heart of knowledge transfer and is also facilitated by a range of different mentoring solutions.

In addition, coping with wicked problems requires focused and continuous action within a dynamic environment. This often indicates the use of small yet calculated steps or experiments to navigate through the unique and complex set of issues being faced. While the cycle of test-study-improve-study may work in some environments, it requires a good deal of risk-taking and persistence because the outcomes of each test may be uncertain, unpredictable, and incremental. On the other hand, using solutions such as group and peer mentoring help build communities of practice that can provide shared risk-taking and sustain momentum better than relying on individual agents of change. The process of problem solving that takes place within knowledge communities provides a vehicle for sharing knowledge, testing out ideas, challenging assumptions, and promoting continuous and deliberate improvements. Camillus summarizes this process as the "science of muddling through"[6] and argues that it is vital for addressing wicked problems. We see the innovative use of mentoring as one approach for building communities that can help with this essential yet challenging muddling-through process.

Lastly, addressing wicked problems requires more than traditional feedback processes within organizations or what is referred to as "feed-forward" processes. Because wicked problems are dynamic and pose challenges that have no clear solution or precedent, traditional concepts of feedback that focuses attention on the past may not be useful by themselves in the current context. Instead of benchmarking the past, wicked problems require envisioning the future. This means shared risk-taking, coupled with continuous environmental scanning as small experiments begin to produce results. An organization's capability to share knowledge in a rapid fashion that is also easily accessible to all employees is even more critical for developing what Camillus calls a "feed-forward orientation."[7] IBM's use of technology solutions, including speed mentoring, virtual or e-mentoring, and the just-in time web-based platform within IBM's Experiential Learning Opportunities portfolio are examples of how mentoring solutions can help provide critical information as organizations address the unpredictability of wicked problems.

Clearly, these are only a few of the ways to understand the key dimensions of and potential mentoring solutions for addressing wicked problems faced by organizations such as IBM. Regardless of the specific mentoring technique used, a critical component appears to be the widespread involvement and engagement of knowledgeable employees across the business enterprise. Prior to mentoring revitalization, IBM was like many other companies that found themselves sometimes ill-prepared to address a range of complex challenges. Mentoring was thought to be a potential tool for helping to bring people together to address these challenges. However, findings of a focus group conducted by members of the IBM mentoring team found that employees perceived that mentoring was for the high-potential and select few employees only. Thus, to promote mentoring as a tool for addressing complex and eventually wicked problems, the company had to expand and then demonstrate that the portfolio of mentoring programs is accessible to all IBM employees. This inclusive approach to IBM's mentoring revitalization has helped stimulate programs that are developed and designed to reach all employees, regardless of geography, flexible or virtual work arrangements, tenure, and demographic segment. In addition, IBM's mentoring portfolio is producing innovative approaches worldwide that extend from the executive office to the manufacturing floor.

To support the notion that mentoring is for all employees, there continues to be a strong push on arming them with the necessary information regarding their roles, responsibilities, and accountabilities in their mentoring relationships. Such an approach enables employees to take charge of their mentoring relationships, to self-identify their particular mentoring solution, and to build strong relationships that can be used to address the organization's challenges. Interestingly, this approach has helped to create collaborative networks that recent research has identified as key factors in an organization's capability to tackle wicked problems.[8]

Clearly, IBM's mentoring revitalization and its various components can be interpreted as a statement of value and commitment to employee empowerment. IBM communicates this value and commitment through consistent education and awareness initiatives that the mentoring team has been engaged in over the course of the revitalization process. The goal of clearly communicating the inclusive approach to mentoring was to stimulate employee-driven answers and personal accountability in the workforce which can help build capacity to address ongoing and emerging (wicked) problems faced by IBM. In addition, it provides a strategic tool for IBM as it attempts to address a core challenge faced by any global organization in today's challenging environment—the ongoing need for global talent development.

Global Talent Management as a "Wicked Problem"

Of the many wicked problems facing IBM, one of the most critical is how to address global talent management within the global war for talent. While talent management is not a new issue facing organizations, the global war for talent represents a complexity of this issue that changes it from being simply difficult to wicked. Once again, a key characteristic of wicked problems is that their roots are complex, unstructured, and interconnected. In addition, wicked problems involve many stakeholders with different values and priorities. As global competition for skilled workers—particularly in the field of science and technology—becomes more intense, companies are working feverishly to attract the right skills and then put development plans in place to escalate the pace at which employees acquire new expertise and develop into the next generation of thought as well as organizational leaders.

However, addressing global talent management must be done within the context of dynamic social, political, economic, and social changes that impact people both locally and globally. Global talent management represents a complex challenge with a high degree of interconnection across multiple policy domains, organizational structures, and levels of government across the globe. The social, economic, and political complexity of global talent management can be overwhelming. In addition, the challenging of equipping people to have the knowledge and skills to work locally as well as build capacity to interact and lead others globally cannot be solved once and for all, despite our best intentions. Changing political environments, new technologies, population dynamics, and demographic shifts, along with the impact of the changing physical environment, mean that addressing one aspect of the issue will have consequences for other related issues as well. Thus, global talent management represents an integrated ecosystem that is complex, dynamic, interconnected, and unstructured.

Clearly, addressing global talent management as a wicked problem requires a multidimensional and fluid approach. It also means that there is a need to draw on broad knowledge bases and develop new knowledge that can be applied to this issue. Because wicked problems are dynamic, there must be continuous transfer and integration of knowledge that helps to address the changing nature of a problem that cannot be quickly solved by one-shot or short-term solutions. To underscore the importance of global talent management as a means for sustaining business growth, Nancy Lockwood argues that, "to sustain outstanding business results in a global economy, organizations will rethink and reinvent their approaches to talent management. Effective talent management calls for strong participatory leadership, organizational buy-in, employee engagement, and workplace scorecards with talent management metrics. Companies that master talent management will be well positioned for long-term growth in workforce performance for years to come."[9] This analysis clearly reflects the complex, dynamic, and interconnected solutions required to address the unique nature of global talent management.

Ongoing talent management should be a priority in any organization's business plan and proactive measures must be taken to develop the skills of everyone, whether they are early, mid- or late-career employees. Employees must be given the chance to apply their skills in challenging and meaningful ways, which is a catalyst for them to build on old skills and develop new ones, based on the vision and mission of the organization. These practices give employees the desire and impetus to engage in building their capability, with the goal of enhancing their value to the organization. However, it has been noted that generally, when organizations encounter financially austere times, the tendency has been to withdraw or shrink the budget for employee training and development. Enduring companies, on the other hand, remain steadfast in their commitment to building talent and intellectual capital that may have short-term costs but can be used to help them with long-term recovery. Global talent development is not just for the good times or for times of financial prosperity; it is for all times, including those of economic challenge and uncertainty. This is how sustainable business impact is created and achieved. If companies fail to follow through on their promise to make employee development a priority, they risk having their employees leave and go to competitors that are unwavering in their commitment to and investment in ongoing career development.

However, a barrier to effectively addressing global talent management can be the very dynamic, unstructured nature of wicked problems. To address ongoing talent needs, an organization reinvents or redefines its business mission and priorities, overlooking the need to keep information fluid between the leaders of the organization and all levels of employees in the business. As the organization reinvents itself, parallel activities should be in place to effectively communicate across all aspects of the business enterprise and then help employees retool their skills portfolio to meet the emerging goals of the organization's new mission. While this may appear simple on the surface, the process of redesign-communicate-retool often takes place at a rapid pace that leaves little room for traditional methods of analysis and assessment. This can lead to an incomplete process where the goal may be clear to organizational leaders, but not clearly communicated to employees throughout the global business. In the same vein, redesign may take place with successful communication, but little attention or effort is placed into retooling a diverse and global workforce to meet the new demands of the organization. As Dychtwald, Erickson, and Morison note, "There are many ways to rejuvenate people and their careers, engendering a fresh sense of accomplishment and renewed loyalty and commitment to the organization."[10] However, defining global talent management as a wicked problem means paying attention to the specific ways in which employees are engaged in finding collective solutions to the firm's ongoing global talent management needs.

Another barrier to be addressed is that some organizations place priority on developing new or high-potential employees at the expense of the rest of the workforce. Employees who show exceptional potential as future leaders must be given the chance to develop the requisite skills; however, if every employee is given the opportunity to learn new skills, the organization stands to build a much more robust talent pool than if all the emphasis is only on the high-potential employees. Development should not be the basis for offering growth experiences to a select few at the expense of the rest of the workforce, but rather all employees, whether early tenured, mid-career, late-career, high-potential, or average, should be given every opportunity to grow and develop new skills. There is a perception that mid- and late-career employees may become disengaged if their company invests most of its time, attention, and dollars in developing high-potential new hires. Dychtwald, Erickson, and Morison address this point by saying that, "Change of pace, the opportunity to learn and the opportunity to apply what's already known in new ways can all reengage mid-career employees, rekindle their ambition, and rejuvenate their careers."[11] This means expanding the traditional approach to global talent management that moves beyond the limited and myopic focus on only emphasizing the development of high potentials to a broader strategy that takes into consideration the growth needs of everyone who represents the organization. The development of human capital must be broad-based and include all employees to show that the organization values everyone to build organization capacity and bench strength.

Organizations can also impede or stall their impact by not fully utilizing the power of mentoring as a means of transferring critical knowledge. Because of the practical learning approach that typically takes place in mentoring relationships at IBM, employees tend to learn and apply their knowledge in an environment that is supportive. Mentoring relationships provide feedback in a constructive and timely manner, and employees can, therefore, gauge how much they have learned and how to tackle the next challenge. This practice has the potential to generate a sense of value and enthusiasm about the idea of learning in an inclusive and collaborative manner. The long-term result is better equipping of the workforce to tackle ongoing as well as emerging wicked problems.

Collaborative learning, whether done through one-on-one mentoring, group mentoring, or communities of practice, supports diversity in many ways. The integration of diversity into the learning process is a healthy way to encourage and instill respect, trust, and collaboration. For example, mentoring relationships that are grounded in the principles of diversity can be powerful organizational tools to help break the glass ceiling, dislodge employees from the sticky floor, create better cultural sensitivity, and help improve the status of under-represented groups throughout the organization. When organizations make a concerted effort to erase barriers to collaboration, they are, in essence, creating great learning opportunities across cultural, age, race, gender, and other diversity dimensions that exist in the workplace. Mentoring that is focused on diversity increases the chances for innovative thinking in approach and ways of getting tasks done. Enhancing diversity through mentoring helps address the range of challenges and growth opportunities versus traditional approached wherein relationships are formed on the basis of sameness or similarity. For example, Clutterbuck and Ragins suggest that, "At its very core, diversity sparks creativity, questions prevailing and limiting assumptions and opens the door to innovation and fresh ideas. Diverse mentoring relationships can be expansive and enriching; they can raise our consciousness and provide a true 'learning lab' for understanding our differences and similarities."[12]

Thus, to break down barriers to global talent management, organizations must develop a broad agenda that engages employees across level, function, and demographic boundaries and integrates these efforts with the overall business strategy. Local talent management typically fails when it is treated as a stand-alone activity. Global talent management as a wicked problem can produce other unanticipated consequences unless it is pursued within an integrated approach or what some call the multiple ripple effects. While there may not be consensus on the cause of the global war for talent, it is clear that solutions must involve multiple stakeholders with diverse perspectives along with an integrated approach that leverages both formal and informal sources of knowledge and skills. Given the pervasive impact of wicked problems, any attempt toward solutions must also be infused throughout the entire business enterprise and not restricted to the executive suite or to a talented few employees to realize sustainable business impact.

Mentoring: On the Manufacturing Floor to the Technical Labs

As IBM began its revitalization of mentoring, it was also looking at ways to support its overall business model that focused heavily on organizational intelligence, innovation, and employee development. Employee development at IBM includes all employees, which speaks to the need for a broad-based mentoring approach. Employees at all levels are encouraged and empowered to demonstrate leadership, make decisions regarding their development, and engage management and mentors through a menu of mentoring options and other career development tools. Nonexempt employees in manufacturing generally work in a continuous workflow operation, yet despite that, they showed creativity in managing their time to the extent that they have been able to participate in mentoring relationships without interruption to the operations.

Nonexempt employees in the manufacturing plant at the East Fishkill, New York site displayed leadership when they formed the initial mentoring program. Samantha Cormulada, senior production specialist who worked the night shift in the East Fishkill manufacturing organization for 21 years, made a commitment to share her extensive experience with her peers by launching a mentoring program for employees in her area. She developed a mentoring model that she anchored on the theme, "Share what you know and teach as you go. Keep it simple." This program began in 2007, and based on the success of the program thus far, plans are underway to expand the scope and reach. In terms of success measurements, the internal data collected showed that morale improved, productivity increased, and employees moved more rapidly up the learning curve. It has been noted that the manufacturing employees are developing a sharper focus on what they need to grow professionally within the organization. An executive for the group endorsed the success of the program and commented that, "The mentoring program inspires and is contagious. It adds to the higher learning environment and assists in making a more united working culture to go after and solve specific working problems. Their dedication to this has fostered value in personal development." Based on this mentoring experience, employees in the manufacturing organization see the potential for their career growth, and they are more focused about increasing their contribution to the business. Infusing a desire for ongoing development and success among workers that may have traditionally been overlooked by such activities is one important element of IBM's use of mentoring to solve the wicked problem of global talent management. We examine two other examples of how IBM used mentoring solutions to address the wicked problem of global employee development: the Black Technical Leaders Forum and the South Africa's Cross-Geography Mentoring Initiative.

Black Technical Leaders Forum (BTLF)

The BTLF was formed in the summer of 2002 by Sheila Forte-Trammell, with the support of Dr. Mark Dean, IBM Fellow. The group was created out of a need for the black technical leaders to come together to support one another and at the same time reach back and pull less-experienced black technical employees through the business. It was rolled out on a pilot basis with the goal of subsequently being introduced to other under-represented groups in technology. Currently, the concept has been implemented by other diverse constituencies, such as the Hispanics, people with disabilities, Native Americans, Asians, and women.

The BTLF was formed under the premise that while the corporation has the responsibility of providing resources and a support system for its employees, the group itself has a personal need to demonstrate "self-help," as well as the personal responsibility to play a role in improving the numbers and success rate of its constituency. It is driven by four beliefs:

- Reaching back and pulling through
- Understanding that knowledge is power
- Trusting relationships accelerate learning
- Developing the need for self-help and self-empowerment

The team defined its strategy and priorities, and articulated how such a group would contribute to IBM's diversity efforts and ultimately to the bottom line. The BTLF strategy was presented to the vice president of Global Workforce Diversity and to the senior vice president responsible for technology—both of whom were encouraging and supportive, which gave the group the necessary momentum to move forward. There are a number of primary and ongoing activities that the BTLF sponsors:

- Opportunities for one-on-one mentoring and group speed mentoring
- Offering roundtables, Technical Cafés and call for technical papers
- Participation in internal technical conferences
- Developmental activities for the black technical pipeline
- Grand Technical Speaker series
- Participation in various panels and external conferences

- Volunteer in Black Family Technology Awareness Initiative to bridge digital divide
- Ongoing career coaching, shadow experience, and rotational assignments
- Education on intellectual property, which helps employees gaining understanding of the patent filings process and inventions creation
- Exposure to members of the IBM Academy and other elite technical forums and organizations within the company

Membership in the BTLF has grown steadily over the years, with members representing IBM's elite list of technologists, drawn from the ranks of IBM Fellows, IBM Distinguished Engineers, Senior Technical Staff Members, Senior Certified Architects, Consultants and Specialists, and highly ranked Research Staff Members. Utilizing this vast array of talent throughout the organization, the Technical Leaders provide peer mentoring and coaching opportunities within the group, as well as extending the opportunity to less-experienced black employees who are in the pipeline.

A series of interviews was conducted to get the perspectives of a few key individuals who are members of the group. Their feedback provides valuable insight into how IBM is using mentoring solutions such as the BTLF to address the wicked problem of competition within a global war for diverse technical talent.

Dr. Mark Dean, vice president of the Almaden Research Lab and an IBM Fellow, was interviewed about his role as a member of the BTLF. IBM Fellows are appointed to this rank, and it is the company's highest technical honor. Fellows are individuals with deep technological knowledge who are selected from the pool of Distinguished Engineers and have a pronounced impact on IBM and the technology industry through their inventions. Because mentoring is a principal purpose of the BTLF, it was important to start the conversation by getting Mark's personal definition of mentoring. He defined a mentor as "someone who is available to listen to your goals, aspirations, and challenges and provide support and candid feedback. A mentor brings awareness to the present state of what's happening and is in a position to offer recommendations on how to react. Additionally, the coaching function of mentoring involves helping mentees figure things out for themselves, in order to become self-sufficient; a good mentor offers suggestions, but should never dictate."[13] Mark indicated that his best mentor was his father. He said that during his early years in IBM he did not have mentors as we know them today. He had access to people who would answer his questions, but there was not an expectation that he would develop a long-term relationship that provided career guidance. These relationships were mutually beneficial and fluid.

Mark also felt that BTLF members function as role models and mentors to the next generation of technical leaders in IBM, particularly for underrepresented groups. A challenge that BTLF members encounter is focusing on their development and future success while at the same time fulfilling their personal commitment to helping others succeed. This is primarily due to time constraints and because there is not a critical mass of black technical leaders to reach back and pull through, thus making the effort quite challenging for those few who are there. For these reasons, Mark encouraged members of under-represented groups to be open to being mentored across diversity lines. Despite the challenges, Mark has seen growth in the BTLF numbers, more black technical resources employees are being mentored, and there have been increased minority appointments into the IBM Academy.

To complement the feedback on the growth and impact of the BTLF, Distinguished Engineer Gary Wright echoed much of Mark's comments. Gary added that the group has recently revisited and redefined its priorities, which fall into three categories:

- **Toward being relevant and visible to our constituency**—Two employees from the technical pipeline are now invited to the BTLF monthly meetings, which gives the technical leaders a chance to personally hear from them and also spotlight their talent and expertise. The BTLF members are also able to assess these employees' levels of technical expertise and identify areas for growth.

- **Toward being a benefit to each other**—The team is now extending the spotlight program internally, which allows BTLF members who are working on significant projects to share what they are doing with the team. Also, the black executives within the group are given time on the agenda to brief the team on topics that have relevance to their growth as well as new activities taking place across the business. The group developed a list of important topics to be discussed, including patent filing, certification processes, ways to gain entry into the IBM Academy, and how to prepare for appointments to higher technical ranks within IBM.

- **Toward being well organized**—This particular call to action assigns two members of the BTLF to be responsible for the meeting agenda and also explore ways to leverage technology to enhance communication and collaboration.

Along with the three focus areas, the BTLF recognized the ongoing challenges faced by IBM in attracting and retaining diverse talent. Thus, it decided to play a larger role in the attraction, development, and retention of black technical employees. Gary also indicated that the team is looking at ways to create a model mentoring program for all black employees in IBM, which will entail extending its reach beyond the technical talent to seek out more black women in technology. Presently, the BTLF initiatives are having an impact on employees in the United States, but attention is now being placed on finding ways to expand their reach to the global community of black employees. Overall, Gary feels that the value proposition to IBM is significant—sharing knowledge and experience with employees in the pipeline strengthens their abilities, and it is inevitable that IBM's capability will thus become stronger. This is a good example of leveraging the knowledge within the BTLF to provide solutions to the broader issues of talent development among diverse employee groups within IBM.

Given the focus of the BTLF on developing and retaining diverse talent within the technical ranks, we conducted an interview with James Macon, Jr., a senior technical staff member, to get a broader perspective of the impact of the BTLF. Jim's personal view of mentoring is that it has helped him get a better understanding of different parts of the business. He has also received practical career advice from multiple mentors, which is much more than any one individual manager could offer. Jim stresses the importance of not looking to just a single source to gain knowledge or career advice. As a member of the BTLF, he has acquired information on some of the keys to success from his peer members. His feeling is that no longer can we afford to learn on an island—learning together is powerful, especially when all the individuals within one's sphere have the same level of motivation and passion for learning. Jim notes that the BTLF sends a message of possibilities to the black employees who are in the pipeline, which shows the up-and-comers that there are blacks in the field of technology who have achieved high levels of success in IBM and helps them realize it can be done and that they, too, can achieve.

Clearly the attraction, retention, and development of diverse talent represent a type of wicked problem that involves many stakeholders and has complex and tangled roots. The engagement of the BTLF has helped to energize and shape IBM's mentoring approach to solving this wicked problem. As we have seen from some of the interviews conducted to review this effort, its impact is growing and being integrated into solutions for other diverse segments of the IBM workforce. The BTLF started with five members that quickly grew to 28, with well over 100 talented technical employees being mentored by the group. Dorothy Leonard and Walter Swap suggested in their book, *Deep Smarts,* that, "It takes at least ten years of concentrated study and practice to become expert (as opposed to merely competent)."[14] The successful growth of the BTLF effort demonstrates how mentoring communities can help facilitate the growth and development of experts with deep smarts in a focused and sustainable way.

The development of the next generation of technical experts within IBM is critical for sustaining its business impact. Thus, the BTLF recognizes that the task at hand is to create more experts and people with deep smarts, which means developing diverse talent in the technical labs into expert levels such as IBM Fellows, Distinguished Engineers, and so on. Obviously, this poses a wicked problem. The impetus of the BTLF is to help the people in the pipeline shorten the cycle for getting to expert level, and the group's motivation is to prepare these future technical leaders to get to the expert ranks much more quickly and in greater numbers. The BTLF represents IBM's use of a mentoring solution to address the wicked problem of accelerating the deep smarts development cycle among diverse technical talent.

The actions that the BTLF has taken to make an impact on diversity throughout IBM's global enterprise reflects George Washington Carver's assertion that, "No individual has any right to come into the world and go out of it without leaving behind distinct and legitimate reasons for having passed through it."[15] Through the BTLF, members can impact the development of employees worldwide, which builds a legacy from which the next generation of IBM employees will reap major benefits. As a result of successful mentoring efforts such as the BTLF, employees in mature organizations are now reaching across the globe to transfer their skills to their colleagues, with special emphasis on those in hyper-growth and emerging countries. Cross-geography mentoring programs are becoming prevalent across IBM and are helping to address the wicked problem of knowledge transfer within high-growth yet turbulent markets, as we examine next within the context of IBM's South African experience.

Building a Global Knowledge Community—South Africa's Cross-Geography Mentoring Initiative

Just as IBM began to make its presence known several years ago in growth markets such as Brazil, Russia, India, and China (commonly referred to as "BRIC" countries), it also maintained its presence in and focus on Africa.

According to the IBM 2007 Global Innovation Outlook, "Many of the conditions that sparked the economic emergence of regions such as Southeast Asia, Eastern Europe and Brazil are beginning to be seen in Africa as well, including growing political stability in some regions, broader access to wireless technologies and increasing investments from other markets."[16]

The economic promise and opportunity that Africa—particularly South Africa—offers are related to the maturing of its Information Technology market and services arena. The growth is especially noticeable in areas where IBM has the capability to add value. Because South Africa is focused on building its infrastructure by developing IT centers of competence in low-cost environments, many international investors are using South Africa as the gateway to the other targeted growth countries in the region.

To have business dominance in these growth markets, IBM and others must use talent as one of their primary competitive strategies. However, this goal poses several challenges in emerging and somewhat capricious environments, such as within the dynamic South African market. Certainly, developing a business presence as well as both local and global talent that can be successful within the South African environment meets many of the qualities of a wicked problem. One of the difficulties facing IBM and other global companies in South Africa is that there's no clear precedent, because the demise of apartheid has both opened up many doors and created numerous challenges. Given the dynamic social, economic, and political environments in South Africa, the issue of global talent development is difficult and changes with each attempt to address it. The lack of diversity in the talent pool within the local environment has roots that are complex, tangled, and involves many stakeholders with different values and priorities.

One of the ways IBM develops global talent is through the cross-geography mentoring program in which employees in growth and emerging countries are matched with employees in mature countries. Several cross-geography mentoring programs exist in IBM today, and over time the practice will permeate the entire global workforce. It was this capacity for cross-geography mentoring that was used to address the wicked problem of global workforce development within South Africa. As IBM South African employees were identified to participate in the cross-border mentoring program, they were challenged to do some introspection and assessment of their interests, skill gaps, and career goals. They were specifically requested to list their current core skills, short- and long-term career needs and the skills and characteristics they would like their potential mentors to possess. This was the basis upon which employees were paired with executive leaders in the United States. The practice that IBM uses in these cross-border mentoring programs does not assume the needs of the employees within the emerging countries. Rather, an open dialogue takes place with the employees and other leaders within their home countries.

IBM finds this method works well because it empowers employees by giving them a voice in their own development. Clearly, this was critical within South Africa's emerging social context. IBM's efforts to develop global and local talent have a variety of both short-term and long-term skills needs as follow:

Some primary short-term skills needs:

- **Global leadership**—Identify quick ways to help employees gain the skills to better function and lead others in a globally integrated enterprise.

- **Client relationship management**—Help IBM employees gain short-term skills to develop partnerships with clients to deliver integrated solutions.

- **Knowledge integration**—Povide assistance to employees that will quickly improve their capacity to leverage and align their tasks and responsibilities with the overall corporate strategy.

- **Global business acumen**—The ability not only to design business strategy for the local market in South Africa, but also to transcend geographic borders and help make South Africa a contender in the global economy.

Some primary long-term skills needs:

- **Global business development**—Enable employees to develop long-term and sustained business growth that builds an enduring enterprise.

- **Global value chain management**—There is continuous focus in IBM to develop ways to support and engage in high-value activities to help the business sustain its position as a premier global enterprise.

- **Cross-cultural competence**—The impetus is to be vigilant in maintaining cultural understanding to open the lines of communication among IBM employees. This awareness of cultural differences will govern the manner in which employees do business with clients and business partners.

- **Marketplace assessment analysis**—IBM expects its employees to develop a strong entrepreneurial attitude and the ability to read both current and anticipated needs and trends impacting global clients.

As IBM began to structure the South African cross-geography mentoring efforts, it needed to articulate specific skills for the mentors who were being asked to address the global workforce development needs of the organization. Some of the key competencies IBM defined for mentors as part of this effort include a mix of technical and relational attributes such as strong analytical thinking skills; proven track record in dealing successfully with clients; broad knowledge that spans business units and geography; as well as strong innovative, problem solving, and leadership skills. Because the need to develop both technical and operational skills was present, the one-on-one mentoring relationships were supplemented with monthly modules covering topics such as IBM's Financial model, how to build horizontal solutions, IBM strategy and Business Leadership Model, managing in a values-based business, and ways to apply the necessary leadership competencies. Employees in the mentoring program formed a cohesive learning group in which they brainstormed ways to apply their newly acquired knowledge to solve ongoing business tasks.

Once the program process was jointly designed with the HR teams in both countries, a formal kick-off program was launched and key sponsoring executives from both countries were on the agenda. Executives from the Global Talent team, Enterprise Learning organization, and the Country General Manager for South and Central Africa attended the initial launch. Shortly after the kick-off session, training was offered for both mentors and mentees. The content of the mentee training included information on how to engage in a meaningful mentoring relationship, roles and responsibility, a commitment to "give back," and how to close stated skill gaps.

Mentor training had a different tone and purpose. This training was conducted by two business executives from South Africa who discussed the culture and history of the country, the IBM business climate, and the economic possibilities there. Participants evaluated the training session very favorably—both groups assessed the session as good to excellent in terms of importance and value. At the close of the seven-month pilot program, participants spoke quite emotionally about the experience as having been most rewarding and having helped them develop new skills and partnerships. The final satisfaction survey indicated that both mentors and mentees rated their mentoring experience in the good-to-excellent range and indicated that they have been applying their newly acquired skills on the job and are also transferring their knowledge to others.

As we delved into the business impact of IBM's mentoring solutions in its South African experience, we interviewed key players within these efforts.

Mark Harris, general manager, IBM South and Central Africa, noted that when you look at emerging markets, one of the key things you realize is that the search for talent is key to being successful. He reflected on the data showing that there is high attrition in many South African companies and noted that "IBM is not excluded from this talent flight."[17] IBM's approach within South Africa is geared toward strengthening its capability to recruit the best available talent, as well as making investments to develop and retain talent. If the business is not able to attract and retain talent, it will fall short in meeting its business goals. In South Africa, the goal is to build and transform both local and global talent.

In attempting to address the wicked problem of global talent development within South Africa, IBM is also building a critical capacity that can be utilized within other global markets. For example, IBM is one of the few multinationals that has put together the necessary training around leadership skills that can be applied on a global basis, especially in emerging markets. While traditional education provides capacity in specific technical areas, the need for developing leadership skills is not as easily met, especially within newly developed or emerging markets. Thus, companies won't be able to quickly bring individuals up to the required stage of leadership development, as the gap between the firm's needs and the available talent pool is large. So creating the cross-geography mentoring program is extremely important, as it helps people start to see role models and the type of leadership characteristics that are needed at the local level.

In addition, building collaborative influence is an important skill that leaders must develop to be effective in their jobs. Within the IBM experience, many of the mentees have good skills, but no amount of education and training can offer the same benefit as talking to real people with real problems and practical experience in the global enterprise. By connecting to these role models and sharing knowledge through cross-geography mentoring relationships, quite a few of the top South African companies are now looking for global growth opportunities to better equip themselves to lead locally. They are also starting to realize that one needs different skills and different ways of thinking to compete globally.

As cross-border mentoring relationships develop, it is important to understand cultural differences. To this end, IBM has invested in global diversity training to give employees and managers the necessary knowledge to operate in IBM's culturally diverse workforce. These training activities and classes are delivered using IBM's blended learning approach, which includes e-learning, classroom study, and role playing. In addition, IBM's global approach to education is tied to its overall corporate values. Thus, employees not only learn the critical skills needed for managing in a global and diverse workforce, but also gain an understanding about the culture and values within IBM itself. Both are important knowledge sets for employees to attain to be effective and successful within the organization. Global firms that don't have such processes in place often find that they hit a wall in terms of leadership development.

For example, one IBM employee who is a mentor in the South African Mentoring Program is Marilyn Johnson, vice president of Market Development. Marilyn has seen an amazing evolution in IBM's mentoring program over the years. In the course of our interview, she reflected that during the 1970s, mentoring was a little-known concept, and where it existed at all, people only whispered about it. At that time, it was neither sanctioned nor supported—so obviously, it has come a long way. Today, mentoring is very structured, formalized, and even encouraged across oceans, latitudes and longitudes, and country barriers. We're finding that mentoring is of strategic importance to talent development. It is embedded into IBM's leadership effectiveness and is supported by using blended tools on the Web and informal network groups based on the different diversity constituencies that exist in IBM. Marilyn concluded her remarks by stating that, "The mentor helps you step out of the comfort zone with confidence. The talent is always there—the mentee doesn't always realize the talent they're bringing, but the mentor puts the spotlight on the brilliance to bring it out."[18]

It's clear that there is something to be learned from IBM's South African experience in terms of raising solutions to address wicked problems. As Camillus writes, "It's impossible to find solutions to wicked strategy problems, but companies can learn to cope with them."[19] He advocates a social-planning process that engages multiple stakeholders and then uses ongoing experiments, or what Camillus calls "robust actions," to examine the impact of various ways to address wicked problems.

Such an approach is illustrated not only by IBM's tactics in South Africa, but also by the expansion of these efforts into other geographic regions throughout the organization. For example, as an extension of the mentoring program, leaders in South Africa partnered with human resources teams in the United States and the United Kingdom to design an approach for strengthening executive leadership skills, managers' capabilities, and employee experience. The program has a range of learning offerings that are intended to address specific talent issues. It entails, for example, training for managers to develop good interviewing techniques for making appropriate hiring decisions. In addition, global leadership skills are being transferred to managers in South Africa, which emphasizes empowerment and skills to achieve personal responsibility. This continuum of training and development starts with attracting employees who bring the right skills into the business in the first place and continues with their ongoing development. The understanding is that employees will develop a strong view and line of sight of the personal career goals they can achieve throughout their time within IBM. Not only is this proof that IBM South Africa values its employees, but it is also evidence of the power of mentoring solutions to facilitate robust actions that can help the firm cope with its ongoing wicked problems.

Lessons Learned–Sustaining Business Impact via Strategic Mentoring Solutions

Global talent development is not a one-dimensional issue, but rather reflects a complex, interconnected set of dynamic issues that cannot be solved by the organization, yet which must be addressed and perhaps even leveraged. Organizations must make it a priority to identify skill needs and skill gaps at all levels of the business and seek different but appropriate ways of addressing the varying career growth needs of its global workforce. However, sometimes organizations run the risk of placing most of their energy on developing new employees and neglect the ongoing development of their other employee segments. Any sustainable approach to talent development has to be holistic, supporting the notion that all employees within the organization must be given the opportunity to grow and acquire different skills that they can apply in ways that will advance the goals of the organization.

Both the Black Technical Leaders Forum and IBM's South African experience underscore the dual needs of addressing employee retention and leadership development. This approach is consistent with what Robert Barner advocates in his book, *Developing the Depth and Versatility of Your Organization's Leadership Talent—Bench Strength*.[20] He makes the point that "Leaders who are able to go beyond managing a set of isolated recruiting, development and training activities are to be able to articulate a viable game plan for capturing and leveraging leadership talent. For their part, organizational leaders are being expected to play a stronger role as coauthors of this game plan."[21] This is explicitly the reason the global leadership development program that is being introduced in South Africa supports the acquisition of versatile leadership skills.

The intellectual bench strength of any organization can be deemed a predictor of how a company performs and sustains excellence, despite the fierce competition that exists in the global marketplace of the twenty-first century. IBM has taken the position that developing intellectual capital has a direct link to business success, and, therefore, the company has a corporate responsibility to enable and empower its global workforce to develop broad critical skills. Having the right skills is a competitive arsenal that IBM uses to sustain its performance in the marketplace, as well as coping with emerging and ongoing wicked problems. Developing bench strength also means that companies must both envision and create the future to sustain business impact. This often requires being open to a set of unexpected and unpredictable possibilities that may cause other companies to withdraw from them, fearing that the risk or level of uncertainty is too great.

During the times of apartheid, IBM was one of the few companies to continue to do business in South Africa and found ways to extend itself to the community at large. Today, the IBM relationship with South Africa and the other countries in Africa is increasingly gaining strength. This has given the company a strategic advantage in terms of employee and leadership development that cannot be easily replicated by other companies who could not envision the post-apartheid future. The ongoing presence within South Africa is now stimulating a host of new initiatives that not only produce business impact but also social impact. For example, IBM has launched a mentoring program called the "Makocha Minds" for students from almost 25 major universities in Africa. This program links students from these universities to technical leaders from several IBM sites in the United States. The intent is to develop the intellectual capital within African countries by exposing these students to experts in the field of science and technology and at the same time help the students gain an understanding of how to function in a global economy and become future global leaders.

Thus, the use of mentoring solutions to sustain overall business impact is producing outcomes that are unexpected, yet strategic, for IBM. This is illustrated in IBM's efforts to build a sustainable business environment as in the example of the South African experience, and through its efforts to engage and develop diverse leadership within core technical areas in partnership with the BTLF. These various efforts form the innovative use of mentoring solutions to solve the ongoing wicked problem of global talent development across IBM's worldwide enterprise.

The BTLF and other such forums within IBM emphasize the importance of innovation and the need to develop key business and technical skills. As a result, many of the other Diversity Network Groups and mentoring teams meet to educate their colleagues about career management, leadership, and business skills, as well as the fundamentals and processes for filing patents. For example, the Women Inventors Community is a think tank whose sole purpose is to encourage, support, and educate its members to "dream up and successfully patent inventions." The impact of these activities is evident by the United States Patent and Trademark Office, which reported in January 2007 that IBM maintained its leading position by the number of patents filed in the United States for the fourteenth consecutive year. "With 3,621, IBM surpassed its own record and earned more United States patents than any other company."[22] This demonstrates that as IBM invests in developing the right skills and in empowering and engaging its employees, the employees will unleash their creative power to help IBM sustain its excellence in the global marketplace.

Some Final Thoughts–The Impact of *Intelligent Mentoring*

Any organization that hopes to realize business impact and maintain competitive advantage cannot become complacent with past success. Enduring companies such as IBM constantly seek to change themselves based on marketplace signals and the need for innovation. Due to the volatile nature of the global marketplace, companies that want to sustain their competitive advantage realize that they cannot use present success to predict and determine success in the future. It is a well-known fact that what got you here will not necessarily get you there. This is especially relevant to organizations like IBM as it attempts to address the ongoing and emerging wicked problems impacting people, processes, and outcomes. Some have characterized wicked problems as relentless. Given this view, organizations and their efforts to address wicked problems must be equally relentless. Firms like IBM must continually seek to retool and reinvent their business strategy while developing and aligning their talent portfolio to meet current as well as future needs. This requires an approach that is dynamic, inclusive, and value-added but can also create chaos, demand trade-offs, and increase risk-taking.

A key assumption throughout the chapters of *Intelligent Mentoring* is that a core characteristic of enduring and successful organizations is their commitment to attracting, retaining, developing, and engaging their global workforce. To better articulate IBM's perspective, Tim Ringo, IBM Global Business Services, and Randy MacDonald, senior vice president, IBM HR, co-authored an article titled, "Unlocking the DNA of an Adaptable Workforce." In this article, they cited some critical points of which companies should be mindful to have business impact and to sustain growth from lessons learned within the IBM experience. To this point they noted, "Our analysis identified four important themes that require the attention and focus of senior executives across the organization, including those responsible for HR functions. These are 1) developing an adaptable workforce—a critical capability; 2) revealing the leadership gap—future growth at risk; 3) cracking the code for talent; and 4) driving growth through workforce analytics. There can be no doubt that winning in competitive and quickly shifting global markets requires responsive organizations."[23] Thus, a core value throughout IBM is a commitment to building and sustaining the capacity of its global workforce as a key tool for creating a responsive organization.

Based on this assumption, we have examined the various ways that mentoring solutions are used by IBM as one approach for achieving its global business strategy. Whether it is developing workforce capability through one-on-one and group mentoring, or leadership development through the use of expert mentoring, or identifying talent in the use of reverse mentoring, all of these techniques are being strategically matched to provide the best fit to the specific challenges faced by IBM worldwide. However, mentoring alone cannot achieve all the crucial outcomes needed by any global company. We have reviewed the unique approach taken by IBM by integrating mentoring solutions within its overall business model as one part of its efforts to build organizational intelligence, strengthen connections across people, and sustain business impact. IBM's mentoring revitalization efforts have developed with a great deal of effort, input, and resources—and have included many successes and some failures. Nonetheless, IBM's mentoring portfolio has emerged as a core element in how it hopes to use intelligent mentoring solutions to sustain business impact as part of its enduring commitment to excellence through people, knowledge, and relationships.

Thus, an important lesson learned from our review of mentoring solutions throughout IBM is that strategic sustainability means being willing to take on wicked problems that may not have a clear "finish-line" insight. In a competitive business environment that focuses on metrics and measures of performance, it can be challenging to make a case for work practices that are difficult to link to specific short-term outcomes. However, using mentoring as a strategic tool for addressing wicked problems challenges traditional perspectives or attempts to define business impact in terms of short-term success. As companies make continuous provisions for addressing specific wicked problems such as global talent management, they must also build a foundation for adaptability given the unpredictable nature of marketplace. What has traditionally been labeled "success" in the past must be replaced with a commitment to building long-term capacity. By developing a strong learning culture through practices such as mentoring in all of its various forms, companies such as IBM become well positioned to build this type of long-term capacity. While the many lessons learned from *Intelligent Mentoring* are examples taken from one organization's journey to build its capacity and address wicked problems, it reflects a set of tools that we feel are not only useful but also vital for any organization.

As we wrote in the opening chapter of the book, we wanted to understand more about the complex nature of mentoring relationships and to strike a balance between mentoring research and real-world applications. The examples we have reviewed and the individuals we have interviewed in telling the story of intelligent mentoring practices at IBM have taught us much about this power tool. The transformation of IBM from meaning "I'm By Myself" into "I'm Being *Mentored*" is in itself an ongoing "wicked problem." Our hope continues to be that the success of IBM's various mentoring approaches, especially its use of a mentoring portfolio that is linked to its global business model, will cause other organizations to take a second look at their menu of mentoring solutions.

We have witnessed the power of mentoring to unlock solutions, develop innovative processes, and support the knowledge that engages communities of employees worldwide. As Camillus writes, "When confronting frustrating problems, an enterprise would do well to recognize that they may be wicked. Moving from denial to acceptance is important; otherwise, companies will continue to use conventional processes and never effectively address their strategy issue."[24] We strongly believe that mentoring provides a diverse array of tools and techniques that can assist global enterprises, as illustrated by the IBM example, to confront, recognize, and address the wicked nature of these ongoing challenges in a way that builds capacity, stimulates innovation, and sustains business impact.

References

[1] Camillus, J.C. (2008). Strategy as a Wicked Problem, *Harvard Business Review,* Product No. R0805G.

[2] Rittel, H.W.J. and Webber, M.M. (1973). Dilemmas in a General Theory of Planning, *Policy Sciences.*

[3] Camillus, loc. cit.

[4] Ibid.

[5] Jackson, S.E. and Ruderman, M.N. (1995). *Diversity in Work Teams: Research Paradigms for a Changing Workplace*, American Psychological Association, Washington, D.C.

[6] Camillus, op. cit.

[7] Ibid.

[8] Weber, E.P. and Khademian, A.M. (2008). Wicked problems, knowledge challenges, and collaborative capacity builders in network settings. *Public Administration Review*, March/April, 334–349.

[9] Lockwood, N.R. (2006). Talent Management: Driver for Organizational Success, Manager HR Content Program, Society for Human Resource Management.

[10] Dychtwald, K., Erickson, T.J., and Morison, R. (2006). *Workforce Crisis: How to Beat the Coming Shortage of Skills and Talent*, Harvard Business School Press, Boston, MA.

[11] Ibid.

[12] Clutterbuck, D. and Ragins, B.R. (2002). *Mentoring and Diversity: An International Perspective*, Butterworth-Heinemann, Woburn, MA.

[13] Interview conducted by Sheila Forte-Trammell with Dr. Mark Dean IBM Fellow and Vice President, Almaden Research Center July 26, 2007.

[14] Leonard, D. and Swap, W.C. (2005). *Deep Smarts: How to Cultivate and Transfer Enduring Business Wisdom*, Harvard Business School Publishing, Boston, MA.

[15] George Washington Carver: In his own words Edited by Gary R. Kremer, 1991, Page 1 University of Missouri Press, Columbia and London.

[16] "IBM Global Innovation Outlook Tackles its Most Ambitious Topic to Date," w3 (IBM Web site) News, June 2007.

[17] Diana Bing and Sheila Forte-Trammell conducted interview with Mark Harris, Country General Manager South and Central Africa IBM August 23, 2007.

[18] Diana Bing and Sheila Forte-Trammell conducted interview with Marilyn Johnson, Vice President General Business—IBM Market Development August 23, 2007.

[19] Camillus, loc. cit., p. 4.

[20] Barner, R. (2006). *Bench Strength: Developing the Depth and Versatility of Your Organization's Leadership Talent,* American Management Association, New York, NY.

[21] Ibid.

[22] "The IBM Fact Sheet, 2008." Article published by IBM China/Hong Kong Limited.

[23] Ringo, T. and MacDonald, R. (2008). Unlocking the DNA of the Adaptable Workforce—The Global Human Capital Study, IBM Corporation.

[24] Camillus, loc. cit., p. 9.

Index

Intelligent Mentoring

How IBM Creates Value through People, Knowledge and Relationships

Audrey J. Murrell
Sheila Forte-Trammell
Diana A. Bing

Foreword by Ted Hoff

FREE Online Edition

Your purchase of **Intelligent Mentoring** includes access to a free online edition for 45 days through the Safari Books Online subscription service. Nearly every IBM Press book is available online through Safari Books Online, along with more than 5,000 other technical books and videos from publishers such as Addison-Wesley Professional, Cisco Press, Exam Cram, O'Reilly, Prentice Hall, Que, and Sams.

SAFARI BOOKS ONLINE allows you to search for a specific answer, cut and paste code, download chapters, and stay current with emerging technologies.

Activate your FREE Online Edition at
www.informit.com/safarifree

> **STEP 1:** Enter the coupon code: CSIQYCB.

> **STEP 2:** New Safari users, complete the brief registration form.
> Safari subscribers, just log in.

If you have difficulty registering on Safari or accessing the online edition, please e-mail customer-service@safaribooksonline.com

Safari
Books Online

Addison Wesley   Adobe Press   ALPHA   Cisco Press   FT Press FINANCIAL TIMES   IBM Press   lynda.com   Microsoft Press   New Riders

O'REILLY   Peachpit Press   PRENTICE HALL   QUE   Redbooks   SAMS   SAS Publishing   Sun microsystems   WILEY